Esther

'North has meticulously researched the myriad details that render this story so true to life and cast a new light on our origins.'
Irina Dunn, former director of the New South Wales Writers' Centre

'Jessica North has really brought to life the story of Esther, the young First Fleet convict who, for a brief period in 1808, became the "First Lady" of the British colony in Sydney Cove.'
Helen Bersten OAM, former Honorary Archivist, Australian Jewish Historical Society

Jessica North has been researching Esther's story for over a decade, discovering intriguing new details along the way. She is a program director at the Australian Research Institute for Environment and Sustainability at Macquarie University, and author of several guides.

Esther

The extraordinary true story
of the First Fleet girl who became
First Lady of the colony

JESSICA NORTH

ALLEN&UNWIN
SYDNEY•MELBOURNE•AUCKLAND•LONDON

Allen & Unwin
83 Alexander Street
Crows Nest NSW 2065
Australia
Phone: (61 2) 8425 0100
Email: info@allenandunwin.com
Web: www.allenandunwin.com

A catalogue record for this
book is available from the
National Library of Australia

NATIONAL
LIBRARY
OF AUSTRALIA

ISBN 978 1 76052 737 2

Map on p. vi is from the Dixson Map Collection, State Library of New South Wales
Set in 11.5/16 pt Minion Pro by Midland Typesetters, Australia
Printed and bound in Australia by Griffin Press

10 9 8 7 6 5 4 3 2 1

MIX
Paper from
responsible sources
FSC
www.fsc.org   FSC® C009448

The paper in this book is FSC® certified.
FSC® promotes environmentally responsible,
socially beneficial and economically viable
management of the world's forests.

For Stephen

Map of Sydney Cove from 1799. George Johnston's initial land grant at Annandale (no. 5) is marked with a star. The Parramatta road ran past the property.

Contents

Introduction

This is the story of a remarkable woman. Arriving in New South Wales as a convict on the First Fleet, Esther Abrahams rose—like Cinderella herself—from the very bottom of society to its top. She had none of the advantages of education and social standing enjoyed by her contemporary Elizabeth Macarthur, and yet she achieved similar success in the management of a large agricultural estate.

Once I had discovered Esther, I was keen to find out more. I read hundreds of books and articles, some of which provided only small threads of detail that, when woven together, created the colourful tapestry of Esther's life. In the process, I discovered several previously unknown documents.

People make history. And it is not until we get to know the people behind historic events that we really understand what they were all about. Esther's life was intertwined with all the major events of the early colony and so, through her, we meet the principal figures of the time—both British and Indigenous—and see how their inter-relationships influenced the historical outcomes.

I relied heavily on personal journals and letters, family and historical records, transcribed conversations, and of course the published work of many wonderful historians. Even the initially daunting volumes of the *Historical Records of New South Wales* became welcome friends, once I was familiar with the people who wrote the letters and reports they contain.

The office in Britain that was responsible for the colonies was initially the Home Office but was later called the Colonial Office, the War Office, and finally the War and Colonial Office. To avoid confusion, I have continued to refer to it as the Colonial Office. I have also called the medical men of the time doctors (rather than surgeons), and have used surnames for men and first names for women.

I have incorporated an accurate timeline throughout the book and have not changed any known facts. Where gaps exist in the records, I have described a possible set of events.

All the people in this story are real. Their names are sprinkled through Sydney's places, and echoes of their characters remain in Australia's egalitarian society. One of the most intriguing of them is Esther. I hope you enjoy meeting her as much as I did.

CHAPTER ONE

Guilty!

Sixteen years old. Frightened. And feeling sick. Esther was standing in the dock at the Old Bailey in London. She was on trial for stealing twenty-four yards of black silk lace, worth fifty shillings. And shoplifting carried a death sentence.

Esther did not look like the women who usually stood in that place. For a start, she was better dressed. Her elegant gown of Indian chintz befitted an officer's daughter, and her dark, wavy hair was gathered fashionably behind her head with wispy curls nestling either side of her face.

Though she felt shaky, she was doing her best to hold her head up and appear composed. She kept her large hazel eyes focused on the wall behind the judge to avoid catching the eye of her father, who sat in the public area to her right.

Major Julian had taken the unusual step of engaging a barrister to defend his daughter's case, and that barrister was pacing to and fro as he teased conflicting details from the second of two witnesses. William Garrow would later become famous for introducing the concept of 'presumed innocent until proven guilty', but in 1786 he had been at the bar for only two years. He called three more people to appear before the court, who all declared Esther to be of very good character, and then the short trial was over.

While the twelve men of the jury huddled in the back corner of the courtroom to decide their verdict, Esther wiped her sweating palms down the side of her skirt. She stole a glance at her father. His head was thrown back, his eyes were closed and his hands were pressed together, with the tips of his fingers resting against his chin.

The jury foreman turned back towards the judge. Esther's heart pounded.

'Guilty of stealing!' the foreman announced.

Esther gasped.

'. . . but not privately.'

That lesser offence, which meant that the shop assistant had been aware of the theft, allowed the judge to at least waive the mandatory death penalty in favour of a lesser one. He sentenced Esther to be 'transported to parts beyond the seas' for seven years. Her father let out a groan.

As a gaoler marched her into the adjacent Newgate Prison and along its dark granite corridors, Esther's mind was numb. The man, who smelt of gin, shoved her into a large cell crammed with more than a hundred other women, and he slammed the door shut behind her.

At first she just stood there in a daze, but after a while she began to take in her surroundings. A few wooden bunks lined the walls of the cell, with several women crammed into each one; most of her cell-mates huddled on the stone slab floor, which was littered with vestiges of straw and crawling with vermin. The women had matted hair and sun-starved, grubby skin. Their filthy bare feet protruded from torn and grimy clothes that hung from their bodies like rags. Esther looked down at her scarlet skirt, which stood out like a splash of blood upon muddy snow. She noticed some of the other women turn, look her up and down, then snigger and murmur to each other.

An overpowering stench wafted around her, and she cupped a hand over her nose. Then she began to retch. Someone shoved her towards a line of chamber-pots, and she made it just in time to disgorge her vomit into one of the half-full vessels. Then she crouched back onto a small square of stone that was stained with blood and damp with urine.

Her distress flowed out in silent tears until a prison guard brought in the three ha'pennies worth of bread provided for each prisoner. As he handed Esther her ration, he stroked the back of his hand down her cheek. She pulled away sharply, and another prisoner took advantage of the moment and snatched her bread. The guard just smiled.

Esther could remember her mother telling her that the more she prayed to God for help, the more He would love her. She whispered a prayer now.

~ 30 August 1786 ~

On that same summer's day, seventy miles away in Portsmouth, George Johnston paced up and down the foreshore, straining his eyes towards the horizon as if willing a ship to sail into the harbour and deliver him from his tedium. He was tall and blond, with clear blue eyes, and he cut a dashing figure in the closely fitting breeches and red jacket of his uniform.

Although only twenty-two, he was already a seasoned officer. At ten years old, he had joined the British Marines to fight alongside his father in the American War of Independence. When twelve, he had been promoted to second lieutenant. Later, after the French had sided with the Americans and declared war on Britain, he had been on a Royal Navy ship fighting them at sea. That was when he had been severely injured and a piece of shrapnel had become lodged in a bone in his leg—an injury that would trouble him for the rest of his life.

After the war was over, only a quarter of the marines were retained—the fittest and the best. Despite his injury, Johnston was one of them, and he now spent his days languishing behind a desk. But if he found the work tedious, he need not have worried. The very war that had taken him from boy to manhood would soon result in the adventure he longed for.

Revelling in their new independence, the American colonies refused to take the thousand convicts a year that Britain had been in the habit of sending them, and British prisons overflowed as a consequence. Old sailing ships, known as hulks, had been tied to moorings and refitted to house hundreds of convicts each. Their pathetic inhabitants lived in dark and damp conditions below deck, where disease and vice flourished. But even the hulks had become hopelessly overcrowded.

Eventually, His Majesty King George III commanded Lord Sydney to instruct the Treasury to begin sending Britain's convicts fifteen thousand miles by ship to a small bay on the underside of the world that had been discovered by Captain James Cook sixteen years earlier.

☙ 15 September 1786 ❧

As summer moved into autumn, some of Esther's cellmates taught her the codes of Newgate Prison. She learned that the luxury of sleeping on the bunks was a privilege heavily guarded by an established hierarchy of prisoners. She discovered that hemp blankets could be hired for a price. So one day she finished painstakingly hand-stitching a new shirt for a guard in return for the comfort of a blanket, but the deprivation of sleep required to protect her prized possession made the custody of it almost unbearable.

☙ 28 October 1786 ❧

The frequent nausea Esther had experienced since arriving in Newgate Prison had just begun to diminish when, one morning, she was led into a small room where a panel of matrons checked the health of each prisoner. To Esther's utter dismay, they declared her to be with child.

As she walked back down the dimly lit corridor, the thought of having a baby in that despicable place horrified her. Suddenly she felt faint and collapsed in a crumpled heap on the stone floor. An older prisoner rushed over to help her. Nelly Kerwin's clothes were gaudy and her flushed cheeks gave her the appearance of an overdressed rag doll, but she was full of kindness.

Nelly helped Esther to sit on a wooden chair where a thin shaft of sunlight penetrated the surrounding dimness. Esther thanked Nelly for her kindness then blurted out her devastating news, before covering her face with her hands and sobbing. Nelly crouched down and gently put an arm around Esther's shoulders.

'Perhaps we can get you to the Master's Side,' she muttered.

When Esther had recovered and was sitting straighter in the chair, Nelly explained that the Master's Side of the prison was a spacious block, separate from the Common Side, with fifty individual rooms. The prisoners who could afford the weekly rent to live there were mostly shoplifters, and they lived in comparative comfort, with good food and bedding. If Esther could find someone to pay her rent, Nelly would be pleased to share her room in the Master's Side. Nelly was with child herself and would welcome the company.

Esther's heart ached when she thought of the shame she had brought upon her father. She had not heard from him since her trial. Now she hesitated to ask for his help, but Nelly persuaded her to try. Like most Jewish girls, Esther had received little education, so although she could read she could not write. It was Nelly who penned Esther's heartfelt apology, the affirmation of her love for her father and her request for his help. But it was Esther's tears that stained the paper as she signed it with a cross. The two women kept her pregnancy a secret.

⟅ 14 November 1786 ⟆

Two weeks later, Nelly welcomed Esther to the Master's Side with a cup of tea and asked her how she had come to be in Newgate Prison. Esther described how she had been brought up in a loving Jewish family in New Folkestone, Kent. But her mother had died, so her father—an officer in the British Marines—had sent her to live with another Jewish family in London. Shortly before her sixteenth birthday, that family's eldest son had won her heart and had later arranged a private marriage ceremony so that they could begin a wedded life together. Esther had been full of happiness the day she had become Mrs Abraham Abrahams, but she had also been confused by her new husband's insistence that they keep their marriage a secret from his parents until he was earning sufficient income to support her away from the family home.

As it happened, Abraham's mother had discovered the union soon afterwards. She had declared it invalid and cast Esther out of the house, accusing her of wickedly seducing her son. Bewildered, hurt and desperate, Esther had sought the assistance of a constable, whose only comment was that it seemed she had been ill-used.

While she was still loitering tearfully on the pavement, unsure of what to do next, a well-dressed gentleman had approached her. Henry Fitzroy had assumed Esther was a young prostitute looking for business; after she had tearfully explained her situation, he had taken pity on her and paid for a night's lodging in nearby St James. She had been grateful, but wondered if perhaps he was just waiting for her to take up the occupation he expected was hers already.

The following morning, Esther had walked through Piccadilly Circus and into Coventry Street, where she had passed the drapery shop owned by Joseph and Charles Harrop. It was then that she had had the desperate idea of acquiring some lace to complete a fashionable hat she had been making, so that she could sell it to pay for her lodging until she could find employment.

However, once inside the shop, her shaking hand had by mistake taken not one but two cards of lace, which she had hidden beneath her cloak. The shop assistant had been immediately suspicious and Esther had quickly left. But the assistant had rushed after her, and accosted her in the street. Esther had tried to proclaim her innocence, but in her panic had lost her grip on the cards, which dropped to the pavement with a clatter.

So here she was, a convicted criminal. Nelly said it sounded like her wedding had been a sham, but suggested that Esther continue using her married name anyway, particularly as she would soon have a child.

In turn, Esther asked Nelly about her own circumstances. Nelly was a businesswoman—and a widow with two children—who had run a boarding house and lent money to sailors. One of those sailors had cheated her out of a large sum of money, so when he died she had forged his will to get back what she felt was rightly hers. Instead, her forgery had been discovered and she had been arrested.

Esther asked Nelly how long her sentence was. Nelly replied that it was only until her baby was born in June, which Esther thought was a blessing . . . until she learned that, following the birth of the baby, Nelly would be hanged for her crime.

⌒ 12 December 1786 ⌒

George Johnston, now a First Lieutenant in the British Marines, reported for duty as cold winter winds whistled around the ships gathered on the River Thames at Woolwich. He was assigned to the *Lady Penrhyn*, which would transport half of the two hundred convict women to the new colony at Botany Bay.

She was a fairly new ship, only a year old, with two decks, a square stern, three masts to hold her many sails, and a painted lady as a figurehead. A barricade topped with iron prongs was being built across her upper deck to separate the convicts from the marines and the ship's crew.

The man chosen to lead the first fleet of convict-laden ships to Botany Bay was Captain Arthur Phillip. This quiet and determined man of forty-eight was instructed to establish, in a land that was virtually unknown, a settlement capable of supporting many future shiploads of Britain's criminals.

When the Pilgrim Fathers had sailed in the *Mayflower* to establish the first European colony in North America, there had been only about a hundred colonists—all of them free settlers—and half of them had died during their first winter. Captain Phillip was taking more than a *thousand* people—most of them already weak, unhealthy convicts—on an eight-month voyage to the other side of the world. The task ahead of him was formidable.

In the new colony, the convicts would be expected to farm the land in order to grow food for everyone in the settlement. No money would be required in such a place, so none would be provided. And no private ships were to be built in the colony. Phillip had strict orders to prevent any contact between the new colony and foreign ports, in case it jeopardised the trade monopoly of the British-owned East India Company. Anyway, that was the plan.

❧ 6 January 1787 ❧

In the new year, all the women in Newgate Prison who were under sentence of transportation were ordered to be transferred to the *Lady Penrhyn*. But because Esther was pregnant, she was left behind.

When the women arrived on board the ship, they were so diseased and covered with lice that Captain Phillip penned a furious letter to the Home Office. He added that they were *almost naked, and so very filthy, that nothing but clothing them could have prevented them from perishing.*

He gave the women some of the clothes that had been packed away for use in the colony, but these were so badly made that they also began falling apart within a matter of weeks.

❧ 11 February 1787 ❧

Esther was now eight months pregnant and terrified at the thought of being transported, particularly as she would soon have a baby to care for. So Nelly offered to help her write an appeal for Royal Mercy. Once again, Nelly wrote out the words that Esther wanted to say, and the appeal was officially lodged.

Then all Esther could do was wait—and pray.

❧ 18 March 1787 ❧

It was the beginning of spring when Esther felt the first of her labour pains. Nelly made her cups of chamomile tea and reassured her that all would be well. As the hours passed, Esther's contractions became stronger and more frequent until Nelly judged it was time to take her to the prison's infirmary, where there were clean rags and fresh water. Esther waddled beside her through the dark, grimy corridors, in a daze of apprehension and astonishment that she was about to give birth.

Not long afterwards, she was squatting upon the birthing stool. Nelly supported her young friend's straining body and offered encouragement, assuring her that her work was nearly done. At last, with a mighty effort, Esther pushed her child into the world.

Nelly lifted up the slippery, wrinkled baby and wrapped it in a cloth. 'You have a lovely little daughter,' she cooed as she handed over the bundle.

Esther looked wearily at the baby. *Her* baby. She kissed its soft forehead, she held its tiny hand, she traced her finger over its rosy lips. And she wondered how on earth she was going to be able to care for such a precious, fragile little life in so terrible a place.

'Have you chosen a name for your babe?' Nelly asked.

'Rosanna,' Esther whispered, 'because she is as beautiful as a rosebud.'

Nelly paused to feel the movement of her own baby, due in three months' time, whose arrival would signal the end of her life.

15 April 1787

But after another four weeks, Nelly went into premature labour. Four hours later she gave birth to her third child—another little girl. The baby, however, survived for only two hours and died cradled in her mother's arms.

21 April 1787

The British Marines were an elite group of special soldiers who were not impaired by seasickness and so could fight effectively at sea— and Lieutenant Johnston was one of the best. But once the convict women boarded the *Lady Penrhyn*, he was faced with a problem he initially found insoluble. His orders were to keep the female convicts strictly separated from the sailors; but some of the women had come from prisons where they had been used to prostituting themselves in exchange for food, and the sailors were happy to oblige them. The women did not realise that they would now receive plenty of food anyway.

Johnston finally ordered the offending men to be flogged and the offending women to be put in leg-irons. Then he threatened to shave the heads of any women who offended in future . . . and order was restored.

∽ 30 April 1787 ∽

By this time, most of the convicts who would travel with the First Fleet had been aboard their ships for many weeks, and most of the ships had left the Thames and sailed down to the Motherbank near Portsmouth, on England's southern coast. But because the ships were carrying over five hundred convict men and fewer than two hundred convict women, Newgate Prison was asked to send some more women to the *Lady Penrhyn*, such as those who had recently been imprisoned.

Esther was just beginning to feel she could cope with the new demands of motherhood. Her days were filled with feeding her hungry baby, walking up and down the corridors to soothe her cries and creeping about while she slept. Despite the fact that Rosanna's presence was a constant reminder of her own lost child, Nelly assisted wherever she could.

Esther had not yet received a response to her appeal for Royal Mercy, so she was shocked when she and her six-week-old baby were ordered to accompany another thirty-six women preparing to join the *Lady Penrhyn*.

Nelly was still being allowed to regain her strength in preparation for her execution so Esther was able to fling her arms around her to say a tearful goodbye. Then heavy iron rings were fastened around the departing women's ankles, and they were shackled together in groups.

Esther clung tightly to her small baby as she clambered up to sit on the outside of a coach which rumbled through London's streets to Woolwich, where the *Prince of Wales* was moored on the River Thames. That transport ship was to take the women down to the Motherbank, where they would finally be transferred to the *Lady Penrhyn*.

∽ 3 May 1787 ∽

After her leg-irons were removed, Esther climbed down through a hatch on the *Lady Penrhyn*'s upper deck to join more than a hundred other female convicts—even though the ship had only been fitted out to take seventy.

Many of the women had already spent months living in the darkness below deck, unable to stand up under a ceiling of only four and a half feet high. Sleeping shelves as broad as a king-size bed had been built into the sides of the hull and mattresses made to fit them, leaving only just enough room to walk between the two rows. Up to four women shared each mattress. There were no portholes, and candles were forbidden for fear of fire, so the only air and light to reach the women came through the single hatch leading to the upper deck.

Once again, Esther was an intruder into a domain that had already been established by others. The most prized positions were those closest to the ladder she had just descended, where a little light and air filtered down, and the stench from the chamber pots was least overpowering. But those places, of course, were already taken.

Crouching low, she made her way through the semi-darkness past impassive faces, and was almost at the end when a smile caught her eye and a small, attractive woman with dark hair held out her arms to hold little Rosanna while Esther settled herself on the mattress. They were quickly joined by a third woman who was heavily pregnant.

The three women introduced themselves. Ann Inett, now cradling Rosanna, was thirty-one and had left her own two children behind in Worcester. Isabella Rosson was twice Esther's age and had been convicted of stealing from her employer. Initially, no expectant mothers had been accepted for the voyage, but the need to boost the number of women had become so great that they were included after all. The women fell quiet and Esther took a long, deep breath as this new phase of her life began.

Apart from the cramped conditions, shipboard life was generally an improvement for most of the women. Lieutenant Johnston made sure that all the women received their ration of food, which included oatmeal, bread, fresh meat and vegetables; and the mattresses were much more comfortable than the bare stone or timber most of the women had become used to sleeping on in prison. They passed the time in the half-light of the lower deck by telling their companions about the lives they had lived before their fateful crimes. It was only when complete darkness surrounded them that they fell quiet.

Each ship in the little flotilla that had been assembled rose gently up and down, surrounded by the refuse that was continually thrown over-board and now swirled around it on the greasy waves. Occasionally a corpse wrapped in canvas bumped against one of the ships as it floated by. On the *Lady Penrhyn*, Esther noticed that the sound of activity on the top deck increased every day as the last of the fresh provisions were loaded onto the ship, and the sails and rigging were prepared for the long voyage ahead. She heard clucking, bleating, quacking, grunting, cooing and honking as various animals were transferred into cages and stalls. She also heard heavy thumps as full water casks were stacked on top of each other.

Then, at last, everything was ready.

CHAPTER TWO
To the Other Side of the World

↔ *13 May 1787* ↔

It was still dark outside when Esther—who had already been woken by her baby twice during the night—was roused again by alarming new sounds. She lay still and listened as orders were bellowed, ropes smacked against masts, and chains rattled. She heard the bare feet of sailors running upon the upper deck, and was startled by the noise of the sails flapping violently as they unfurled, filling with wind. The ship lurched to one side, and there were shouts as the sails were adjusted. The ship lurched again, but the movements gradually steadied into a rhythm as a new sound—of water whooshing against the wooden hull—filled the lower deck, and the *Lady Penrhyn* moved away from Portsmouth to begin her epic journey in the company of the other ten ships of the First Fleet.

There were two armed warships: HMS *Sirius*, commanded by John Hunter and carrying Arthur Phillip, and the smaller HMS *Supply*, commanded by Henry Ball. There were also six ships to carry the seven hundred and fifty convicts: the *Scarborough*, *Friendship*, *Alexander*, *Prince of Wales*, *Charlotte* and *Lady Penrhyn*. The final three were store-ships loaded with supplies: the *Fishburn*, *Golden Grove* and *Borrowdale*.

Esther was travelling with over a thousand other people to an unknown future in an unknown land. She sat up and clung to a nearby post to keep her balance as the *Lady Penrhyn* rocked from side to side in the swell. She had never been on a ship before and now that they were actually on their way, her mind raced. Would the ship manage to stay afloat in the immense depths of the ocean? Would she and her small baby survive the voyage? Would she be attacked by savages at Botany Bay? Did she face a life of slavery in the new colony?

But those worries were soon overwhelmed by the more immediate problem of seasickness. If Esther, Ann and Isabella weren't lying on their mattress groaning, they were vomiting into a bucket. Unlike the sailors' hammocks, which hung steadily as the ship rolled and bucked around them in the swell, their sleeping shelf swayed through every sickening movement. Finally, after several miserable days had passed, their bodies adjusted to the motion and they began to feel less nauseated.

Esther's shipboard life soon settled into a routine. Each morning began with the aroma of freshly baked bread, and the clanging of the ship's brass bell. Every day, if the weather was fine, she was allowed to climb through the hatch to be in the fresh air on the upper deck. Along with some of the other convict women, she was assigned to laundry duty, washing the clothes of everyone on board. Sometimes she would also wash the linen clouts she used for Rosanna's nappies, but usually she just scraped the worst of the mess into a chamber pot before drying the cloth rags out and using them again.

While she worked, she kept an eye on baby Rosanna, who was tucked into a nearby corner of the decking. She could see other women scrubbing the decks with salt water or emptying the many chamber pots into the sea. Every now and then, Ann or Isabella would come over to coo at Rosanna and jiggle her small hand.

While on the upper deck, everyone used the ship's heads as their lavatory. Esther would lift up her skirt and petticoats and (not having any other undergarments) would then sit on the open wooden platform which hung out from the bow, high above the water, and hang on desperately as she was swung up and down by the waves. Then she would clamber down and rinse off from a bucket of seawater. Those women who were menstruating had to beg the sailors for old clothes which they could rip up, as nothing had been provided for them.

Once a week Esther and Ann would drag their mattress and bedding up on deck to be aired in the sunshine, then Isabella would help them scrub their sleeping shelf clean with seawater. From time to time Esther would have to cover her baby's ears when sailors exploded gunpowder between the decks to cleanse the air of disease.

Their food at sea consisted of rice, peas, oatmeal and 'hardtack' crackers, as well as salted beef and pork. The Abrahams family had observed very few Jewish customs, but they had at least followed God's commandment not to eat pork. Esther wondered what to do at first, but then gave herself dispensation, believing that God would prefer that she and her baby survive the journey. Nevertheless, she couldn't help feeling a little disgusted each time she swallowed it.

⬱ 31 May 1787 ⬰

It was in the dark, early hours of the morning when Esther heard Isabella softly groaning. She whispered to her friend, asking the cause of her discomfort, though she had already guessed that it was because Isabella's baby was coming too early.

Esther gently moved the still-sleeping Rosanna to the furthest corner of the mattress. By now Ann had woken as well, and she and Esther did all they could to comfort their suffering bunkmate. As the other women woke, many gathered around to offer help and advice.

Isabella's labour continued through the following hours. With no birthing stool available, she walked up and down the small pathway between the sleeping shelves, crouching down with each contraction. When the baby's birth seemed imminent the convicts' doctor, Dr John Altree, arrived to assist. Isabella, kneeling on all fours, finally pushed her baby into the world.

Isabella called her daughter Mary, and the women rejoiced at her safe arrival. But Mary was so very tiny and weak, Esther could see that life itself was a struggle for her.

After they had been sailing for three weeks, Esther noticed a sudden change in the ship's routine. She and the other convicts were kept below while once again orders were shouted, ropes squealed, sails flapped and bare feet pattered about the upper deck. Then one of the convict women near the hatch called out that they had arrived at the port of Santa Cruz. The smacking of waves against the wooden hull eased as the *Lady Penrhyn* entered the calmer waters of the harbour, but then a large cable roared like a monster when it dropped the anchor through the clear water to bite into the harbour floor. After a final tug, all was quiet. They were at the island of Tenerife, off the west coast of Africa.

As soon as Esther was allowed back on deck, she saw that fires had been lit beneath large cauldrons so that she and others could wash the officers' clothes in the fresh water that was brought on board in wooden casks. The salt water used for laundering at sea had caused fabric to chafe uncomfortably—a particular problem for the officers in their tightly fitting breeches.

The women had nothing more than the clean water, so they bullied the dirt out of each soaked item by beating it against the timber deck. Esther paused to flick water towards a small terrier called Jack that belonged to Lieutenant John Watts. Jack raced up and down, biting at the splashes of water and barking with excitement.

When Esther had finished washing, and every available piece of rigging was hung with dripping clothes, she leaned against the ship's railings and watched the sailors load empty casks into boats. The boats ferried the casks to the shore, to be returned later to each of the eleven ships, replenishing their supplies.

Esther rocked her baby from side to side and looked out at the bustling harbour, while her long dark hair danced in the brisk sea breeze. She could see white houses with blue roofs dotted along the base of the hills, a castle in the distance and a mountain whose peak was lost in the clouds. Then she looked down at her sweet daughter, now eleven weeks old, and was rewarded with a heart-warming smile. She beamed back and kissed Rosanna's little fingers. When she returned her gaze to the harbour, she couldn't help thinking of Isabella's tiny baby, who seemed to find it difficult even to breathe, and she whispered a prayer for her.

During the week they spent in port, Esther and the other women sweltered in the heat. But they enjoyed wonderful treats as well. Their daily ration now included fresh mulberries and luscious figs. Even better for Esther, the salted pork had been replaced with fresh beef. She took her time eating it, savouring the familiar flavour, which could be enjoyed guilt-free. She squeezed some of its juices onto Rosanna's small lips and laughed at the amusing expression she made.

One evening, as she lay on her bed in the dark, she could hear the voices of the nearby *Sirius's* crew floating over the water as they sang around a piano that the ship's doctor had brought with him. The old songs reminded some of the other convict women of happy times in the London drinking houses and several of them softly joined in. When the singing finally stopped, the only sounds Esther could hear were the empty ropes knocking against the masts, and the gentle lap of water against the ship's hull.

≈ 8 June 1787 ≈

Dr Altree had become ill, so Arthur Bowes Smyth, the ship's principal doctor, took over the care of the convicts on the *Lady Penrhyn*. Esther was on the upper deck enjoying the cool breeze when she noticed him descend the ladder to the convicts' deck. He emerged again soon afterwards, carrying a wrapped and motionless bundle in his arms. With a shock Esther saw that he was followed by a distraught Isabella and she realised that tiny Mary's fight for life must have come to an end. She rushed over to put her arm around Isabella's shoulders as Dr Smyth murmured a few muffled words and then tossed the wrapped bundle into the sea.

≈ 9 June 1787 ≈

Esther and the other women were once again confined below as the sailors on the *Lady Penrhyn* prepared to weigh anchor and set sail from

Tenerife. But instead of sailing down the west coast of Africa, where there was a greater risk of becoming becalmed, the fleet swung out across the Atlantic Ocean to catch the trade winds on their way to Rio de Janeiro.

Out in the open ocean once more, the sweating convicts were called up for their daily exercise. Lieutenant Johnston stood by the ship's wheel and cast a watchful eye over the bedraggled women as they clambered up the ladder. Esther's time in the Master's Side of Newgate Prison had allowed her to keep her clothes clean and in good repair, and they stood out against most of the other women's rags. Her behaviour was also noticeably more modest than that of her deck-mates. Surrounded by their coarse chatter, she sat quietly on a coil of rope in the shade of one of the sails, and rocked her baby from side to side on her lap, delighting in Rosanna's sweet smiles. When she looked up she saw the slowly retreating mountain of Tenerife—whose snow-covered peak was now clearly visible.

❧ 12 June 1787 ❧

Sometimes the progress of the fleet was slow, and one afternoon the ships seemed to be hardly moving at all. From the upper deck, Esther saw one of the sweating sailors dive into the cool water below. Some of the women screamed and rushed to look over the side of the ship, expecting to see him disappear beneath the waves. Esther looked too, but there he was, bobbing up and down in full sight. The women cheered at his ability to keep afloat in seas of unimaginable depth, and soon other sailors leapt over the side to show off their own prowess.

Little Jack ran up and down the deck, barking through the railings at all the bodies in the water. But a call of 'Shark!' from the top of the mainmast caused an abrupt end to the fun. Esther watched anxiously as one by one the sailors clambered up the rope ladders and trium-phantly stood dripping on the deck.

❧ 15 June 1787 ❧

As the fleet crossed the Tropic of Cancer, heavy rain prevented the convicts from being allowed on the top deck. Esther crept about in the dark, bent over beneath the low ceiling, and feeling faint from the humidity and lack of air. At night, rats and cockroaches scuttled over the floor and Esther didn't dare step off her sleeping shelf to use a chamber pot.

Violent squalls now battered the fleet, and the women were hurled about below while deafening cracks of thunder rumbled through the ships. The ever-present stench became even more overpowering. Mingled with the odour of stagnant bilge water, rotting food and hundreds of unwashed bodies, there was the pungent reek of overflowing chamber pots, soiled clouts and stale menstrual rags. The air was stifling, the tar between the ship's timbers became sticky in the heat, and tempers frayed. Ann Smith, transported for stealing, picked a fight with the prostitute Charlotte Springmore, transported for throwing acid over a rival, but came off second-best and retreated to her shelf with a bloodied nose.

ᴥ 5 July 1787 ᴥ

Their passage slowed even further as they entered the doldrums. This notorious belt of calm that encircles the earth, just near the equator, is where hurricanes are born. The heat made Esther constantly thirsty. She was sweating heavily and losing even more water in the milk for her baby. Dr Smyth had ordered a small extra cup of water to be sent down for any nursing mothers; but, just as Esther crept back to her shelf, carefully holding her full cup, Ann Smith snatched it for herself. Esther turned to retrieve the cup but, at that moment, they heard Jack barking up above.

'Someone should toss that yapping mutt overboard!' snarled Ann. Then she glared at Esther so menacingly that Esther decided to return to her shelf empty-handed.

ᴥ 14 July 1787 ᴥ

A week after the ships had crossed the equator, Esther was sitting on her favourite coil of rope when a large whale, as long as the ship itself, rose majestically out of the water only twenty yards away. Everyone stopped what they were doing to watch the magnificent creature swim alongside the ship, spouting water high into the cloudless sky. Then its enormous tail towered above them as it slowly disappeared beneath the waves. Esther turned to Lieutenant Watts.

''Tis a shame that little Jack missed the spectacle,' she said. But her smile quickly faded when she saw his face.

'It seems some malicious creature thought fit to toss dear Jack into the sea,' he replied. By the time their voyage was over, four more dogs would be lost overboard from the *Lady Penrhyn*.

⌘ *2 August 1787* ⌘

The ships were buffeted by strong winds and heavy seas as they continued sailing southwards. Esther's dress whipped about her body as she struggled to make progress along the top deck, leaning forward into the wind and clinging to the ropes and rails. But they soon reached their next port: Rio de Janeiro. They would stay a month in this pleasant place, anchored opposite the steps leading to the magnificent Royal Square, while the ships were caulked, their sails repaired and provisions restocked.

Once again, the convicts were treated to fresh meat, along with a wonderful assortment of bananas, yams, lettuces, limes and guavas. Esther had never tasted such delights! And the benevolent Captain Phillip bought soap for the convicts out of his own money.

Sympathetic local African slaves belonging to the Portuguese colonisers paddled through the blue water in canoes shaded by jaunty red-and-white awnings; they carried oranges, which they generously threw up onto the ships for the convicts to eat. For Esther, as she sucked on the delicious golden fruit, this land seemed full of vibrant colour—so different from the drab streets of London. The daily tinkling of convent bells added an almost magical quality to the air and for a moment Esther could forget that she was a convict with an uncertain future.

⌘ *21 August 1787* ⌘

While they were in port, it happened to be the Prince of Portugal's birthday, and as the women lay on their bunks that night they could hear the distant crackle and pop of festive fireworks. The next day

Esther saw Lieutenant Johnston arrive back on board carrying a potted geranium plant—the vibrant green of its leaves contrasted with its spheres of bright red blooms and reminded her of the fireworks she had imagined the night before.

⇜ 4 September 1787 ⇝

It was time to weigh anchor again. Baby Rosanna screamed when a twenty-one-gun salute was fired from the port in honour of the fleet, and was returned by the guns on the nearby *Sirius*. The fleet then headed out across the Atlantic Ocean for Cape Town, with dark and ominous clouds heralding a stormy crossing.

It wasn't long before mountainous seas rocked the ships. The convicts were kept below for days on end, and Esther was cut and bruised from being violently tossed about. A sudden deafening crack shocked the chattering women into silence—the gale-force winds had blown a boom clean off the *Lady Penrhyn*. Tensions rose among the imprisoned women and Esther found it increasingly difficult to protect her rations while dealing with a squirming six-month-old baby. She lost weight and began to look gaunt.

⇜ 13 October 1787 ⇝

After nearly six weeks of howling gales, the fleet finally arrived at the Dutch colony of Cape Town at the bottom of South Africa. When the frenetic work of bringing the ships to anchor had finished and calm had settled, Esther ventured on deck. Cape Town was a disturbing sight after the elegance and gaiety of Rio. Gallows and implements of torture stood along the shore, including huge wheels for stretching and breaking bodies. Esther could even see the mangled remains of unfortunate wretches who had died upon them—some with their right hands cut off and nailed to the side of the wheels.

This would be the fleet's last port of call before Botany Bay, and the provisions bought here would be the most important of all. More than five hundred animals were crammed onto the ships—sheep, cattle, horses, goats, ducks, geese, turkeys, chickens and pigs. The

Lady Penrhyn began to smell like a farmyard as the animals' urine seeped through gaps in the timbers. Potted sugar cane and strawberry plants and young trees of fig, apple, pear and quince were strapped to the sides of the narrow corridors and bales of hay were piled high in every corner. Extra water for the animals was stowed in barrels; rice, barley and corn to eat and to sow were stacked in sturdy burlap sacks which could be used later to make clothing; and wine and spirits were tucked into corners and crevices to give courage to the new colonists.

∾ 11 November 1787 ∾

As the ships departed Cape Town, Esther knew they were leaving behind the last vestige of civilisation and were now heading for a small empty bay that they wouldn't reach for another two or three months.

Many convicts were now given extra tasks caring for the animals on board the ships, and it wasn't long before a marine asked Esther to follow him up through the hatch and down another, then along a narrow passageway to a corner where a carpenter was fitting up stalls. The marine pointed to a white goat tethered to a post and told Esther that it belonged to Lieutenant Johnston. The goat needed to be fed and milked each day, and its stall kept clean for the remainder of the voyage. If she were prepared to undertake this extra task, she could drink half the milk herself.

Esther couldn't believe her good fortune! Each morning she clambered up and down the ladders to the goat pen. She would nestle Rosanna—now seven months old and able to sit up—into a corner, then sit down herself on a rickety stool before gently taking hold of the goat's soft warm teats. At first, it took her a long time to coax the frothy milk into her wooden bucket, and her fingers ached afterwards. But she gradually grew more proficient and was soon able to perform her task quickly. When she finished, she would sit back and carefully pour half the milk into a wooden bowl.

It had an oddly sharp flavour, but she soon became used to it and looked forward to taking her time to enjoy its warming sustenance, far away from the snatching grasp of the other convicts. After indulging in the peace and quiet for as long as she thought prudent, she would clean the stall, fetch fresh water and hay for the goat, then pick up Rosanna— who had been busily putting pieces of straw into her mouth—and re-join the other convicts.

On this, the longest and final leg of their journey, the ships were driven across the great Southern Ocean by the strong westerly winds known as the Roaring Forties—and into the worst storms of all, with bitterly cold winds and huge seas. When thick fog shrouded the fleet, the convicts could hear the eerie boom of guns being fired and bells rung, to signal the ships' positions to one another. And when hail and snow covered the decks, the officers wore greatcoats over their flannel waist-coats. But Esther still had only a single blanket to protect herself and her baby from the cold, so she huddled close to Rosanna, Ann and Isabella.

❧ 29 December 1787 ❧

Another treat awaited the women at the end of December when, still filled with Christmas cheer, Dr Smyth gave each of the *Lady Penrhyn's* convicts some sago pudding made with brown sugar from his own stores. Its sticky sweetness reminded Esther of the rich puddings her mother had made.

❧ 1 January 1788 ❧

As the fleet battled its way into the New Year, a storm was at its height. Startling cracks of thunder shook the ships, and waves crashed over the side of the *Lady Penrhyn*, flooding into the decks below. As the ship mounted the crest of each massive wave she would lurch forward and begin a terrifying descent until she slammed into the base of the next one. The force of the blow would shudder through the timbers and on one occasion it sent Esther and her baby hurtling into the icy water mixed with overflowing commodes and vomit that sloshed around the floor. Esther struggled quickly to her feet, but she and Rosanna were already miserably wet and cold. As the night ached past, Esther could hear chicken coops breaking their fastenings and crashing into the walls above, and larger animals tumbling about in their pens.

By morning, a pink tinge suffused the thinning clouds and the returning light raised the officers' spirits. They decided it was time to reassert their dominance over the seas, so Esther and the other women were given mops and buckets and ordered to return the salty water to its source. Gradually order was returned and the routines of shipboard life were re-established. The following night luminous jellyfish lit up the sea's surface, and the Aurora Australis flew across the heavens in glowing, dancing streamers of red, orange, yellow and white.

The passage from the Cape had been slower than expected, and the hay to feed the suffering animals was now exhausted. The only feed left for Esther's goat was stale bread. One morning, when she arrived at the goat-pen, she saw that a nearby sheep had starved to death. Each precious sheep, cow or chicken represented the beginning of stocks that would be needed to feed the thousand colonists, and every loss was a significant blow.

7 January 1788

After nearly two months at sea, the lookout on the *Lady Penrhyn* shouted that he could see Van Diemen's Land. When Esther emerged from the hatch the following morning, she saw a rocky coastline and a land that was uniformly green. The *Lady Penrhyn* rounded the southern tip of Van Diemen's Land and began her run north up its coast towards the mainland, but powerful northerly winds bore down upon her, slowing her progress.

20 January 1788

It took ten frustrating days for the ships to make their way up the coast to where they finally swung into a bay after travelling fifteen thousand miles from their homeland. Captain Phillip had sailed on ahead with the faster ships—HMS *Supply*, *Friendship*, *Scarborough* and *Alexander*—to begin building shelters at Botany Bay, but he had arrived only a couple of days earlier. Lieutenant Ball from the *Supply* rowed out in a long boat to guide the *Lady Penrhyn* to a mooring, and the officers all cheered for the safe arrival of the whole fleet.

When the convicts were allowed onto the upper deck, Esther over-heard the officers congratulating each other on the success of the voyage—during the whole eight-month journey no one had succumbed to scurvy and not a single ship was ever out of sight of the others in its group for more than an hour. Across the fleet, a total of forty convicts had died (many of whom were in poor health before the voyage). *Lady Penrhyn* had lost only two of its convicts plus Isabella's baby, Mary. Now the voyage was finally over, Esther could hardly believe that she and her baby had survived the journey, with its cramped con-ditions and terrifying storms. She bounced Rosanna on her lap and quietly whispered a prayer of thanks.

Botany Bay. For so long it had been just a name, but now here it was, a place as real as any other. It felt so very far away from England, so unfamiliar and strange. There were no busy towns, no farms, no colour. All was green and brown, except for the piercing blue sky above.

Esther learned with surprise that an Englishman already lay buried on the shore. A sailor named Forby Sutherland, who had been on the *Endeavour* with Captain Cook eighteen years earlier, had died of tuberculosis while they were moored in Botany Bay. Cook had named the south point of the bay in his honour. The bay itself had apparently been named after the many plants Joseph Banks, the ship's botanist, had acquired there.

Esther felt a mixture of excitement and apprehension at the thought of her new life in this strange land. While she watched the bustling activity on the shores of the bay—where marines were busily cutting grass, fetching fresh water and netting fish—she imagined walking along the shore herself. But, as her eyes followed the line of rocks, she instinctively stepped back from the ship's railing when a native man appeared from among the trees. He was dark-skinned, slender and completely naked, with short dark, curly hair. And he held a long spear with a bone point.

One of the sailors had told Esther that all the native men were missing a front tooth—as a sign of their manhood. Coincidentally, Captain Phillip had also lost a front tooth, so that, when the native men came close enough to see his smile, they saw what seemed to them the reassuringly familiar symbol of an initiated man.

When the British officers had first rowed ashore, the native men had shouted at them and brandished their spears. But Captain Phillip had offered them beads and indicated that he was looking for water. The native men had then shown him where a bubbling stream emptied into the bay.

❧ 21 January 1788 ☙

Lieutenant Johnston was working his marines hard: clearing land, pitching tents, constructing a saw-pit and building shelters for the starving animals still on board the ships. They were making good progress, so he was disappointed when he received orders from Captain Phillip to join him with a small party of marines to explore the next bay to the north in case it proved more suitable. Captain Cook had marked the bay on his map, naming it Port Jackson, but not entered it.

Captain Phillip had not been impressed with Botany Bay. It was too shallow for ships to anchor close to the shore; the fine meadows that Cook had described were nothing but boggy marshland; the freshwater creeks were not large enough for the long-term needs of a growing colony; the black sandy soil did not promise to be very fertile; and the bay was exposed to the fury of the south-easterly winds.

When one of the sailors aboard the *Lady Penrhyn* told the women about the delay, Esther's heart sank. Ann Smith rushed towards the sailor, beating her fists against his chest with frustration. They had all counted the days until they could step free of the cramped and unpleasant conditions on board, but now they would have to wait even longer. In the oppressive heat of summer, this unexpected setback seemed intolerable, although Esther was also nervous about what would happen when they finally did move ashore.

The explorers set off in three small boats rigged with sails. They travelled up the coast, carefully keeping clear of the wild surf that crashed against the high sandstone cliffs, while they searched for a gap between them. As they went, they passed groups of natives who shouted angrily: 'Warra, warra!'

Then, just as Cook had marked on his map, they saw an opening more than half a mile wide. The boats swung round to pass between the massive heads and into a harbour that stretched before them for many miles. It was, according to Captain Phillip, *the finest harbour in the world, in which a thousand sail of the line may ride in the most perfect security.*

Johnston saw a string of bays to the left, each with a crescent-shaped beach of white sand peeping from behind its protective headland. To the right, wide inlets ran away into the hinterland. When the boats passed one of the northern bays, a group of natives waded out into the water, unarmed, to meet with them. Captain Phillip was so impressed by their 'confidence and manly behaviour' that he immediately named the bay Manly Cove.

The officers camped for the night on a small beach to the south of the heads, and the following day they rowed further down the harbour. The green land slipped by on either side until they rowed past a reedy bay to one that had a fresh stream flowing into it and a shore that fell away so steeply that ships would be able to anchor close in. Captain Phillip named it Sydney Cove, in honour of the British Home Secretary, and decided to pack up the whole fleet and move the settlement to its shore. The explorers didn't waste time going ashore but returned immediately to the ships in Botany Bay.

∽ *24 January 1788* ∾

Esther and the other women were once again confined below while the *Lady Penrhyn* was prepared to set sail early on the next day. Not long afterwards, she heard the sailors above shouting—two unfamiliar ships had come into view on the horizon. The sailors began speculating about the reason for their arrival. Were they storeships from England, already bringing extra supplies for the new colony? Was one of them HMS *Bounty* with Captain Bligh, who had planned to visit the colony on his way to Tahiti? Or were they Dutch ships, sent to prevent a British landing?

The British flag was hurriedly hoisted at Point Sutherland.

CHAPTER THREE

A New Beginning

The following morning, Lieutenant Johnston set off in the speedy *Supply* with Captain Phillip, Lieutenant Philip King from the *Sirius*, some marines and a few convicts to make a start on establishing a settlement at Sydney Cove. Although they sailed at daybreak, a strong gale slowed their progress and they didn't arrive until late in the evening, so they spent the night on board the ship.

As the morning sunlight tinged the leaves at the top of the gum trees, the officers climbed into boats to row ashore. The convict James Ruse jumped out near the water's edge to carry Johnston on his back across the mud flats, setting him down as the first officer ashore.

Soon afterwards, the morning's peace was disturbed when one of the convicts began hacking into a gum tree with his axe. The thuds resounded around the cove until they were overcome by the sound of tearing timber as the tree toppled over. Then another tree was felled, and another, until a small area had been cleared on the eastern side of the stream.

At the edge of the new clearing the marines erected a flagpole, and Captain Phillip formally took possession of the land for King George III.

Britain's flag was raised to the top of the pole and it slowly unfurled in the warm breeze, flashing its garish colours to the surrounding countryside. Although the flag had the red cross of St George for England and the diagonal white-on-blue cross of St Andrew for Scotland, it did not yet include the red saltire of St Patrick for Ireland.

As the sun set below the unknown horizon, the officers and marines gathered in the clearing. They drank toasts to the King, to the Royal Family and to the success of the colony, and then they gave three hearty cheers, which were echoed by the sailors still on board the *Supply*. Between each toast, the marines fired volleys into the air. The surrounding animal life was shocked into silence, but the men, so preoccupied with the hope and promise of their new colony, were unaware of the unnatural stillness that surrounded them. From that moment, the tranquillity of the cove was forever transformed by the busyness of an ever-growing settlement.

Back at Botany Bay, the mysterious ships turned out to be French, under the command of the Comte de La Perouse. He had lost some of his boats and fourteen men when they were massacred by natives in the Navigator Islands in the South Pacific Ocean. So he had fled to Botany Bay, where he had expected to find an already established settlement, to build new boats. The British officers still there had welcomed him as guests of the British Government, and left him to his tasks while they moved up the coast to Port Jackson.

At seven o'clock in the evening the last of the fleet from Botany Bay entered Port Jackson, and by eight o'clock they were all safely anchored off the small cove about four miles in from the heads. Still below deck, Esther was unsure whether to look forward to walking along its shores or to cherish every last minute of her time in the safety of the *Lady Penrhyn*.

⍛ *27 January 1788* ⍛

Many of the male convicts who were unloaded from the *Scarborough* the following day were stepping onto dry land for the first time in over a year. They outnumbered their marine guards and could have run away if they had wanted to. But where would they go? They had no idea how to survive on their own and were completely dependent on the food given to them by their guards. And the marines, in turn, were dependent on the convicts' labour to build the settlement and establish the farms that would provide everyone with food.

Captain Phillip had only three months to unload everything from three of the convict transport ships, the *Lady Penrhyn*, *Charlotte* and *Scarborough*, because those ships were contracted to the British East India Company and due to leave for China. Six of the other ships would have to depart eight weeks later, leaving only the navy-owned *Sirius* and *Supply* to serve the colony.

There was so much to do. The cows, horses, sheep and goats that had survived the voyage needed to be lowered by rope into boats and rowed ashore; crops had to be planted; storehouses built for supplies; fences set up to contain the livestock; a hospital built for the sick; and tents and huts erected to house all the colonists before winter set in. It was all urgently required by the fledgling colony and there was no one to do the work except the convicts, few of whom possessed any useful skills for building a settlement.

Among them were twelve carpenters, but only a couple of farmers: James Ruse, the man who had carried Johnston ashore, and the brewer, James Squire. Instead, there were stocking weavers, milliners, watchmakers, ivory turners, pin-headers and book binders. Whatever their previous trade, all the men were now handed axes and saws and ordered to begin clearing the land. To make matters worse, the commander of the marines, Major Robert Ross, refused to allow his men to be used to supervise the convicts' labour, arguing that their only role was to protect the colony. So Captain Phillip had to appoint overseers from among the convicts themselves, a move that established a new culture in which those in authority were considered to be not much different from anyone else.

And so the work began. The few axe thuds that had so unceremoniously disturbed the peace on the first day were followed by sustained attacks on the surrounding forest. Before long a team of tree fellers walked around the point into a pretty, crescent-shaped cove that was sacred to the Gadigal people.

The Gadigal was a clan of about sixty people whose land lay along the southern side of Port Jackson. The cove was where Gadigal boys became men—in an intense two-day ceremony that included having deep parallel lines cut across their chests with sharp shells. The long strip of skin between the lines would be peeled off and the skin pinched together to make a prominent and glorious scar. In the highly charged atmosphere at the height of the ceremony, each boy would have a front tooth knocked out of its socket.

When the sun rose above the ridge the following morning, causing the dewy leaves of the eucalypts to sparkle, the young men would walk proudly through the cathedral of glittering trees, carrying their new spears and smiling through their pain to prove their manhood.

But on this day the convict workers were ordered to clear the land of trees to make space for planting crops. They started at the sandy beach and steadily moved inland, cutting down everything that stood in their way.

Trees that were hundreds of years old were sliced through until all that was left were their stumps, bleeding red sap into the earth. The trunks were dragged away by teams of convicts hauling on chains. The birds and animals of the forest fled in panic. The devastating advance continued to a rocky ridge, stopping short of a pair of forest red gum saplings.

⌁ 28 January 1788 ⌁

The twenty-eight marine wives and their seventeen children were brought ashore next, but Esther was still kept on board with the other convict women. After so long a journey, they were forced to remain confined in their cramped and smelly prison, even though they could hear the bustle and activity of the settlement. Esther's only respite was when she was allowed to scramble up and down the ladders to milk Johnston's goat each morning. The stiflingly hot days often ended in violent thunderstorms, with terrifying cracks of thunder that made Esther even more anxious about moving ashore.

❧ 30 January 1788 ❧

The chattering in the semi-darkness below deck quietened one morning when a marine climbed down the ladder and called out a list of six names—the last belonging to Esther's friend, Ann Inett. The chosen women were taken back up the ladder and disappeared.

Half an hour later Ann returned looking flushed and excited. She had been asked to go to a place called Norfolk Island with Lieutenant King to establish another colony there. He was taking twenty-four people, including fifteen of the best-behaved convicts, and enough stores to last them for six months. It seemed a good opportunity for advancement to Ann, so she had agreed to go; one of the other women had declined, not being able to face another voyage so soon.

Esther asked Ann how far away it was. A thousand miles! Ann said that apparently Captain Cook had reported it had tall pine trees suitable for making ships' masts, and good supplies of flax to make clothing and ropes—all of which made the island a valuable possession. So Captain Phillip wanted to claim it for Britain. She added excitedly that they would be leaving in ten days' time.

❧ 1 February 1788 ❧

Meanwhile, Captain Phillip sent Lieutenant King back to the French visitors at Botany Bay with an offer to send their letters and reports to Europe with the returning ships of the First Fleet. The Comte de La Perouse gladly accepted Phillip's offer and sent all his dispatches to Port Jackson before his two ships departed.

It was a fortunate decision. A few weeks later, both French ships were wrecked on a coral reef in the Pacific Ocean and the men were never found, but La Perouse's valuable reports were safely delivered to the French Ambassador in England, and they finally reached his homeland and his king.

❧ 5 February 1788 ❧

After most of the animals had been landed from the ships in Sydney Cove, the convict women were at last allowed on the upper deck and

Esther could begin to make sense of her new home. A stream flowed into the cove, dividing the land in two. It rose from springs in swampy ground further south and flowed down through a thick forest of gum trees, across mud flats at the water's edge and out into the cove.

On either side of the stream gentle hills sloped up to form a shallow basin. Captain Phillip had chosen to live on the eastern side of the cove, together with most of the officers. His portable timber-and-canvas house immediately became the focus of the colony. Lieutenant Johnston had pitched his own round campaign tent a little further uphill, where it commanded an expansive view of the motley settlement and the grand harbour.

Across the stream on the western side, which was steeper and rockier, the two hundred and fifty marines had made their camp. The neat line of tents fronted a track which became the first road in the colony, known as High Street. The main female convict tents were being set out a little further to the north. The male convicts had been given a length of canvas and told to fend for themselves. Their rough shelters, now strung between the trees, littered the hillside in an area that quickly became known as The Rocks.

The day was already warm and a heady scent wafted across the water from the crushed leaves of the many felled gum trees. Esther took deep breaths, delighting in the clean, fresh fragrance after the below-deck stench. Against a sky of brightest blue, colourful birds flew overhead with raucous cries, and pesky flies buzzed around her perspiring face.

Despite the oppressive heat, there was activity everywhere—some men were felling trees, others were sawing timber; some were dragging loads of provisions, and yet others were building a blacksmith's forge. Tents and cooking fires speckled the landscape, and there was a clamour of shouted orders. Most of the ships' boats were being used to ferry stores to the shore, but Esther could see a few further out in the harbour where men were hauling fishing nets. When they returned to the shore, Esther watched as some native men helped to drag the nets ashore and were rewarded with part of the catch. She hoped that she would soon be given some fresh fish to eat herself, instead of more repugnant salted pork.

While they waited to be allowed on shore, Esther and the other convict women washed their hair and most of their belongings in buckets of sea water which they hauled up over the side of the ship. They took turns to comb out each other's tangled hair while they laughed and gossiped. Some, like Esther, had been allowed to bring some extra clothes with them and these were now retrieved from the stores below. But most had only the rags they were wearing and were now given new convict dresses from the government supplies. The feisty Ann Smith tossed hers onto the deck, vowing she would wear no prison garb as she intended to escape as soon as they were let ashore.

Five women considered to be of good character were chosen to work as domestic servants for the government officers. They were disembarked and rowed over to a special tent that had been set up for them on the eastern side of the cove. Esther sighed. She held little hope of attaining such a respected position, especially with a young child to care for.

❧ 6 February 1788 ❧

The following morning, when Esther climbed up the ladder to milk the goat, she found the stalls for the animals all empty, and a nearby sailor told her they had been landed the previous day. And at last, after eleven long days, everything was ready for the remaining female convicts to disembark. Beginning at six o'clock in the morning, the whole day was spent ferrying the two hundred women and their belongings to the shore.

The camp buzzed with chatter as the marines led the women to the clean, white communal tents that had been erected for them between clumps of trees at the base of the rocky western hillside.

Esther stepped gingerly onto the shore carrying Rosanna, who was nearly one and the first free Jew in the land. Esther walked up the beach and looked around, still gently swaying. Two older women, each of them holding a young child of her own, arrived on shore from the *Charlotte* at the same time.

Gentle Susannah Holmes was twenty-four. She had been convicted of stealing clothing and silver spoons from her employer, and been sent to Norwich Castle Gaol, where Harry, her two-year-old son, had been born.

The more daring Mary Broad was twenty-three, with brown hair and soft grey eyes. She had been convicted of highway robbery in Devon and imprisoned on the *Dunkirk* hulk. The guards on the hulks would sometimes withhold food to gain sexual favours—and Mary had been pregnant when she had been taken aboard the *Charlotte*. The five-month-old daughter she now held in her arms, named Charlotte Spence, had been born during the voyage to Botany Bay.

The three young mothers were naturally drawn to each other and they followed a marine across to one of the tents, where they settled their few belongings together. Esther had kept some of that morning's ration of bread to give to Rosanna during the day, but the bully Ann Smith snatched it from the folded shawl by Esther's feet. Esther took a deep breath and realised she would have to remain vigilant.

By the time the last of the convict women had stepped ashore it was six o'clock in the evening. The stiflingly hot day was cooling, clouds grey as gunmetal were loitering in the south, and thunder rumbled through the heavens. The first heavy drops of rain splattered down upon the scarred land as Esther and her new companions collected their evening meal which included some delicious fresh fish.

For some of the male convicts, after so long in prison conditions, the sight of the convict women—with their bright smiles and new dresses, so happily put on that morning—was simply irresistible. For a few women used to trading their favours, this was an opportunity to take advantage of the sexual desperation around them, and they sought alliances with men who they thought might improve their situation. With six men for every woman, they could afford to be choosy.

Then it began to pelt with rain and sailors came ashore with rum to spare. As the ground rapidly turned to slush beneath their feet, couples scattered in all directions in an attempt to find shelter among the bedraggled canvas. The remaining men prowled the settlement in search of other willing women. If the few marines had tried to prevent the couplings, they would likely have proved incapable of controlling the many hundreds of prisoners, so no restraining orders were given.

Esther stayed in her assigned tent with Susannah, Mary and some of the other convict women. More than once, one of the wandering men slunk in to grab one of the women. But the others would rush over, screaming, beating and kicking until he gave up and was driven away.

The drains dug around the tents had been designed to divert the kind of light runoff that the misty showers of England produced, but this was not the gentle rain of home. This was a cascade to mock the feeble attempts men had made to control its flow. This rain belonged to a land where flood and drought dominated the landscape. It beat down relentlessly upon the cleared ground, creating rivulets which eroded the sandy soil into crisscrossed runnels of water that bled down to the shoreline to be lapped up by the waiting waves. It soon seeped under the women's tent from all sides, and they huddled together in the centre to stay dry. To Esther, it felt as though the pounding drops were intent on drumming the canvas into the ground and washing away the intruders who clung to the shore.

At midnight, a massive thunderbolt struck a tree in the midst of the camp and, with a deafening crack, split the tree in two, killing the pig, six sheep and two lambs that were penned beneath it. It was a confronting beginning to Esther's new life.

ᴄ᠊ 7 February 1788 ᠊ᴄ

When Rosanna's hungry cries woke Esther in the morning, the sun was already warming the tent and steam was rising from the sodden ground outside. With her baby fed, Esther combed her long dark hair with her fingers and plaited it loosely down her back. Then she picked up Rosanna and stepped out into the early morning sunshine to find Johnston's goat.

The cove was a slushy morass and even though she stepped gingerly across the sludge, the edge of her skirt was soon caked with mud. To make her way across the gurgling stream, she had to find the row of large stepping stones that had been placed in it for this purpose. She came to a group of marines who were dragging the dead animals away from the still-smouldering tree. Looking anxiously at each animal, she was relieved to see that Johnston's goat was not among them.

Esther searched further up the hill until she finally spotted her goat tied to a stake up near Lieutenant Johnston's round tent. She hesitated to venture so far from the main camp, but she could hear the goat's distressing bleats, so she picked up her skirt with her free hand and strode up the hill.

She saw the red geranium Johnston had bought in Rio de Janeiro sitting in its pot by the tent's entrance, its showy flowers blooming daringly against the earth-splattered canvas. But Johnston himself was absent. Esther settled Rosanna nearby and set to work on the poor goat, whose udder was painfully distended from missing the previous day's milking.

When she was finished, Esther took a peek inside the large tent. It was dry and spacious, with all that was required for daily comfort—a table, chair, writing desk, two wooden chests and a straw mattress made up with clean bedding. She smiled as an idea formed in her head. She poured half the milk into a wooden bowl on the table, then picked up Rosanna and launched back down the hill.

She walked up to the first marine she came across and explained to him that she wished to offer her services as a domestic servant to Lieutenant Johnston, including the task of milking his goat—a duty at which she had already proven herself proficient. The marine promised to convey her proposal to Johnston.

When Esther arrived back at the women's tent, she found that everyone had been ordered to witness the formal establishment of the colony. So she walked down to the flagpole with Susannah and Mary.

The neatly dressed marine wives stood together in the clearing. The female convicts gathered behind them, together with all the bewildered children, while the male convicts slumped beyond them, groggy with liquor and lack of sleep. Suddenly the raucous laughter of a native bird broke out and reverberated around the cove.

The regimental flag, with its elegant wreath of thistles and roses on a white background, fluttered proudly in the warm breeze as the four companies of marines formed ordered lines behind it. Esther saw Lieutenant Johnston take his place at the front of his men. Lieutenant King would soon be leaving for Norfolk Island, and Captain Phillip had chosen Johnston to replace King as his aide-de-camp.

Johnston's black shoes were highly polished; tightly buttoned black leather gaiters hugged the calves of his long legs; clean white breeches fitted snugly beneath a red jacket that hung in tails at his back and was decorated with gold braid and shiny brass buttons. A snowy cravat nestled about his neck and a red sash was tied around his waist. Each of his shoulders was decorated with a gold fringe that quivered with his every movement. His sword swung at his side, and he stood tall and proud—a king's man doing his duty.

The drums and fifes of the band burst into a tune as the marines formed a guard of honour for Captain Phillip, dipping their flag as he approached. He removed his hat in salute and took his place before the assembly, praising the marines for their commendable behaviour since they first boarded the ships a year earlier. The convicts were ordered to sit down and the marines moved to encircle them.

Two red leather cases rested on a camp table. They contained commissions from King George III appointing Captain Phillip as Governor of New South Wales and setting out the legal structure of the new colony. They were solemnly read out by Captain David Collins, the colony's judge advocate—even though he had no legal training.

As their new governor, Phillip stood before the crowd in his neat blue naval uniform and carefully explained the rules that were necessary for their survival. The time had come to assert his authority and bring order to the colony. To begin with, from this day forward, any man who entered the women's tents at night would be shot. And because their food was so precious, any theft of food or animals would be punishable by death. It was vital that everyone should work towards the establishment of the settlement; any able convict who did not work would not be given food. He added that no one would be asked to work beyond their capacity, and he intended to reward convicts who proved themselves trustworthy and industrious. He believed they could all look forward to a promising future. Three volleys were then fired into the air, with the band playing 'God Save the King' between each one.

With the ceremony over, the convicts scattered about the cove and the officers dined with their new governor. But the many flies had already infested the mutton with maggots. There was much the British needed to learn about this new country.

∽ 8 February 1788 ∾

The following morning Esther again walked up the hill to milk the goat, and this time Johnston was sitting on a stool by the side of his tent. He thanked her for milking the goat the previous morning, and told her that he had received her offer of services—but would she be able to manage the work in addition to caring for her child? Esther insisted that she could. In that case, Johnston said, he was glad to agree to her proposal, adding that he would arrange for her to move to the closest tent on the eastern side of the stream where the other female servants lived.

Esther held Rosanna up and twirled with happiness as she made her way back to the women's tent.

∽ 10 February 1788 ∾

On the first Sunday after the women had disembarked, the colonists gathered together for a religious service and the first marriage ceremonies in the colony. Everyone, whatever their religion, was required to attend the Anglican service. Five convict couples became legally wed that day. Esther watched wistfully as pretty Susannah Holmes married Henry Kable, the father of her toddler—both signing the register with a cross. The pragmatic Mary Broad married William Bryant, a Cornish fisherman whom she knew from both the *Dunkirk* and the *Charlotte*.

Each male convict had been allocated to one of the many tasks necessary to build the settlement. Some of the female convicts were assigned as cooks—they roasted meat or made damper on shovels they held in the fires (which ruined the shovels for digging). Others took turns to sew or wash clothes, gathering each day along the sides of the stream to thrash the muddy garments against the rocks before rinsing them in the clear water and lying them along the bank to dry in the hot summer sun. As huts were gradually built, housekeepers were assigned to keep them in order for the small group of convict men who shared each one of them.

William Bryant was already planning a promising future for himself and his new bride. He explained to Governor Phillip that the colonists would need plenty of fresh fish to survive until the livestock increased in number. Of course, that would require proper management of the fishing activities—and he was the very man for that task. The governor agreed, and ordered a hut to be built for Bryant around the point in the farming cove so that he could keep an eye on all the fishing equipment and the boats. As Bryant's wife, Mary would take on his housekeeping duties.

✎ 18 February 1788 ✎

Many convicts were already getting sunburnt. As Esther had some experience with making hats, she was asked to try weaving one out of the fronds of the cabbage tree palms that grew prolifically around the cove, and to teach the skill to Susannah Kable. After some experimenting, which had both women in fits of laughter, Esther finally came up with a functional pattern. She plaited the leaves into flat strips which she could then sew into ever-widening circles, to create a dome, and then a wide brim.

The two women sat under the shade of a large tree while Esther taught Susannah how to replicate the design. Rosanna stood on her wobbly legs, holding onto Esther's shoulder and pointing at Harry as he toddled about over the rough ground, bringing leaves and twigs back to his mother.

While they worked, Susannah told Esther about her time in Norwich Castle Gaol. Her new husband, Henry Kable, had also been a prisoner there and they had become close. Kable had applied to marry her three times, but the prison governor had always refused to give his permission. Nevertheless, Harry was conceived and born while they were both still imprisoned.

Eight months later, Susannah had been chained to two other women and put with her baby on the outer seat of a coach. They had travelled with a gaoler named John Simpson three hundred miles to the *Dunkirk* hulk, where they would be kept until they could be transported to Botany Bay with the First Fleet. To Susannah's great distress, Henry Kable had not been permitted to go with them.

When they had finally reached the *Dunkirk*, its captain had refused to accept baby Harry because there were no papers for him. Susannah had been standing on the damp wooden deck, still chained to the others, when the captain had nodded to a guard who stepped forward and wrenched her baby from her arms.

John Simpson had asked if the child might remain with his mother until the matter could be resolved, but the captain had flatly refused. So Simpson had reluctantly accepted the squirming baby and climbed back over the side of the hulk, into the waiting rowboat. Overcome with grief, Susannah had sunk, sobbing, to her knees.

She learned afterwards that when Simpson reached the shore, instead of returning directly to Norwich, he caught the next coach to London and sat with baby Harry on his lap, rocking and jolting all the way of the two-hundred-mile journey. As he travelled, he stopped at inns along the way to coax a little warmed milk or oatmeal pap past the baby's lips and empty its nappy.

When Simpson finally reached London, he left the baby with a woman he knew there and went straight to the office of the Home Secretary, Lord Sydney, demanding a meeting. At first Simpson was refused, but he waited outside until he caught sight of Lord Sydney and insisted on speaking to him.

By the end of their meeting, an order allowing baby Harry to join his mother had been duly signed, as had another requesting the child's father join his family on their journey to Botany Bay. A letter was also despatched to the *Dunkirk*, informing Susannah of the decision. Simpson had then travelled with baby Harry all the way back to

Norwich Castle Gaol to collect Henry Kable and then escort them both back to the *Dunkirk*. Because of his kindness, the little family had finally been reunited.

Susannah then explained to Esther that a generous woman named Mrs Jackson had read about their plight in the London papers and had raised twenty pounds (equal to about two-thirds the annual wages of a farm worker) on their behalf. Mrs Jackson had spent the money on books, clothes and farming tools she thought would be useful to them in the new colony. Then she had wrapped them all in a hessian parcel, which had been given to Captain Sinclair of the *Alexander* to be handed to Susannah after their arrival at Botany Bay.

But Susannah now feared that Captain Sinclair had plundered the parcel. Apart from a few books, he said he couldn't locate any of the other items. Henry Kable had approached him several times about it, but the captain had sent him away. Sinclair had even boasted that, as Kable was a convict, there was nothing he could do about the missing items.

➣ 20 February 1788 ➢

When Esther arrived to milk the goat the following morning, Johnston was sitting under the shade of a nearby tree, scraping some mud from his boots. He told her that he had been exploring further up the harbour with Governor Phillip. Esther asked if they had come across any fierce savages.

Johnston replied that the natives seemed to be a friendly people who had shown no animosity towards them. And why should they? He believed they would derive great benefit from the arrival of the British— they did not yet even have the wheel. They had to hunt daily for food, but he was certain that once they saw the British farming practices they would be astonished by such productive management of the land.

'They *look* fierce,' insisted Esther. That was a good thing, Johnston explained, as it might stop convicts from straying into the woods. Ten had escaped already, including Ann Smith. Most had straggled back into the settlement after having walked to Botany Bay in the vain hope of gaining passage on the French ships. They had been turned away with a day's food for their return journey and had brought the disturbing news that La Perouse had been forced to fire at the natives, to prevent them stealing from the French camp.

Before she left Johnston's tent, Esther mentioned Susannah's missing gifts, and he offered to look into the matter.

✐ 23 February 1788 ✐

Good catches of fish confirmed the importance of William Bryant's work, and in accordance with his wishes a two-room hut had been built for him at Farm Cove. From her new home Mary could see the grapevines and apple, orange and pear trees that had already been planted in the government farm. They added a familiar aspect to the otherwise strange landscape.

✐ 27 February 1788 ✐

Most of the convicts behaved well in their new open gaol. They felt a great sense of relief to be off the ships, and to have something meaningful to do. But a few could not break their old thieving habits, and by the end of their first month on land three men had been convicted of stealing food from the stores. True to his word, Governor Phillip ordered them to be hanged.

At five o'clock that afternoon all the convicts were ordered to gather to witness the punishment, in the hope that it would deter future thefts.

The afternoon sunshine was still warm as Esther and Susannah stood together at the edge of the crowd to watch the condemned men be marched by marines over to a tree between the convict camps. Harry and Rosanna sat on the ground by their mothers' feet, playing with stones. There was a hum of whispers as everyone waited for the first man to be ordered up the ladder to the hangman's platform.

But then the murmuring stopped abruptly. A marine with a piece of paper in his hand ran splashing across the stream to reach Major Ross, the marine commander. After Ross had read the order, he announced that Governor Phillip had delayed the execution of Henry Lovell and Joseph Hall for twenty-four hours while he examined their records.

But Thomas Barrett, who had also been caught forging coins out of officers' buttons during the voyage, was to receive no such reprieve. Just eighteen years old, he was already the colony's most troublesome criminal. He climbed the ladder and turned deathly pale as he waited on the platform.

However, the convict who had been assigned as hangman could not bring himself to place the noose around Barrett's neck. The stream gurgled beside the silent crowd.

Major Ross shouted at the hangman to proceed, but he stood there, looking down at his feet. Still sitting by his mother, Harry began hitting two stones together.

Click. Click. Click.

Major Ross's voice rang out once more, declaring that if the hangman did not perform the deed that very instant, the marines would shoot him dead.

Click. Click.

Ross motioned impatiently for a marine officer to step up and take over the task. As the noose was finally laid around Barrett's neck, the condemned man blurted out a confession. The chaplain uttered a final prayer and Barrett called for everyone to take warning from his unhappy fate.

Then he dropped, twitching and writhing as his life was wrenched away. Barrett's body was left to hang for an hour before it was cut down and buried near the gallows.

⟫ 28 February 1788 ⟪

The next day everyone gathered again for the hangings of Lovell and Hall. But almost every convict in the settlement had signed an appeal for clemency, and Governor Phillip instead banished the two men for life: Lovell to Norfolk Island and Hall to a small, barren island in the middle of the harbour, where a boat delivered rations to him once a week—earning the island the name of 'Pinchgut'.

Later, another offender, with the rope about his neck, was offered a pardon on condition that he took over the post of hangman.

CHAPTER FOUR

A Hut to Call Home

The soil around Sydney Cove was proving to be too sandy for growing crops, so Governor Phillip decided to spend a few days exploring a bay to the north of Port Jackson in the hope of finding better farming land there. Esther took Rosanna down to the cove to see the exploring party, which included Lieutenant Johnston, set off up the harbour in the governor's cutter and a long boat.

As it was a Sunday morning, at ten o'clock the drummer boy summoned everyone, dressed as well as they might, to gather beneath the trees for the Sunday service. As usual, everyone was required to attend the Anglican services, whatever their religious beliefs. Esther met up with Susannah and Mary. While they waited for the service to begin, they watched some native women fishing from canoes out in the bay. The canoes were made from long sheets of stringybark gathered at each end and tied with vine, large sticks wedged across the centre to keep them open. They floated low in the water and the women had built small fires on mounds of clay at one end so that when they caught a fish they could cook and eat it immediately.

One of the native women, who had a young child sitting on her shoulders, was singing to the fish. Mary explained that they didn't use any bait when they were fishing, but made hooks in the shape of a crescent moon out of pieces of shell, which they jiggled up and down to lure the fish to bite. She dropped her voice to add that they also cut off the top two joints of a little finger. Apparently, spiders' webs were wound around the joint when they were little girls, and after a time the end of the finger dropped off. But she didn't know whether it was done to help them wind their fishing lines, or as some sort of ceremonial way of 'giving back'.

ᴒ 3 March 1788 ᴐ

The next morning Esther left her tent early to milk the goat. The surrounding settlement was still silent in its sleepiness as the now familiar morning chorus of birds rang throughout the cove and the gum leaves hung sugar-frosted with dew. Esther took a moment to stand still and admire the glassy water of the harbour, which reflected the pale pink sky.

Her initial apprehension about being able to cope with life in this strange land was beginning to dissipate. Now that the settlement was established, she felt a little safer, and her work for Johnston seemed manageable.

Rosanna squirmed in her arms and brought Esther's thoughts back to the task at hand. Esther set her daughter down and watched her crawl purposefully across the dusty ground. Rosanna was nearly a year old and could walk a few steps if she held her mother's hand. Esther scooped her up again and continued up the hill.

After Esther had milked the goat, she tidied the inside of Johnston's tent, then searched the nearby scrub for a fallen leafy branch she could use to sweep the tent's earthen floor. When she had finished, she tied the door flap securely closed before returning to the main camp. All she had to do now, until Johnston returned, was to milk his goat each day.

ᴒ 9 March 1788 ᴐ

The expedition into Broken Bay was not as successful as Governor Phillip had hoped. They found no suitable farming land and could not even find the river that emptied into the bay. But they did discover another natural harbour, which Phillip described as the finest piece of water he had ever seen. He named it Pitt Water in honour of the British Prime Minister, William Pitt the Younger.

When they returned, Johnston described to Esther what fine mimics the native men were, and how the officers had often roared with laughter at their imitation of them. Because they lacked beards, the gender of the British men continued to confuse the locals, and Johnston had twice ordered a marine to drop his breeches to settle the matter.

His tone became more serious when he told her about an aspect of the local culture which he feared would cause problems. They left their weapons and tools all about the place, quite confident that they would be there when next required. Their children were taught never to steal, but that ideal was not shared by all of the British people, least of all the convicts. Governor Phillip had issued strict orders prohibiting anyone from touching items belonging to the natives, but the convicts knew there were willing buyers for such contraband among the sailors, who would soon be returning to England and were assured of a good price for them back home.

◇ 15 April 1788 ◇

Johnston was off again in April. He explained to Esther that it was imperative they find better grazing land. Six of the remaining sheep at Farm Cove had been killed by dogs belonging to the natives. Without more stock they would remain dependent on England, and they could never be sure when a supply ship would arrive—there were many potential hazards on such a long voyage. They needed to become independent as soon as possible. Esther helped him pack his knapsack with a blanket, canteen, gun and food, and then she tied his kettle to one of its sides.

This time the exploring party set off from Manly. They trudged inland (through today's French's Forest to Pennant Hills) and observed a chain of mountains thirty or forty miles away, running north to south. The oil rising from the thousands of eucalypt trees that covered the wide coastal plain tinged the mountains a hazy blue. The northernmost peak was higher than the rest, and the governor named it Richmond Hill. During their travels they saw beautiful black swans, with white wingtips and a six-foot wingspan. They were again disappointed not to find better farming land, but the sight of the mountains gave them hope, as they suspected a river would flow from the peaks to the sea and be flanked by rich river flats.

◇- 5 May 1788 -◇

Early in May, Esther joined a crowd that gathered on the shore to wave goodbye to the *Lady Penrhyn*, which was on its way to China. It was a year since it had left England. When the ship disappeared up the harbour, Esther felt somewhat more isolated, now that her physical link with England had gone. The *Charlotte* and the *Scarborough* followed over the next two days. Autumn continued with heavy rains; fish became scarce and the harvest of crops, as they had feared, proved scanty. Even the natives appeared hungry, now that their fish stocks were so diminished. They would gather round when a net was being drawn in, grateful for the gift of fish that followed.

Esther noticed that some of the colonists were showing the first signs of the dreaded scurvy—their skin was covered with red blotches, crops of pimples appeared around their mouths, and their teeth were becoming loose. Everyone was encouraged to eat as many fresh green vegetables as possible and to make tea out of the native sarsaparilla vine which grew across the rocks near the settlement and tasted of liquorice.

While the unloading of supplies from the ships remained a priority, carpenters who belonged to the vessels that were waiting to leave were recruited to help build the huts, storehouses and hospital so desperately needed by the settlement before winter. Most of the convicts still lived in tents, but whitewashed huts for the more important inhabitants were appearing all around the settlement. Each one had a central front door and a window on either side, giving it the cheery appearance of a face. Sydney began to look like a quaint village nestled around the stream, bustling with the activity of a thousand people living and working in a space of little more than a square kilometre.

A mile or two through the woods south of the Sydney Cove settlement was an area known as the Brickfields, where convicts shaped and fired clay bricks. These were stacked onto carts and dragged by teams of twelve harnessed convicts all the way to the building sites of the first significant public buildings. To fix the bricks together the builders needed limestone to make mortar, but there was none to be found near the colony, so some of the female convicts were assigned to gather the thousands of discarded oyster shells that littered the shoreline so they could be ground down and burnt to provide the necessary lime for mortar.

The first real Government House also began to be built. It started off with only three rooms, but soon became a grand two-storey stone building when another three rooms were added on top.

⟨⟩ 21 May 1788 ⟨⟩

Two weeks after the *Lady Penrhyn* had sailed, Esther was shocked to see a convict crawling into the settlement with a spear sticking out of his back. Marines rushed to his aid and were told that another convict had been beaten to death by natives. Then the bodies of two more convicts assigned to cut rushes in a nearby bay were found lying in the bushes. They had been speared many times and one of them had a smashed skull.

⟨⟩ 31 May 1788 ⟨⟩

The day after the bodies were discovered, Governor Phillip took Johnston and ten other men to investigate the murder scene. But they didn't find anything helpful. The tent, clothes and provisions belonging to the convicts were all still there, but their tools were missing. There was no trace of any natives, so the investigators travelled on to Botany Bay, where they spent the night on the beach. They met many natives along the way, but none of them behaved unusually and they found no sign of any of the missing tools.

As they made their way back along the coast, about two hundred armed warriors suddenly appeared, but they seemed equally as surprised to see the white men. Johnston ordered his men to halt.

Then Governor Phillip held out his arms to show that he was unarmed and he began walking slowly, alone, towards them. Everyone else stood silent and still . . . and then all at once the natives put down their spears and moved forward to greet him.

Later investigations found that it was quite possible the rushcutters had provoked the attack on them—it seemed they had stolen a native canoe a few days earlier. The natives could also have been taking revenge for the murder of one of their own. Major Ross was establishing a small farm across the bay to the west; recently, when some natives had been passing through it, one of them had picked up a marine's jacket. When he refused to give it back, the marine had sliced his knife across the man's belly.

Governor Phillip concluded that the natives had not been hostile until they themselves had been attacked by first the French and then the British. He understood that they saw the British as intruders, and that convicts had been stealing their spears, shields and fishing lines to sell to sailors on the returning ships. In any case, there was no proof that any natives had been involved in the recent murders. The fact that the convicts had been killed by native spears did not prove that those spears had been thrown by native hands, even though that was most probably the case.

Phillip decided that he could not punish indiscriminate groups of natives without proof of their involvement. He offered a free pardon to any convict who could prove who the murderer was, but no one came forward. And so the matter ended.

◁ 4 June 1788 ▷

It was King George III's birthday, a time for celebration! The *Sirius* and *Supply* fired twenty-one-gun salutes at sunrise, noon and sunset; the marines were given extra porter to toast the King's health; and even the convicts were given half a pint of rum for each man, and half that amount for each woman.

At midday Esther joined the happy throng in the cove for the formal festivities. The marines marched down with their flags flying, and fired a volley into the air. Then the band launched into 'God Save the King' and the colonists' lusty voices joined in. Another volley crackled through the air, and again the band struck up. A third volley was fired, and the band began once again. The governor declared three days' holiday—amid mighty cheers—and the convict who had been banished to the tiny island of Pinchgut was pardoned.

Afterwards, Johnston and the other officers joined Governor Phillip for a luncheon banquet of pork, mutton, duck, fish, pies, salad and pre-served fruits. They even tasted the meat of one of the native animals, a kangaroo that one of them had shot. Their feast was complemented by fortified wines, and the men stood to raise their glasses in a toast to 'the Governor and the Settlement', followed by three hearty cheers. Phillip thanked them for the honour, drank their health, said he wished for harmony throughout the settlement, and promised that he would do everything possible to promote it. Meanwhile, the convicts sat about the cove, shouting toasts to everything they could think of. Until their rum was gone.

As evening fell, everyone gathered around an immense bonfire. Esther was standing nearby when Major Ross arrived next to Johnston. She heard Johnston talk to him about the governor's plans for the colony, and she could sense his enthusiasm. But the disagreeable Major Ross did not share his optimism. He didn't think the place would ever be suitable to settle in or, if it was, it would take another hundred years. He thought it would be cheaper to feed the convicts on turtle and venison at a London tavern than to send them to Sydney Cove. In his opinion, the country did not supply anything useful and there wasn't a man among them who didn't wish to return home.

Johnston had to admit that almost all the seeds that had been put into the ground had rotted and, while the pigs and poultry were doing well, the sheep were not thriving. It was true that, for the time being, they would need to make do with salt meat and the dwindling fish, and that all their other supplies were running down. But a supply ship from England was expected any day, and Johnston was sure that the stores she brought would give them the time they needed to become independent. And once the essential buildings were complete, there would be plenty of labour available to cultivate farming land.

The men's conversation ceased as the assembled crowd burst into songs around the bonfire. And when Governor Phillip arrived, the convicts gave him three more cheers before everyone raised their voices to sing 'God Save the King' . . . again.

⇌ 25 June 1788 ⇌

Work continued as usual after the holiday, but the fortunes of the colony did not improve. As the winter's chill began to bite, a careless convict shepherd lost all the colony's cattle—a bull and five cows— in the woods, and though several search parties were sent out to find them, none were successful. It was a major blow. Without the cattle to breed from, an essential source of meat had been lost.

The harbour's fish stocks were also now heavily depleted, and hungry natives snatched fish out of the convicts' nets as they were pulled in. To make matters worse, of the hundred sheep that had been purchased at the Cape—intended to be the beginning of a growing flock—only twenty-nine remained.

Then one morning, when Esther arrived at Johnston's tent, he angrily told her that someone had killed his goat! He had managed to catch two convicts red-handed down by the shore, but they swore they had found the goat already partly butchered, and they only took some of the meat because one of them was to be wed the following day. It was devastating news to Esther. She had grown to love the goat, and to rely on its precious milk. But now she would have to manage without it.

By the end of June the *Alexander*, *Prince of Wales* and *Friendship* transports and the *Borrowdale* storeship were ready to leave, each carrying formal dispatches urgently requesting further supplies for the colony. But before Governor Phillip gave the captain of the *Alexander* permission to leave, he made an insightful decision that would influence the unconventional evolution of the colony's society.

The legal powers of the Governor of New South Wales were unique, and Phillip was able to apply only as much British law as he saw fit. Back in England, anyone who had once been sentenced to death was considered already dead in the eyes of the law, and so could never again own property, enter into a contract, or indeed sue anyone else for damages.

But they were not in England. And Governor Phillip had vision. He wanted the convicts to become productive citizens once they had served their sentences, and he believed that if the Kables brought a successful case against Captain Sinclair for Susannah's missing items, it would show the convicts that their property rights would be upheld in future, and he hoped *that* would encourage them to build good, honest lives for themselves.

1 July 1788

Susannah Kable (who was expecting another baby) was now a married woman and so everything she owned was her husband's property. Therefore, a writ was issued in the names of both Henry and Susannah, and a warrant ordered Captain Duncan Sinclair to appear before the court the following day to answer a charge in the first civil law case in New South Wales.

The court consisted of the judge advocate, Captain David Collins, the Reverend Richard Johnson and Dr John White, the colony's principal doctor. Esther waited with Susannah outside the small hut that was being used as a courtroom. The court found Captain Sinclair guilty and ordered him to pay to the Kables fifteen pounds, the approximate value of the still-missing items.

Susannah was astounded and jubilant. She thanked Esther over and over for bringing the matter to Johnston's attention. News of the ruling quickly spread among the convicts, many of whom began to believe they could have a promising future in this strange land.

14 July 1788

With the debt settled, the colonists waved goodbye to the familiar ships, leaving only four still at anchor in Sydney Cove: the two naval ships, HMS *Sirius* and HMS *Supply*, and the last two transport ships, the *Golden Grove* and the *Fishburn*.

It was now Johnston's turn to have a hut built for him to live in, and Esther kept a close eye on its progress. A small team of convicts placed a cabbage tree palm trunk at each corner of the new building then filled in the walls with a weave of thin wattle branches they had collected from Blackwattle Bay. Then they packed clay over both the inside and outside of the walls and covered the eave-less roof with a thick thatch of rushes. The hut had two rooms—a living room graced with a fireplace, and a bedroom—and a wooden front door hung on leather straps.

The only panes of glass in the colony were waiting to be set into the windows of Government House. So, like everyone else, Johnston's hut had open windows with shutters made from woven twigs. The twigs helped provide some privacy but did nothing to stop flies, mosquitoes and other insects from sharing the home.

When it was finished, Rosanna 'helped' Esther remove all the sticks and stones from the earthen floor, and to sweep it clean, before the few pieces of furniture were moved in. Johnston ordered a convict to dig a garden on one side of the hut. He offered to share with Esther any vegetables she could grow in it. She sowed potatoes, pumpkins, corn and turnips. She also planted the red geranium next to Johnston's new front door.

∽ 22 August 1788 ∾

The temperature fell to freezing, and August was frosty and wet. But, despite it being the middle of winter, all the trees looked curiously similar to when the colonists had arrived in mid-summer—none of them had shed their leaves. It was as though the landscape was mocking their notion of seasons.

Still keen to explore this new land, Governor Phillip took Lieutenant Johnston, Dr White and seven marines on an expedition to the coastal area around Manly; this time they were to proceed from there on foot, rather than by boat. After landing at Manly Cove they walked along the coast to a large lagoon where an elderly native showed them a ford they could cross. Shortly afterwards they shot a duck for their dinner and camped for the night.

Due to the freezing weather, Johnston had suggested that Esther and Rosanna stay in his hut while he was away, so they could be warmed by the fire. So now Esther had a door which she could shut against the icy winds and noises of the night. The original roof of thatch had already collapsed in a storm and had been replaced with wooden shingles, which made the little house seem even more secure.

To get the fire going, Esther gathered some dried leaves and twigs and laid them carefully beneath the chimney. Then she reached for the small round tinder box, which she emptied onto the floor beside her. After fluffing up the tinder, she struck the flint against the steel above it so that sparks rained down upon it, making it glow. Then she blew on it gently and touched it with the sulphur-tipped spunk to cause a burst of flame from which she quickly lit a small candle and, from that, the pile of twigs. It was a Friday evening and, though she had only the one candle, it somehow felt right to her to light it before sunset to signify the beginning of the Jewish Sabbath. It was part of a childhood memory she had of her mother, and it made her feel close to her. Esther embraced the light then covered her face with her hands, but she couldn't remember the words of the blessing, so she just welcomed God and the Sabbath into the house.

Outside, the August winds whistled around the hut, and the white crests of wind-blown waves formed white horses out on the darkened harbour. But the hut was filled with the soft, golden light from the flames, and Esther settled contentedly in their warmth, with Rosanna asleep on her lap. She realised that she missed Johnston more, each time he went away.

23 August 1788

The next day the explorers walked to the tip of a narrow peninsula, and camped part of the way back. Then they returned to Manly Cove, where they gave gifts of their brass buttons to the local natives.

◆ 10 September 1788 ◆

'We are sending Captain Hunter back to Cape Town in the *Sirius* for supplies,' Johnston told Esther on his return. He added that everyone's ration would be reduced until John Hunter returned a few months later.

On the other hand, Johnston continued, the *Supply* had brought good news of farming prospects on Norfolk Island, so the *Golden Grove* would take another forty settlers there with supplies for eighteen months, to reduce the pressure at Sydney Cove.

That in itself would be a risky business. The surf at Norfolk Island was so rough that, when provisions had previously been landed from the *Supply*, five men had drowned after their boat was overturned.

The *Sirius*, on her way to the Cape, and the *Golden Grove*, heading for Norfolk Island, sailed out of Sydney Harbour together, leaving only the little *Supply* to defend the settlement. When the *Golden Grove* returned from Norfolk Island, she and the *Fishburn* would sail for home, and the *Supply* would become the struggling settlement's only link with the outside world.

◆ 5 December 1788 ◆

The crops in Farm Cove were still not thriving, so Governor Phillip hoped to establish a more productive farm on better soil he had discovered sixteen miles up the western river at a place he called Rose Hill. The grass was so high there that the local kangaroos could only be seen when they bounded off in fright.

Lieutenant Johnston was ordered to take ten convicts by boat and settle them in a camp with marines to guard them so they could begin clearing the land. Esther had returned to the servants' tent after Johnston's previous expedition, but he again suggested that she stay in his hut while he was away. This time he said it was to protect their growing vegetables from theft.

One night she and Rosanna were woken in fright by a violent knocking at the hut's door. It was Henry Kable, and he was holding Harry. He told Esther that Susannah had been in labour for most of the day and the birth of her baby now seemed imminent. Could she come? Esther dressed hurriedly and grabbed some precious rags. Then she hurried down the hill, leaving Kable to look after the children.

Inside the Kables' tent, Susannah's sweating face was illuminated by a brightly burning candle. The remaining hours of the warm night passed slowly, and a pale light that gave no colour to the landscape showed through the tent flap before Susannah brought forth a new baby. Smiles and tears of happiness greeted the little girl, whom Susannah named Diana after Henry Kable's mother.

This time, when Johnston returned from his travels, Esther and Rosanna did not go back to their place in the servants' tent. They both stayed living with Johnston in his hut.

⟶ 31 December 1788 ⟵

Soon afterwards, Governor Phillip had yet another, more unpleasant task for Johnston. Since it was now clear to the local natives that the white settlers intended to stay and continue damaging their hunting grounds and fish stocks, they had tried to protect the rest of their land by attacking unarmed settlers who wandered away from the settlement.

Few natives visited the colony and, although Governor Phillip had tried to persuade some of them to live among the colonists and teach them their native language and customs, none would agree. So, reluctantly, he ordered Johnston and Lieutenant Ball, commander of the *Supply*, to capture a native man by force.

On the last day of the year Johnston and Ball set off on their mission, taking a small group of marines in two boats to Manly Cove. The natives came forward to meet them as usual and, at Johnston's signal, the marines suddenly seized two of the men. One escaped by dragging his captor into deep water but the other, a strongly built man about twenty-four years old, was caught by a rope thrown around his neck. He was held by several of the marines and was tumbled, while shouting and struggling, into one of the boats.

The captive was tied to the thwarts while the marines pulled desperately away from the shore to avoid the spears that rained down all around them. Johnston ordered his men to fire over the heads of the enraged natives, who fled long enough for the boats to get away.

After the joys of forming friendships with the native men on his many explorations—eating and laughing with them by day, and dancing and singing with them at night—Johnston felt sick at the treachery he had just performed. He recognised the fine young warrior, Arabanoo, who now lay still and resigned to death at the bottom of the boat. Johnston held out some cooked fish he had brought with him and tried to comfort the captive, speaking gently and encouraging him to eat.

Arabanoo looked at him incredulously. Why had he been captured, if not to be killed? And why offer him fish to eat before his death? But he could see no malice in Johnston's expression, no sense of victory in his movements. Arabanoo reached out and took the fish, but when Johnston patted him encouragingly on the shoulder, he winced and drew back.

By the time they had rowed back across the harbour to Sydney Cove, Arabanoo had accepted that he was not to be murdered and the white men had some other reason for his capture.

Esther was among the group of people waiting for the boats to return. She had never been close to a native man before and, although she considered him likely to be a murderous savage, she noticed that he stood very straight and held himself with dignity. He walked with Johnston towards the governor's new house—the two-storey stone building still being constructed—repeating in a soft, musical voice the English words Johnston taught him along the way. As they passed Esther, Johnston pointed to her.

'Woman,' he said.

'Wo-man,' repeated Arabanoo with a nod. But Esther quickly ducked behind others in the crowd, not wishing to be identified by the savage.

They reached Government House and one of the officers rang the bell that hung next to the door. Arabanoo jumped in fright at the sound, but Johnston patted his shoulder again, speaking soothingly, and took him up to the bell so that he could jiggle it himself and understand what had made the sound. Arabanoo laughed at the harmless cause of his fear and then rang the bell delightedly himself.

When a curious servant looked out of the second-floor window, the native man shouted in disbelief at how tall he must be. Then Governor Phillip, who many of the natives respected as the leader of the white men, appeared in the hallway and Arabanoo willingly followed him into the house.

Later, back at his hut, Johnston described to Esther what had happened next. Arabanoo had dined heartily, although he could not be persuaded to take any wine. He seemed to understand at last that the white men wanted to learn his language and teach him some of their customs. When he had wiped his fingers on his chair at dinner, he had been handed a napkin, which he had then used diligently for the rest of the evening.

Johnston then described how Arabanoo had struggled into a shirt, but then had backed towards the warmth of the fire and had caught his shirt tail alight. For a moment they had lost him to panic before they could quench the flames. Subsequently, he had been quite nervous when they had wanted to cut his hair and shave his beard, until he had seen the actions performed on someone else. Then he had readily obliged them.

In the end, the whole procedure had turned into fine entertainment. Arabanoo had shouted with glee as insects had tried to escape from his hair—and he had eaten them with relish, until the officers had showed their disapproval. Afterwards, he had pointed to a portrait of the Duchess of Cumberland which hung on the wall and had declared her 'woman'. He had seemed very eager to please the officers, which Johnston thought was truly admirable, considering the manner of his capture. Johnston told Esther that he hoped Arabanoo would forgive his treachery, once he understood the motives behind it.

And so it was, that a native man dressed in a shirt, jacket and trousers sat in the drawing room of Government House conversing, in a manner, with the Governor of New South Wales.

CHAPTER FIVE

Hunger

The following day, Johnston rowed Arabanoo back to Manly Cove to show his people that he was safe and well. As their boat approached the shore, native men moved cautiously out of the trees and onto the beach, and Arabanoo called to them in his rapid, liquid language. But he was still a captive. An iron ring had been riveted around his left wrist, with a rope leading from it to his convict guard; leg cuffs had also been attached to prevent his escape during this excursion. Johnston then took him back to the settlement, and Arabanoo's friends returned to the woods, as free as the snow-white cockatoos that flew squawking overhead.

Despite the indignity of his restraint, the native warrior was remarkably tolerant towards his captors and came to accept his new life in the settlement, graciously consenting to his role of teacher. He lived with Governor Phillip, and was gradually freed from all restraint. He happily drank tea, but would not touch the spirits that were routinely offered to him.

On most evenings, after dinner, Johnston and the other officers would gather around him so he could teach them some of his native words, and correct their faltering pronunciation. And they would teach him some words of English. Arabanoo mastered English much more quickly than they managed to learn his language.

Johnston enjoyed the company of the gentle native man. On Sunday afternoons he would lift Rosanna (now nearly two) onto his shoulders and carry her down to visit him—much to Esther's disapproval. Rosanna would eagerly toddle towards Arabanoo and he would crouch down to her height, beaming with welcome. He would then hold out a large brown hand into which she would put her small white one, and he would murmur to her in his melodious voice. If he were eating, he would hold out the choicest piece of his food, which she would take gladly, leaning against his strong body while she ate it.

Then, 'Wombat!' Rosanna would shout delightedly, watching while he transformed his body into the shape of a wombat, deftly mimicking its movements as he ambled over the ground. Then a call of 'Kangawoo!' would result in another transfixing display.

Rosanna would look for Arabanoo whenever her mother took her to the cove. One morning, as she and Esther left their hut, Rosanna stumbled over the geranium plant and knocked off one of its bright red flowers, which she picked up before hurrying after her mother. As they approached the cove, she saw her large friend crouching on some rocks by the water, hitting one stone against another just as she had seen her smaller friend Harry do. As soon as Esther was engrossed in conversation with Mary Bryant, Rosanna ran over to him.

'Boo! Boo!' she called.

'G'day, Rodie,' and he extended his palm towards her in welcome, as usual. She laid the bright red flower into its brown expanse and looked eagerly into his eyes, seeking the delight that was always so obvious whenever he was pleased. He beamed back at her.

'Rodie wait,' he said, and turned back to his work with the stones. Esther called to her sharply, but Rosanna hesitated until Arabanoo placed one of his stones into her small hand and folded her fingers over it. '*Boodjeree* tone [good stone],' he said. It was smooth and dark with shiny flat surfaces and one thin, sharp edge.

Esther called again, and this time her daughter came running, feeling Arabanoo's comforting spirit travel with her.

When they came back to their hut, Rosanna pulled at her dress and asked Esther to put a pocket on it. Both Johnston and Esther had a number of pockets on their clothes to carry the many small items they needed during the day, and Esther was keen for Rosanna to learn to be helpful, so she agreed to sew a small pocket onto the ragged dress that she had made for her daughter from a burlap sack.

Rosanna dropped her stone into the pocket and carried it with her everywhere. Whenever she felt anxious she would plunge her hand into the pocket to feel the stone's smooth sides and think of Arabanoo.

◇ 4 February 1789 ◇

Johnston strode towards their hut with a frightening scowl that distorted his face. Rosanna ran behind the house and stroked her stone as he went inside, and she heard him explode in a tirade about William Bryant, who had apparently been stealing from the daily catch of fish.

Johnston paced around the room in exasperation while Esther sat pale-faced on the chair. It seemed the ruse had been going on for some time and, to Johnston's added frustration, it confirmed all that Major Ross had been saying about the convicts: once a thief, always a thief. Johnston wiped his hand across his brow.

'What will become of him?' Esther asked in a small voice.

Johnston explained that their situation was too perilous to allow such an offence to go unpunished. The laws had been quite clear from the outset.

Esther covered her mouth with her hand. There had already been six executions in the colony, and she couldn't bear the thought of seeing the body of someone she knew so well twitching and writhing on the end of a rope.

She sat silently for some time. When she spoke, she reminded Johnston that the success of the settlement must surely remain the priority. He had already told her they couldn't be sure when a relief ship would bring more supplies. Surely, then, the fishing skills Bryant possessed were paramount to their survival.

That evening, Johnston went to Government House as usual, and the following day Bryant's case was heard before Captain Collins, the judge advocate. He was found guilty. But he was not sentenced to hang. Instead, he was ordered to be turned out of his hut; to be given one hundred lashes; to lose the leadership of the fishing enterprise . . . but to continue fishing.

As usual, the convicts were summoned to the head of the stream to witness the flogging. Many of them had long envied Bryant's life of relative freedom—in a hut of his own, and with nothing more strenuous to do than a bit of fishing. When his wife arrived at the flogging tree, the other convicts shuffled aside to keep their distance. Only Esther and Susannah stood by Mary's side as the marines beat their drums and Bryant was led to the tree.

Two marines removed his shirt and tied his hands to the tree, above his head. The flogger dragged the cat-o'-nine-tails out of its bag; he shook free its long leather strands, stiff and hard with dried blood. There were knots tied along each strand, to give better purchase against flesh.

Esther stared at the ground in front of her. Then she heard the swish of the lash through the air, and the sharp crack as it whipped across Bryant's bare back. A muffled grunt was forced from his body.

'One!' called a marine.

Swish . . . crack. 'Two!'

After twenty lashes, Esther risked a peek. The skin on Bryant's back was lacerated, and lines of blood were trickling down to his trousers. She quickly looked down again.

After fifty lashes, a cry accompanying each stroke, Esther's hands were clammy with sweat. She dared not look again, but she knew that by now his flesh would be cut through to his shoulderblades.

At eighty lashes Bryant became silent. The weight of his body hung from his slack wrists, and it swayed with each blow. Shreds of bloody skin were torn off by the knots of leather and flung through the air, splattering onto the ground. Mary stood silently, but Esther noticed that the dust at her feet was mottled with tears.

Finally, the marine called out, 'One hundred!'

Bryant's quivering body was cut down and left on the ground. The rest of the convicts moved away to continue their day's work, leaving the three women standing in the hot sun. In a choked voice, Susannah offered to take the children away, bending down to wipe her damp cheeks with her dress. Mary walked over to her husband's body. The flesh on his back had been reduced to a jelly.

Esther stood rooted to the spot. Had she contributed to this terrible suffering? Would it have caused Mary more agony to have seen her husband's body now swinging lifeless from a tree than witness this cruel horror?

To ease her guilt, she longed to be helpful; she ran to her hut and snatched up some rags and a wooden bucket of water. When she returned, Mary was kneeling beside her husband. Ants were already carrying off prized pieces of bloody flesh. In silence, Esther and Mary dipped the rags into the water and gently bathed Bryant's back.

ꝏ 6 February 1789 ꝏ

The colonists had now spent a year at Sydney Cove. Everyone was encouraged to grow as much food as possible, but even the stunted vegetables that usually resulted were often stolen in the night. Esther spent many hours with her lively daughter collecting wild celery, native spinach and small wild figs to supplement their meagre diet.

Captain John Shea, who was in charge of one of the four companies of marines, died of tuberculosis. As a result, just before his twenty-fifth birthday, Johnston was promoted to Captain-Lieutenant and took over command of Shea's company. With his promotion came the duty to join the other officers rostered to sit as magistrates on the bench of the colony's young court. The ripple of promotions that cascaded through the ranks ended with the appointment by the crotchety Major Ross of his own nine-year-old son to the rank of Second Lieutenant.

∾ 9 March 1789 ∾

As autumn arrived, sixteen convict men working at the Brickfields banded together to walk to Botany Bay intending to steal fishing tackle from the natives there. But they caused such a racket as they marched through the trees, jubilant in their defiance and waving their tools as weapons, that the natives had plenty of warning of their intention. As the convicts came over a small rise they were suddenly faced with fifty fearsome warriors charging towards them. The panicked convicts scattered into the woods. One was killed and seven were wounded before the marines were alerted and raced out to bring the rest of them back to the safety of the settlement.

Governor Phillip was incensed by the convicts' behaviour. He ordered those involved to be given one hundred and fifty lashes each and to be put in leg-irons for a year. The incident was carefully explained to Arabanoo and he was brought to the flogging tree to witness the punishment so that he might understand that it was against the white men's law to attack his people.

But what the mighty warrior saw that day he did not perceive as justice. It was not his people's way to assault a defenceless man, and the sight of the convicts bound to a tree, unable even to face their assailant, filled him with horror and disgust. Governor Phillip had not, on that occasion, managed to convince Arabanoo that the white men's ways were just.

Three weeks later, six marines were found guilty of stealing food, alcohol and tobacco from the public store. Though it was painful for Johnston to accept, the colony's court had no choice other than to sentence them to death.

∾ 15 April 1789 ∾

There was trouble enough in the white men's settlement, but now a terrible blight crept through all the native clans living nearby. Just after Easter, Johnston heard about a native family which was suffering in a nearby cove. Phillip took Arabanoo and Dr White to visit them. They first found the dead body of a young girl. Then a man and a boy aged about ten who were both gravely ill, with pustules all over their bodies. The boy was gently pouring water from a shell onto the man's feverish head.

Dr White took the man and boy back to the hospital, where he and his assistant, Dr William Balmain, could care for them. Arabanoo stayed behind to dig a small grave in the sand with his hands. He lined it with soft grass and then solemnly laid the dead girl's body into the hollow. He covered it with more grass, then built a mound of sand over the top. Later that evening, two officers found the mother's body and buried her next to her daughter.

Back at the hospital, Johnston asked Dr White what he thought might be the cause.

'I am afraid it is the smallpox,' replied the doctor.

Over the following weeks, the mysterious illness swept quickly through the native population with devastating effect. Half of those living around Port Jackson succumbed, their bodies found exactly as they had died—some sitting on the ground with their heads between their drawn-up knees, others leaning against a rock. Hundreds fled the area to escape the pestilence, and the coastal country became eerily empty, with not a single canoe in the harbour.

Many ill natives were brought into the hospital, and Arabanoo moved in to nurse his people. The young boy Dr White had taken to the hospital, who was named Nanbaree, eventually recovered, by which time Dr White had become so fond of him that he and his convict mistress adopted him as their own child. An orphaned girl named Boorong was also adopted, this time by the Reverend Johnson and his wife.

⇆ 19 April 1789 ⇆

It was a Sunday in mid-April, and the settlers had been on reduced rations for many months. As usual they gathered to offer prayers for the safe return of Captain Hunter and the *Sirius* with its cargo of precious supplies. They didn't know if he had even yet reached the Cape, but they hoped and prayed that by now he was well on his way back to Sydney Cove.

On that Sunday morning, Hunter was in fact just reaching the southern tip of Van Diemen's Land and heading into gale-force winds. The weather was so bad during the following three days that he could not see the sun or any star to determine his exact latitude. He could only peer through the thick fog and driving rain in an attempt to see land and get his bearings. The violent wind split three of his sails, and the waves tore off the ship's figurehead, roundhouses and head rails.

Every sail the *Sirius* was capable of carrying was raised in an effort to push her safely past the point of land. At midnight, a solid blackness rose from the horizon and Hunter guided his ship safely past it before rain obliterated his view once more. He hoped that they had now passed the southern tip of land, but some hours later the steep and rocky point of Tasman's Head (Bruny Island) loomed into view, the foaming sea crashing against its base and the gale threatening to dash his now leaky ship against its jagged rocks. Fortunately, the fierce wind suddenly changed direction and dragged the *Sirius* away into the expanse of open sea. The exhausted crew let out a cheer and the ship continued to limp northwards to the safety of Port Jackson. Hunter believed that divine providence had saved his ship.

28 April 1789

Over a thousand miles away, Captain William Bligh was also proving his seamanship and sailing into legend. His crew on the *Bounty* had mutinied, put him and eighteen loyal men into an open boat, and set them adrift in the ocean. Bligh had a sextant and a pocket watch, with enough food and water to last only a few days. With no map, he was navigating his small boat across three thousand miles of ocean to Timor, unaware that there was now a British colony on Norfolk Island, only a quarter of that distance away.

9 May 1789

Seven months after he had left Sydney Cove, Captain Hunter at last returned to it. He brought with him four months' worth of flour, wheat seed, many items purchased on behalf of the officers, and a year's supplies for his crew. But he did not bring news that any other supply ship was on its way from England.

Johnston was one of the officers who had placed an order with Hunter, and he now handed Esther a small package of tasty delights: spices, brown sugar, raisins and sago. And there was more: a colourful assortment of fabric remnants, needles and thread. Esther was elated! The first thing she planned to make was a new dress for Rosanna from some pretty blue cotton patterned with yellow daisies.

◇ 11 May 1789 ◇

But the blessings were brief. Arabanoo began to show the symptoms of smallpox. He confidently allowed doctors White and Balmain to care for him, and they used the best treatment they knew: they bled him of his infected blood and administered their many medicines. But seven days later the gentle warrior's spirit joined those of his ancestors.

The following day Johnston explained to Rosanna that Arabanoo had gone.

'Boo gone?'

'Yes.'

'Rosie go?'

'No, Rosie.'

'See Boo!'

Johnston explained to Rosanna that Arabanoo was now a spirit and that his people believed their spirits became part of the sky.

'Up?' She pointed.

'Aye, up there.'

'Boo in sky?'

'Aye.'

'And Rosie tone,' she said, matter-of-factly.

He laughed. 'I suppose a part of him must be in that, too.'

Rosanna thrust her hand into the pocket of her new blue dress and gripped the stone in her small hand.

A shadow of gloom descended over the whole settlement at the loss of the good-natured native man. Governor Phillip—for whom Arabanoo had become a respected friend—arranged a sombre funeral and then buried his companion at Government House.

While the settlement mourned Arabanoo, on the other side of the world Lord Sydney was finally acting on the requests Governor Phillip had sent with the seven ships of the First Fleet that had now returned. And he did it in style. He arranged for HMS *Guardian* to be fitted out as a storeship to carry to the colony another two years' supply of food, wine and clothing, plus sixteen chests of medicines, blankets and other bedding for the hospital, and tools for building and farming.

Seven horses were loaded into the ship to provide transport in the colony. Eighteen cattle, plus sheep, goats and deer were taken on board to provide meat, milk, cheese and butter. Sir Joseph Banks supervised the construction of a special storehouse on the quarterdeck to house ninety-three pots of growing vegetables and herbs, plus one hundred and fifty fruit trees from Kew Gardens, ready to plant straight into the ground.

Then twenty-five convict farmers and craftsmen—bricklayers, carpenters, smiths and stonemasons—boarded the vessel. Seven non-convict overseers were added to supervise the work gangs, two of whom were royal gardeners from Kew Gardens, personally chosen by Banks. The fourteen-year-old cousin of Prime Minister Pitt joined the crew as a midshipman.

ᵔ 4 June 1789 ᵔ

Meanwhile, in Sydney Cove, the King's birthday in June offered a reason to celebrate once again, and the convicts decided to put on a play—*The Recruiting Officer* by George Farquhar. Esther helped to decorate one of the huts with colour-stained paper, and placed twelve candles stuck in bottles around its mud walls. Henry Kable played the lead role and Mary Bryant took a minor part. The audience consisted of both convicts and officers, and the performance concluded to enthusiastic applause.

6 June 1789

Shortly afterwards, when Johnston was off exploring again, Esther became aware of a familiar feeling of nausea. She stopped what she was doing and placed her hand on her belly. She wondered how Johnston would react if she had another child.

At the time, Johnston was with Governor Phillip, Captain Hunter and two others on expeditions to Broken Bay. Phillip suffered from kidney stones, and every now and then their progress was slowed when the pain in his side made it too difficult for him to walk. At times, Johnston was also troubled by pain from the shrapnel lodged in his leg.

Nevertheless, they finally found the river that emptied into the bay. Phillip named it the Hawkesbury, and they rowed up its length as far as Richmond Hill. Huge cliffs towered on either side, some with logs wedged thirty or forty feet up the cliffs, signifying there had been large floods over the years. But there was also rich soil on the flats, which looked very promising; they dug in some potatoes, corn and melon seeds.

The marine in command at Rose Hill, Captain Watkin Tench, was disappointed not to be able to join the governor's expedition parties, and was inspired by them to do some exploring of his own. He travelled twenty miles to the west and to his great delight discovered a deep, wide river running north, which Phillip later named the Nepean.

7 August 1789

When Captain Cook had discovered New South Wales it happened to be during a wet autumn, but the settlement at Sydney Cove was established during a powerful El Nino event, which caused severe drought. At this time, the earth around Farm Cove, now bare of shade, baked dry beneath the winter sun, and the crops withered.

Thefts of food from all the farms and gardens became such a major problem that a convict suggested a night-watch of trusted convicts be established to patrol the settlement and detain anyone they found outdoors after the drums had sounded the nightly curfew.

His plan was accepted by Governor Phillip, and so the first Australian police force was established—made up of twelve convicted criminals.

◇ 1 November 1789 ◇

The colony now had only enough supplies to last a further four or five months, so the men's daily rations were reduced again, to two-thirds of their original amount. Governor Phillip could not bring himself to reduce the women's rations any further, as they were already only two-thirds that of the men's, and many of the women were suckling babies.

At least there had been good harvests of wheat, barley, oats and corn from the two hundred acres of land that had been cleared at Rose Hill. However, while there were still rations of salted meat in the stores, the whole harvest had to be kept as seed to sow the following year.

Esther's thin arms already contrasted disturbingly with her large body, as she was now heavily pregnant with her second child. Gnawing hunger was a constant companion, and she longed for a supply ship to arrive. Some days she couldn't help wondering if England had forgotten the struggling colony altogether. Or maybe it had been defeated in a war . . . or could its population have perished from a plague? There was no way to know.

◇ 21 November 1789 ◇

Could an industrious man ever become self-supporting in New South Wales? And if he could, how long would it take? These were questions for which Governor Phillip needed answers. James Ruse, the convict farmer, had been a diligent and honest worker at the government farm. Phillip believed he could reward Ruse's good behaviour as an encouragement to others, and at the same time test whether he could support himself from the land.

So Phillip established Ruse on a farm near Rose Hill with one and a half acres of ploughed land, five more acres cleared of trees, and a small hut. He also gave him tools for digging, grain to sow, two pigs and six chickens. He promised that if Ruse could support himself he would be given the land to keep as his own. Ruse called the property

Experiment Farm, and the colony buzzed with conflicting views of his chances of success.

During the smallpox epidemic most of the natives had fled from the coast, but now the worst of the disease seemed to be over, and a few began returning to the harbour's pretty coves to gain access to their fish. Governor Phillip had orders from King George III to use all possible means to open communication with the natives and win them over so that all the King's subjects could live in harmony, but progress on that front had come to a halt with Arabanoo's death. Phillip also wanted to know if there were any sources of wild food the colonists could be utilising. So he once again ordered the capture of a native man. This time he chose Lieutenant William Bradley from the *Sirius* for the task.

Bradley led a group of marines down the harbour in boats until he saw two native men walking on a beach near South Head. As they got closer, he could see the scars of smallpox on their faces. He offered them some fish and the hungry men came willingly to the boat to receive their gifts and cheerfully talk to the marines. At a sign from Bradley, his men knocked their legs from under them and tumbled them into one of the boats, lashing them down. Nearby natives screamed and wailed at the treachery, but the boats pulled clear of the shore. It was, according to Bradley, by far the most unpleasant service he was ever ordered to execute.

Johnston and Esther were among the crowd waiting for their return at Sydney Cove. Nanbaree, the boy who had been adopted by Dr White, explained to Johnston that one of the captives was a Gadigal chief, his own uncle in fact, whose name was Colbee. The younger man's name was Bennelong, a warrior from the Wangal clan whose lands lay west of the Gadigal's, up the harbour. Nanbaree told Johnston that neither man had a wife or child. Although it was true that Bennelong's first wife had recently died, Nanbaree didn't know that Bennelong already had a new wife, an older woman called Barangaroo.

Johnston asked Nanbaree to explain to his elders that they would be well treated and allowed to return to their people later, but the two captives remained sullen. Like Arabanoo, they were washed, shaved and clothed, and an iron ring was riveted to one ankle with a rope spliced to it.

ᐁ 12 December 1789 ᐁ

A couple of weeks after his capture, Colbee managed to undo the rope and make a dash for freedom when his convict guard wasn't looking. Bennelong tried to follow, but his guard caught him before he managed to escape. After that, Bennelong's rope was replaced with a chain attached to his guard's wrist. Governor Phillip's hopes now rested upon this one man.

Bennelong was slim and muscular, about twenty-five years old. After Colbee's escape he noticeably relaxed and began to enjoy being the centre of attention in the white chief's house. He quickly learned some English words and, unlike Arabanoo, he was eager to experiment with all the unfamiliar food and drink placed before him, happily accepting the continual offers of wine.

Bennelong became the star attraction at Government House dinners, singing and dancing to an appreciative audience. After dinner, the officers would point to one of the many scars on his robust body and he would launch into an animated explanation of its glorious cause. When asked about a scar on the back of his hand, Bennelong had grinned widely and explained that when he had once captured a woman from another tribe and was dragging her off by force, she had bitten deeply into his hand to try to get away. But he had knocked her down, beaten her unconscious, and dragged her home victoriously, as was the custom of his people.

ᐁ 16 December 1789 ᐁ

After valiantly reaching Timor in his small boat, Captain Bligh and his crew were taken by ship to the Cape of Good Hope on their way home to England. Five days earlier the *Guardian* storeship had left the Cape to begin the last leg of her long journey to New South Wales. She was commanded by twenty-six-year-old Lieutenant Edward Riou. At the age of thirteen Riou had sailed with Captain Cook in the *Endeavour*, and later with both Cook and Bligh on the *Resolution*. Bligh and Riou were two of the best seamen in the Royal Navy—one had just demonstrated his skill and courage, and the other was about to do so.

∽ 24 December 1789 ∽

The heavily laden *Guardian*, with three hundred people on board, was sailing southeast from Cape Town, into the freezing waters of the Southern Ocean. On Christmas Eve, twelve days after leaving port, Riou and his crew saw a large iceberg, twice as high as the ship's mast. They launched their boats to collect some of the nearby floating ice chunks to melt for fresh water for the many plants and animals they had on board. It was dark by the time the boats were hoisted back up, and a thick fog had begun closing in.

Lookouts posted all around the deck strained to see through the frosty air as the ship slowly moved through the waves. Just before nine o'clock, a huge, eerie whiteness appeared, and Riou turned his ship into the wind to clear the mountain of ice that stretched up out of sight. However, beneath the water's surface, a pointed ledge jutted out from the iceberg. The timber ship crunched straight into it.

The fierce wind swung the ship around and off the ice, but her rudder was torn away and her rear cabins shattered, leaving a gaping hole though which the icy water gushed. As the gale strengthened, the shivering sailors worked frantically to save their ship, taking turns to work the pumps throughout the night. But the vessel sank deeper every hour.

In the wild dawn of Christmas Day, Riou lowered boats over the side and helped his men pull a rolled-up canvas sail into the water. They opened it out and spread it over the hole, tying it closely to the hull in order to stem the rushing inflow of water. The ship was now rolling so wildly that water gushed into the portholes, so Riou ordered all the ship's guns to be thrown overboard to lighten her load.

Riou coolly sat down on the sodden deck and wrote a letter to the Admiralty, which he placed in one of the boats: *Sir, if ever any part of the officers or crew of the* Guardian *should ever survive to get home, I have only to say their conduct after the fatal stroke against an island of ice was admirable and wonderful in everything that related to their duties, considered either as private men or on his Majesty's Service.*

As time went on, the ship's precious cargo also began to be jettisoned. While Riou struggled to help his men, a barrel fell on top of him, crushing his hand. But he continued to work on the deck, finally issuing an order for the terrified animals to be hurled into the icy sea, where they struggled, bellowing until they drowned. An eerie silence then surrounded the broken ship as it lurched on through the mist.

On Boxing Day Riou gave permission to abandon ship. But the five life-boats could not carry everyone on board, and sixty-two people had to stay behind, including all the convicts, three overseers and one of their daughters. Riou declared he would go down with his ship.

The jolly boat was the first one lowered into the waves. So many panicked passengers scrambled down the ladder to cram into the boat that it was quickly swamped by water and everyone in it drowned. The other four boats were launched successfully, but one had to push away from the ship before receiving any provisions to avoid being sunk under the weight of extra men who were jumping into it.

Of the boats which rowed away into the coldest ocean in the world, all were lost at sea except the one carrying Riou's letter, which was miraculously rescued fourteen days later by a French ship that had been blown off its course.

With his injured hand cradled in a makeshift sling, Riou continued working to save his ship and the people still on board. The sail covering the gaping hole was torn away by the waves, but again and again Riou and his men dragged another one under the hull to replace it. They also rigged up a temporary rudder so Riou could steer the ship. All the other men took shifts on the pumps, in the slim hope that they would stumble upon another ship or an uncharted island. To give them encouragement, Riou promised that any convict who survived would be given a free pardon.

For nine agonising weeks they worked the pumps continually, but the water in the hold was never less than sixteen feet deep, which caused the ship to sit low in the water, like a log, only a few inches above the point where it would inevitably sink.

Suddenly, out of nowhere, a whaling ship appeared! The exhausted men shouted and waved their arms, desperately seeking a sign that the whalers had noticed them. And then it came. The whaler turned towards them, and they knew they would be saved.

The whaler led the listing *Guardian* all the way back to the Cape of Good Hope. Captain Riou and his courageous crew (including Thomas Pitt), and all the convicts, had survived. But most of the people and provisions destined for the starving colony at Sydney Cove were lost to the ocean's depths.

By the time the *Guardian* arrived back at the Cape, Bligh had already left for England. One of his crew had gone mad from his ordeal in the open boat, but the others helped to salvage the last provisions from the *Guardian* before she was abandoned. As they worked, everyone knew that Captain Hunter had already returned to the Cape in the *Sirius* to buy emergency provisions for the struggling colony at Sydney Cove, and they wondered if the colonists would survive.

CHAPTER SIX

An Island of Surprises

◇ *12 January 1790* ◇

Esther lay groaning on her bed. 'I . . . can't do this,' she moaned, as she felt her starving body bear down once again. Susannah patted a cooling damp cloth across her forehead, while Mary crouched at the end of the bed.

With a little more encouragement from Mary and one final mighty push, Esther's new baby entered the world. A little boy. How would Johnston react?

He was ecstatic! Now that he had a son, he felt a greater purpose to all his endeavours. While Esther rested, he gathered up the soft, warm bundle of his swaddled child and carried him out into the bright daylight. He strode with new pride up the hill to the site he had chosen for his tent when he had first arrived in the new land. Lifting his baby high above his head, Johnston rejoiced.

Esther lay back on her bed with relief and allowed herself to imagine a promising future for her son in this new land.

◇ *28 February 1790* ◇

A few weeks later, when Esther had finally managed to soothe her baby to sleep, Johnston strode in from a meeting at Government House. She looked up wearily.

ESTHER

'We're off to Norfolk Island, Hetty!' he announced. He proceeded
to explain how Sydney Cove, even with everyone on half rations, only
had enough supplies to last for two more months; Norfolk Island, on
the other hand, had proved to be fertile and productive, with good
supplies of fish. So Governor Phillip had decided to split the colony
in two.

A thousand miles away! Esther could hardly bear to contemplate
the idea of packing up their belongings and setting sail once again—
this time with *two* young children to care for.

But Johnston's eyes were shining at the prospect of a new adventure.
Once the *Sirius* and *Supply* had safely delivered all the newcomers to
the island, Captain Hunter would sail the *Sirius* to Batavia for more
supplies. He would take with him Lieutenant King, who would make
his own way back to England so he could personally explain their
predicament to the Home Office. And Major Ross would take over as
governor on Norfolk Island.

Esther knew that Johnston was not on the best of terms with Ross
and regarded him as obnoxious, but he explained to her that Phillip
probably wanted to put as much distance between himself and Ross
as possible.

'When do we leave?' she asked.

'In six days' time.'

At this news she turned quickly away so Johnston wouldn't see the
tears that welled in her eyes. In their little hut, her life had become
settled and she was beginning to feel she could just about cope with the
demands of a new baby. But dealing with another sea voyage seemed
just too much.

⇔ *5 March 1790* ⇔

As hundreds of convicts and marines began loading provisions and
livestock onto the two waiting ships, the *Sirius* and *Supply*, Sydney was
now all bustle and activity. It was the day before they were to set sail
and Esther, having wrapped her baby in the finest fabric she could find,
followed Johnston to a large hut, where several marine officers and

78

their wives were gathered to see the baby christened with his father's name, George. Susannah Kable and Mary Bryant waited outside with small bouquets of ferns and wildflowers, which they gave to Esther to mark the occasion.

Esther had never attended a Jewish naming ceremony but, nevertheless, knew that for boys it involved circumcision. She pragmatically accepted the customs of Johnston's religion.

The morning after the christening, Esther lingered to take a last look around the small hut that had been her home for the past year and a half. She blinked more tears away, took a deep breath, then pulled the wooden door closed behind her. Then she bent down to break off a piece of the geranium plant which she stuck into a wooden cup of soil.

After the little family boarded the *Supply* and settled into one of its tiny cabins, the two vessels sailed up the harbour, leaving Sydney Cove empty of ships and totally isolated. Esther felt the familiar movement of the ocean swell as they passed the cliffs of North Head and sailed into the open sea. Once again she stood on the top deck gazing out at the vast expanse of water and wondering what lay ahead for her.

ᴖ 13 March 1790 ᴖ

Landing at Norfolk Island was always a treacherous affair. On this occasion the ships sailed around to Cascade Bay on the far side of the island, where at half-tide their boats could row in backwards and let their passengers jump off onto a large rock that jutted out from the shore. Johnston and his marines were set down first so they could find Governor King and explain to him what was happening.

Esther's heart raced at the thought of managing the landing manoeuvre with her two small children, but there was no other way to get ashore. She climbed awkwardly into the boat with Rosanna and baby George, clinging to them tightly while they waited for several other women to clamber in as well. Then they were on their way, buffeted by the contrary waves and rocking from side to side as their boat neared the coastline.

When they were only a few feet away from the landing rock, a large wave swamped their boat and forced it back. The women screamed and were sternly ordered to keep still while the boat was rowed in close again. Nearer . . . nearer.

Esther held her breath and scrambled onto the rock with one arm holding her baby and her free hand yanking Rosanna behind her, until finally they all stood upon solid ground.

But powerful winds now forced the ships back out to sea before any provisions could be landed. Meanwhile, Esther—bedraggled, but thankful to be safe—set off with her children up a steep hill for the four-mile walk across the island to the small settlement of Kingston. Rosanna trotted along beside her, her excitement echoing Johnston's optimism. When they reached the township, Johnston was waiting to lead them to a small hut where Esther could breastfeed her crying baby.

↪ 19 March 1790 ↩

The gusty conditions continued for several days, and so all the supplies had to remain on the ships. Esther struggled each day to feed her family from the one wooden bowl that Johnston had borrowed from the resident marines.

Then she finally heard with relief that the ships had managed to heave to outside the reef about a quarter of a mile off Kingston, and were launching their boats to carry the luggage, livestock and barrels of supplies over the wild surf to the shore. Esther knew it would be an awkward task in the rough seas and she was keen to see Johnston's trunk travel safely to shore from the *Supply*. So, even though it was beginning to rain, she stood with her children beneath the shelter of a large pine tree uphill from the beach to watch the unloading through Johnston's spyglass.

She hadn't yet spotted his trunk when she noticed that the strongly running tide was gradually sweeping the *Sirius* towards a reef of rocks which lay off the west point of the bay. She shouted and waved her arms at the ships, but no one took any notice of her and she realised they could not hear her.

At last, Lieutenant Ball on the *Supply* grasped the situation and frantically waved his hat at Captain Hunter over on the *Sirius*, while pointing to the reef. Esther watched as Hunter raised his sails and tried to tack away, but the wild wind made it impossible, and she gasped at the sickening sound of breaking timbers as the ship's stern struck the reef.

The rain was now whipping beneath Esther's tree, but she couldn't take her eyes away from the drama unfolding in the wild seas. She saw Hunter shout orders. The sails dropped and the sailors feverishly sliced the hemp ropes with knives and chopped down the masts with axes, until both the sails and the masts tumbled onto the deck. Other men were frantically unloading the supplies to lessen the ship's weight so it might lift and float free from the reef, but the surf became so rough that the boats could no longer come alongside. Water was still cascading into the hold, so all hands were ordered to move the supplies out of the flooded depths and onto the top deck.

Esther grabbed Rosanna's hand and turned to run to tell Johnston what was happening. But word had already flashed around the settlement that the *Sirius* was in trouble and she saw Johnston and his marines hurtling through the now driving rain towards the beach. Out on the creaking wreck, Captain Hunter tied a rope around an empty cask and threw it overboard to be pushed by the raging surf to the waiting marines, who used it to pull to shore a thick cable which they tied to a large pine tree. Hunter hung a metal grating from the cable and tied two ropes to either side of it to make a pulley, so that it could be hauled from ship to shore.

As the afternoon waned, three or four sailors at a time would climb aboard the grating and be pulled over the jagged rocks by the marines. Often the sailors would disappear momentarily beneath the churning waves, before they arrived bruised and choking onto the beach. But in the end everyone came safely ashore from the stranded vessel.

However, most of the livestock and barrels of supplies—which were so vital for the township, where the population had just tripled in size—remained on the wreck until the following morning, when two convicts went back via the pulley to push the animals over the side, either to drown or to swim desperately through the crashing waves to the shore. Pigs, goats and chickens were all tossed into the sea.

As the pounding waves gradually broke the ship apart, the two men loaded casks of supplies onto the grating, some of which were washed off along the way while others were dashed to pieces by the submerged rocks. Yet fortunately most of them reached Johnston and his waiting marines.

Esther knew that the loss of the *Sirius* was truly awful. This was the ship that was supposed to sail on to Batavia for desperately needed food. And now the little *Supply*, which could carry only fifty people, was the one remaining ship for the two settlements—their only defence, and their only link with each other and with the outside world.

◇ 21 March 1790 ◇

Two days later, and still worryingly thin, Esther walked through the bustling township to find Ann Inett, her friend from the *Lady Penrhyn*. Ann was looking well fed and happy—indeed, it was obvious to Esther that everyone on the island had fared much better than their Sydney counterparts. Ann took Esther's hand and led her into the small Government House, where a bonny one-year-old boy was playing with his convict nurse. Ann nodded to the nurse, who put the baby down and left them alone.

Ann explained that this was the governor's little boy, named Norfolk; he had been the first baby born on the island—and he was her son.

Esther picked him up. 'Do you mean that you . . . and Governor King?'

Ann said that the governor had invited her to live with him as soon as they had arrived on the island. She knew that, if she declined, he would most likely just choose someone else, and she didn't see why she should miss out on the privileges that would surely come with the position.

As it turned out, the governor was devoted to his son *and*—Ann patted her belly—she already had another one on the way. She was only sorry that they would now be returning to Sydney, as she and the children would have to wait there while King travelled all the way to England and back.

⌐ 24 March 1790 ⌐

The *Supply* sailed back to Sydney Cove with King and his family, and Major Ross took over as governor on Norfolk Island. Esther gathered with all the other islanders around the flagpole to hear Ross declare that half rations would have to be introduced immediately until he could confirm what had been salvaged from the *Sirius*. He called for three cheers for their future, and everyone followed him in a line to pass beneath the flag as a sign of their voluntary oath that they would follow the new law.

But Esther's heart sank as she walked around the flagpole with her children. She had thought that coming to Norfolk Island would at least mean they would have plenty to eat. Now she would be on half rations again, while trying to feed her hungry baby, and the gnawing pangs of hunger she knew so well would continue.

But the balmy island hid a pleasant surprise. Five miles long and three wide, it was breathtakingly beautiful, with lush vegetation and huge pine trees. The surrounding blue sea, though treacherous where it crashed into the land, was at least abundant with fish—and Esther soon learned that there was yet another bountiful, if more unusual, source of food.

Twice a week she would leave her children with a convict maid and set off with a group of others for the four-mile walk up to majestic Mount Pitt, where thousands of petrels nested in burrows. The group would reach the nesting sites just as the sun was setting and the birds were returning from feeding out at sea, hovering above their heads in huge chattering flocks. Esther and the others held up their flaming pine knots. The birds, which had never developed a fear of people, were attracted by the light and flew in so close that she could easily catch them in her net.

So many birds nested on the island that the hunting parties caught thousands every night until the breeding season ended in July. The settlers gave the birds various nicknames, including flying sheep, mutton birds and birds of providence. The petrels were the size of fat pigeons; although they had a fishy flavour, Esther was grateful for the change from the usual salted meat. They went well with the small heads of palm trees, which reminded her of cabbage.

Now the sound of hammers and saws provided a constant backdrop to Esther's day as dozens of huts were built for the newcomers. At the end of May she and Johnston moved into a newly built cottage where she planted the geranium with its bright red flowers in the rich brown soil by its door.

⮌ 2 April 1790 ⮌

While Esther was enjoying the bountiful harvests of fish and birds on Norfolk Island, at Sydney Cove starving Susannah Kable covered her face and burst into tears when the *Supply* arrived with news of the wrecked *Sirius*. Here there were no flocks of petrels to ensure their survival; here the shortage of food had become critical.

With only enough salted pork to last a few more weeks, Governor Phillip had reduced the pitiful daily rations to less than a quarter of their original amount. Everyone, including the governor himself, received the same meagre amount of food: a little flour, some weevil-infested rice or peas, and a small piece of salted pork.

As a last resort, he reluctantly sent the *Supply* to Batavia to hire another ship to bring emergency supplies to the colony and to set Lieutenant King on his way back to England. Phillip estimated that by the time the *Supply* returned, the only food left in the colony would be flour and biscuits.

He ordered a flagpole to be erected at South Head so that if a ship was ever sighted out at sea, the men stationed there could raise the flag as a signal to the settlers in Sydney that a ship was arriving. Every boat in the colony was delegated to fishing, and William Bryant was again ordered to supervise the whole operation. He and Mary were even allowed back into their hut. But Mary felt no pleasure from their situation. To her, the whole place was hateful.

Bennelong was the only person in the colony given plenty to eat, so he would not realise their desperate situation and perhaps alert his people that the new settlers were vulnerable. So each day, wearing a smart red jacket with silver epaulettes, he ate his way through more than a week's ration of food. His shackle was removed as a sign of trust, and Governor Phillip even gave him the dagger that he usually wore at his side whenever Bennelong was with him—which was most of the time.

But Bennelong grew bored. The novelty of being such a celebrity among the white men faded, and he was worried about what was happening with his wife. Barangaroo was an attractive woman, older than Bennelong and admired by both the native and British men. If he was away for too long, she might find herself another husband. So one night he tricked his guard by pretending he was sick and pleading to go out into the fresh air. But once outside, he leapt over a low fence and escaped back into his bushland home.

A few days later, a thick morning mist swirled around Farm Cove. Here kangaroo grass entangled the seedlings that were struggling between the eucalypt stumps that stood as gravestones for the majestic trees that had once graced the bay. And standing among them was Bennelong. He was indeed astonished by the white men's management of the land. Their present suffering, which was only too obvious to him, seemed a natural result of their irresponsible behaviour and stupidity.

His people never needed to destroy the landscape to bring food from the country. The food was already there, waiting to be sought out and plucked from the bushes, dug from the ground or hunted through the trees; to be brought back and shared with others. They had little sense of ownership, because everything they required was within easy reach. In place of work, they had play; in place of greed, they had generosity; and in place of want, they had plenty. But the white settlers, many generations past living in harmony *with* the land, were blind to the bounty that surrounded them. They strove relentlessly to clear away the food-laden shrubs, to rip up and lay bare the bountiful earth, and to drive away the animals that provided such welcome meat. As a result, their farms and gardens lay dry and barren.

Yet, although the two cultures lived so differently, the cycles of their lives were just the same. And so it was, that in an atmosphere of hopelessness and dejection Mary Bryant gave birth to a son, whom she named Emanuel.

◠ 3 June 1790 ◠

'The flag is up!' Susannah Kable, in her tattered dress, pounded on the door of Mary's hut.

The door opened and Mary stood holding her small baby. She beckoned Susannah inside.

Mary suggested that it must be the *Supply* returning, but Susannah reminded her that the *Supply* was not due back for months.

Meanwhile, the township was alive with people shouting and scurrying in all directions. On that cold winter's afternoon, the emaciated settlers at Sydney Cove were absolutely jubilant. Women covered their children in kisses, and men shook each other by the hand.

Mary and Susannah soon learned that a large ship flying an English flag had entered the harbour. But the weather was so rough that she had to wait for three long days before she could make her way down to Sydney Cove. They discovered that she was the *Lady Juliana*, with a cargo of over two hundred female convicts, who arrived bright-eyed and well fed, decorating the township with their smiles and their curves.

But the *Lady Juliana* only had a few provisions left over from her voyage. Even worse, there were apparently another *thousand* convicts due to arrive within the next few weeks. Of course Britain assumed that the well-stocked *Guardian* would by now have delivered enough provisions for all those people.

For the time being, news from home—in the form of letters, newspapers and plenty of gossip—made up for the lack of supplies. The settlement fairly buzzed with chatter. Susannah told Mary what she had found out about the devastating loss of the *Guardian*, and they both felt sick at the thought of that floating treasure trove of provisions being lost in the deep, icy waters. If only the *Guardian* had arrived, they would never have lost the *Sirius*.

Mary was particularly interested in news of the *Bounty*'s mutiny, and the fact that Captain Bligh had managed to sail a small boat all the way to Timor. Susannah noticed her asking everyone she could about it.

Mary told Susannah she had found out that a new corps of the British Army was due any day to replace the marines, who would then return to England. And they both wondered what that would mean for Esther.

What neither of them knew at the time was that a loaded storeship, the *Justinian*, had reached New South Wales the day before the *Lady Juliana*; but the strong winds had forced her north so she didn't arrive until a few days later. When she turned up at last with her welcome supplies, full rations were finally restored. Oh, how busy everyone was now! So many provisions to unload and store, so many more huts to build.

The winter skies turned blue and Susannah's spirits lifted. But Mary remained despondent and preoccupied with her thoughts.

◈ 5 June 1790 ◈

On Norfolk Island, Esther knew nothing of the new army corps on its way. Her little cottage was comfortable and her life was as pleasant as she had known since before her ill-fated marriage. She devoted most of her time to the care of her children and the development of her gratifyingly productive garden but, like everyone else, she and Rosanna also gathered pine nuts and other wild food to supplement their rations, and picked caterpillars off the growing corn.

With over five hundred people now on the island, new farming lands were needed. So Johnston left Esther and the children in Kingston and took his marines and some convict labourers to a picturesque valley where they set up a farm named Charlotte Field after the Queen.

While he was away, Esther made clothes for herself and her children from more of the fabric remnants Captain Hunter had brought from the Cape—which made her by far the best-dressed woman on the island. She also made cushions for her convict-made wooden furniture and curtains for her windows, so her home was as comfortable and colourful as her clothes. Only her shoes remained shabby.

The marine wives, who had travelled out on the First Fleet and then on to Norfolk Island, were respectable women who could not approve of Esther's social position; but they were also fascinated by her fashionable elegance, so an invitation to tea proved just too irresistible.

⬱ 26 June 1790 ⬱

A few days after the arrival of the *Justinian* at Sydney Cove, three transport ships turned up—the *Surprize*, the *Scarborough* and the *Neptune*—bringing the expected thousand extra convicts.

Susannah and Mary took their children down to the cove to watch them disembark. They waited patiently in the winter drizzle while the Reverend Richard Johnson was rowed out to the ships to welcome them to Sydney, but they were surprised to see him hastily return, his face pale, holding a white handkerchief to his face as he pushed through the crowd on his way to Government House.

They soon understood why. They watched in dismay as boatloads of dead and dying people were brought ashore. Even compared with the very thin settlers, the newcomers were frighteningly emaciated—covered in their own filth, disfigured by scurvy, rotting with gangrene and crawling with lice. Few were able to stand. Their near-naked bodies were dumped at the water's edge and they crawled, like hideous bony insects, up the shore.

Other settlers going about their business nearby stopped what they were doing and slowly walked in disbelief towards the shore to stand beside Susannah and Mary. Then those further away came over to see what was so compelling and, like a wave washing back across the settlement, hut after hut emptied as their occupants walked to the water's edge and looked silently at the ghastly scene. An eerie hush floated over the cove.

Then all at once, the united compassion of the assembled crowd asserted itself in the face of the atrocity confronting them and, like a flock of birds, they moved as one—convicts and marines together— and ran down to the water's edge, flinging their arms around their fellow countrymen and dragging them up the hill towards the hospital. The men splashed waist deep into the water, reaching into the boats to lift their pathetic passengers onto their backs.

Some of the new arrivals took their last breaths on the ships' decks as they waited to be landed; others died in the boats as they were rowed ashore; many perished in the arms of their rescuers. Because the colony's hospital overflowed within the first couple of hours, dozens of tents had to be hastily erected. Four patients were placed in each one, but they had to share a single blanket between them to protect them from the winter's frosty chill.

Susannah and Mary felt helpless in the face of such suffering. They joined others in gathering grass and bracken to create makeshift bedding; they then attended to the sick and dying convicts, some of whom were the survivors from the wrecked *Guardian*, whose courage had been acknowledged and caused them to be recommended for pardons. The sunken eyes that stared up at the women seemed hardly human; it was as though their minds had retreated to distant depths, seeking sanctuary from their torture.

As a lucky few began to recover, they told Susannah and Mary about their voyage. The British Government had paid a fixed sum for each convict who embarked in England, to cover their transportation plus sufficient food for the voyage. But the ships' captains had instead kept most of the food back so they might sell it at high prices in Sydney Cove. To them, dead convicts were more profitable than living ones.

The convicts had been kept in the dark holds for almost the entire journey, chained together in groups that had to move as a single unit. When one of them died, the starving convicts who were chained to him would conceal the death so they could take the dead man's rations, until the rotting corpse, being gradually stripped of its flesh by rats, was finally detected.

When the ships had stopped at the Cape and learned of the wreck of the *Guardian* and the shortage of supplies in the new colony, their captains had confined the convicts to an even smaller space so they could take on more goods for sale. The heavily laden ships then took in so much water during the rest of the voyage that the wretched convicts were waist deep and had to remain standing for days on end or drown in the filth that washed around them. A quarter of the convicts who had embarked on the voyage had died along the way and half of the remaining ones were gravely ill.

For the first few days, Susannah and Mary saw a dozen corpses carried from the hospital each morning, sometimes lying on the foreshore for several days before they could be rowed across to be buried on the north shore of the harbour. Even more gruesome were the bodies the captains had had thrown overboard as they entered the harbour and which now began to wash up on the pristine beaches, naked and swollen.

While the dying convicts lay in their tents on the cold ground, the captains of their ships set up shop on shore to sell their goods at exorbitant prices to those who had the means to pay for them. The promissory notes used as currency within the colony were not acceptable anywhere else, but the marine and civil officers could draw bills of exchange on their salaries.

Susannah and Mary were appalled to see the captains profit from such abominable cruelty—nevertheless, the necessity was so great that their boxes of food, glassware, hats, perfume and paper goods were soon empty.

A few weeks later, the *Scarborough* and the *Neptune* left Sydney Cove, bound for Canton to collect a cargo of tea for the British East India Company. The other two ships would meet them there, after first delivering supplies and some of the surviving convicts to Norfolk Island.

∽ *16 August 1790* ∽

At Kingston on Norfolk Island, the bountiful sea birds had migrated north, the surrounding cabbage trees had all been eaten and there were only enough supplies to last another twelve weeks. Then, one day, after the rations had again been halved, Esther heard shouting and ran outside to see what it was about. The *Surprize* lived up to her name as she came into view across the ocean, accompanied by the *Justinian*.

∓ 17 August 1790 ∓

The difficult matter of unloading the ships through the fierce surf began once again. Johnston was already down at the beach directing his marines when Esther and Rosanna joined the crowd of five hundred people gathered to welcome the new arrivals.

One boat crammed with convict women and casks of salt meat was making for the shore when a series of large waves appeared from nowhere and smashed it against the reef. Only twenty yards away, Esther watched helplessly as the women tried desperately to snatch gulps of air while being tumbled by the choppy surf. Johnston and his marines splashed out through the waves to reach the struggling bodies, but three women and a child all drowned before her eyes.

As two more apparently lifeless women were pulled onto the shore, Esther ran over to help them. As she approached, one of the bedraggled women started crawling up the sand before slumping back down.

'Nelly Kerwin!' cried Esther. 'Can it be you?'

Her dear friend and cellmate from Newgate Prison turned to face her before bursting into tears of relief. Esther dropped to the sand and cradled Nelly in her arms while tears flowed down her own face. She asked a nearby marine to carry Nelly to her cottage, where she gave her some dry clothes, settled her among cushions that matched the cloudless blue sky outside, and made her a strong cup of tea.

Nelly explained that after her baby died, her execution was stayed, awaiting a decision from the King. For two long years she remained in Newgate Prison, not knowing whether she would live or die. Then, when the King had recovered from a period of insanity, he celebrated by pardoning some of the convicts who had been sentenced to death. Nelly was one of them, on condition that she be transported for the term of her natural life.

Esther clasped her hands together in joy. 'I can't believe you are sitting here with me!' she said.

Another passenger on the *Surprize* was a twenty-eight-year-old doctor named D'Arcy Wentworth, whose presence caused quite a stir among the marine wives. They buzzed with gossip about him when they visited Esther. They told her he had been charged with highway robbery *nine times* and had faced four trials at the Old Bailey.

'He is a convict then?' asked Esther.

No indeed. There was the mystery. Apparently his guilt could never be proven, even though some of the stolen property was found in his possession. As he was from a noble family, the talk was that his influential relatives must have swayed the courts, and he had decided to travel to the colony while he was still free to get away. The London newspapers had called him *notorious*, the wives explained, and reported that he had lived under false names in London and had cohabited with all sorts of women.

The marine wives told her how admirably tall he was, and handsome as well, with an appealing Irish accent that made them want to keep him talking. One of them added in a hushed voice that, apparently, he had bedded a seventeen-year-old convict girl during the voyage to Sydney Cove.

Apparently the girl had given birth to their son just as they arrived at Norfolk Island. Dr Wentworth had attended the birth himself and then washed his own newborn baby.

Esther's curiosity about this daring highwayman was roused, and she suggested to Johnston that they invite him to dinner. On the allotted day, she was calling Rosanna to come inside when her maid informed her that the two men had arrived back from their walk to Charlotte Field.

Esther plucked a red geranium from the garden and slid it behind her ear so that its vibrant colour would accentuate her glossy dark hair. She wore a pretty shawl she had made from one of the fabric remnants Captain Hunter had brought from Cape Town, and she pinched her cheeks to give them extra colour before taking Rosanna's hand to walk inside.

The daylight was fading and the room already glowed with soft candlelight as Johnston presented Dr D'Arcy Wentworth to her. Esther's face flushed further as their guest strode forward with a broad smile.

'This is an unexpected pleasure, Mrs Abrahams,' he said.

She bobbed a curtsey as he lifted her hand towards his lips.

The two gentlemen fell into easy conversation while Esther's heart pounded and she tried to decide whether to tell Johnston that she already knew Dr Wentworth. Because leaning against her sky-blue cushions was the gentleman she knew as Henry Fitzroy, who had found her a place to live in St James.

As the conversation moved on, she decided to say nothing.

CHAPTER SEVEN

An Uncertain Future

From her garden in Farm Cove, Mary Bryant could tell that something was wrong. The governor's boat was being rowed aggressively towards Sydney Cove and the officers aboard it were shouting frantically. By the time Mary had run around the point, she could see that the governor himself was in the boat. He was lying across Lieutenant Henry Waterhouse's knees and a spear was sticking up out of his body.

When the boat finally pulled in to the shore, Dr Balmain rushed down to meet it. He instructed the officers to carefully carry the governor up to the hospital. As Mary watched, a blood-soaked Phillip was gently lifted out of the boat and she could see that the spear had gone right through him—in near his collarbone and out through his back. Susannah arrived to see what all the shouting was about, and the two women followed everyone else to the hospital to learn of the governor's fate.

Mary told Susannah that she heard Governor Phillip had been visiting Bennelong at Manly Cove, to thank him for a gift of whale blubber, when another native man had apparently hurled his spear straight through him. Susannah said the attack must have been caused by a terrible misunderstanding, but Mary said she wasn't so sure.

Because the Bryants were always fishing in the harbour, they had become very friendly with the natives, who abided by a strong system of payback. Mary explained to Susannah that the natives might have purposely arranged the attack on Governor Phillip, as retribution for all the troubles they had experienced since the settlers had arrived. The whole episode might even have been arranged by Bennelong. He had made no attempt to stop the man from throwing his spear—never said a word, apparently. But it could mean that, now that the sufferings of his people had been atoned, the two communities could start afresh, on equal terms.

Eventually, Dr Balmain emerged from the hospital to announce that he had removed the spear and that the governor was still alive. Though in agonising pain, Phillip had ordered that there be no retaliation for the attack.

❧ 17 September 1790 ❧

As a token of his continuing friendship, Phillip sent a gift of freshly caught fish to Bennelong, who was still camped on the north shore. But Bennelong would not return to Sydney until the governor had first come to him to show that he held no anger towards him.

So, ten days after the attack, Governor Phillip gingerly lowered himself into a boat to visit his native friend and convey his wish that one day Bennelong would agree to come back to the settlement voluntarily.

❧ 6 October 1790 ❧

About three weeks later, William Bryant was fishing near the north side of the harbour when he saw Bennelong preparing to visit Government House. Barangaroo was pleading with him not to go. She tearfully stamped her foot and began tearing out her hair. But Bryant knew that Bennelong would go, whatever Barangaroo said. He wouldn't be able to resist the opportunity to show off to his friends how much he knew about the white men's ways.

The chaplain and his adopted native daughter, Boorong, were rowed over to stay with Barangaroo, to reassure her that this time no one would be captured. Nevertheless, as soon as Bennelong had left, Bryant saw Barangaroo furiously break her husband's prized fishing spear against some rocks.

Good relations with the British were restored by Bennelong's visit, and the natives eventually 'came in' to Sydney. From then on they could always be seen about the town. They bartered spears, clubs and fishing tackle for hatchets, knives and jackets. Governor Phillip hoped that such collaboration would encourage harmony between the two cultures.

Even Barangaroo began visiting Government House with Bennelong, although she steadfastly refused to wear any clothes, except for a decorative bone pushed through her nose. Sometimes she turned up bleeding and bruised, from having been beaten by Bennelong; at other times it was obvious that they were close.

Once, when Barangaroo sat beside the governor's fire complaining of a stomach-ache, Bennelong blew on his hand to warm it before gently placing it on her naked waist. Then he leant over to bring his mouth close to the pain while he sang a healing song for her.

In the meantime, Governor Phillip arranged for a small cottage to be built for Bennelong on a prominent point below Government House that could be seen from many places on the harbour. The cottage was twelve feet square and constructed of brick and tile.

The governor also arranged the building of a second Government House at Rose Hill, where he could stay when he visited that settlement. When it was completed, he invited Bennelong and Colbee to accompany him on a visit there.

⇜ 7 December 1790 ⇝

Phillip and Colbee sat in the governor's boat with Bryant—who would be rowing them up the river—while Bennelong dashed back to his cottage to collect a possum-skin cloak to take with him. But Bennelong didn't return. After a while, the others started off without him, but then they saw Bennelong scrambling over the rocks on the point near his cottage, pursued by an infuriated Barangaroo.

Bryant drew the boat close, so that Bennelong could get in. As he climbed aboard, he shouted to his wife that he would be gone for only one night. But as Bryant pulled away again, the men saw Barangaroo run to a new canoe Bennelong had made for her and drive its paddles straight through its bottom. Then she flung the paddles out into the harbour and ran back towards the cottage, presumably to find other items to damage.

Governor Phillip tactfully suggested they return to the shore so that Bennelong could get out, and the mighty warrior accepted his advice. The governor and Colbee continued on to Rose Hill, and the following day Bryant rowed Colbee back to Sydney Cove.

The day after that, Bryant set off again for Rose Hill. This time, Bennelong and Barangaroo were both in the boat with him, laughing and talking happily together, off to visit the governor in his new house. They were served a hearty lunch, but Barangaroo then announced that she didn't want to stay the night after all, and she must return home. Bennelong explained to Phillip that she would cry if he didn't take her back.

So Bryant picked up the oars once again and rowed Bennelong and Barangaroo all the way back down the river to Sydney. He had to return to Rose Hill the following day to collect the governor.

⌐ *17 December 1790* ⌐

Susannah and Mary stood together outside the Bryants' house, watching the Dutch ship *Waaksamheyd* sail up the harbour. She had been chartered from Batavia by Lieutenant Ball of HMS *Supply* to bring provisions to the colony, and the decks were loaded with beef, pork, flour, sugar and rice. It was a wonderful sight. And, like the others who were lining the shore, Susannah and Mary waved and cheered as she sailed past.

A few days later, Susannah mentioned to her husband that she didn't like the look of the ship's captain, Detmer Smit, although Mary was apparently happy to do all his washing for him. Kable told her that the Bryants' friendship with Smit might not be as innocent as it appeared.

Bryant's sentence was soon due to expire and he had recently drunkenly boasted to some sailors that he was going to try to get a place on Smit's ship when it sailed, leaving Mary and the children behind. Kable, who had been made a constable in the colony's police force, had been asked to keep a watch on him until the ship had sailed.

⊱ 23 December 1790 ⊰

Just before Christmas, Colbee's gentle wife, Daringa, brought her two-day-old baby to show Mary. Daringa was the half-sister of the clan leader, Moorooboora. She had walked all the way from Botany Bay, where she had given birth, so that Colbee could present his child to Governor Phillip and they could stay the night at Government House.

Mary noticed that Daringa's hair was matted with blood, and Daringa explained that Colbee had beaten her with his wooden sword.

⊱ 25 February 1791 ⊰

On the small Rose Hill farm that Governor Phillip had given him to work, James Ruse was reaping the rewards of his careful farming practices. To him the land was a precious gift that gave him freedom, purpose, reward and the beginning of a new life filled with hope, so he treated it well. He burnt the felled trees and mixed the rich ash into the soil. He dug deep pits into which he threw straw, food scraps, seaweed, manure and anything else he could find that would rot and feed the starving soil—and the land responded with bounty.

When he visited the governor to announce that he had collected his last ration from the government store and could henceforth support himself from his farm, Phillip was overjoyed. Here at last was proof that the colonists *could* become self-sufficient. He gave Ruse the title to his land, as promised, with an additional parcel of thirty acres—the first grant of land in the colony.

⊱ 27 March 1791 ⊰

At the end of March, Susannah was relieved to see that both Mary and William Bryant were among the crowd waving goodbye to the

Waaksamheyd as she sailed away. She had been chartered by Governor Phillip to take the shipwrecked crew of HMS *Sirius* back to England. HMS *Supply* was at Norfolk Island once again, so the cove was empty of ships.

⮎ 9 April 1791 ⮌

On Norfolk Island, Esther was packing the last pie into a handmade basket when Johnston strode in to tell her that their picnic would have to be brief. There was trouble at the barracks and he would have to sort it out that afternoon. He explained that, since the rations had been cut, the marines considered themselves worse off than the convicts, who could supplement their food with vegetables they grew in their gardens. If the marines wanted vegetables, they had to buy them from the convicts.

So now the marines were refusing to collect any rations at all until their portions were increased—something that couldn't be done because Governor Phillip had issued strict orders that everyone was to receive the same amount.

Esther was puzzled. Couldn't the marines grow vegetables themselves if they wanted to? Of course they could, Johnston told her, but it seemed that Major Ross's attitude had convinced them that any work other than defending the settlement was beneath them.

That afternoon, as planned, Johnston ordered the troops to fall in. He explained to them Governor Phillip's orders regarding equal rations for all; he also pointed out the valuable operation they were undertaking, establishing a new outpost for the British Empire. Their roles needed to remain flexible to achieve success in this unusual situation.

He asked them what they thought would happen if the island colony failed—because they all knew the French were just waiting to take possession of it. He reminded the men that they had each been chosen as the very best of the hundreds of marines who had volunteered to join the First Fleet, and that every person in the colony was depending on them. More than that, their king was depending on them—and Johnston expected every man to do his duty to the King.

He walked along the line and looked each man in the eye. Then he ordered them to pick up their ration bags and accompany him to the store to collect their provisions. He turned on his heel and strode out the door. He didn't look back.

After initial hesitation, a couple of men collected their ration bags and followed him out of the barracks. Then, gradually, each of the remaining men did the same.

'I expected nothing less,' Johnston told Esther later, sounding rather more confident than he had felt at the time.

⌖ 2 May 1791 ⌖

Colbee's wife, Daringa, was respected as a kind and gentle woman. So, when a convict in Sydney stole her fishing tackle, Governor Phillip called all his native friends together to witness the justice of British law in action. The convict was flogged in front of them, bound and helpless; but rather than being gratified, they were just as horrified as Arabanoo had been at such unfair treatment of a fellow human being.

Daringa covered her face and wept into her hands. Barangaroo, always more passionate, snatched up a stick and began beating the flogger himself.

⌖ 8 May 1791 ⌖

The marines on Norfolk Island were now due to return to Sydney. The ships of the Second Fleet had brought new soldiers—the New South Wales Corps—to replace all the marines in the two settlements. The soldiers were army men, and the corps was made up of recruits of a much lower calibre. Unlike the overwhelming response when marines had been invited to volunteer for the First Fleet, the army could not find enough men to fill the ranks of the New South Wales Corps, so extra soldiers had been enlisted from army deserters and those who had previously been court-martialled.

Marines usually enlisted for life, and most of the ones in New South Wales would now return to England. But those who were not officers could instead accept a grant of land and remain in the colony as free settlers. Johnston told Esther that he had asked Governor Phillip for a civilian role so he could remain in New South Wales.

The day before they were due to leave Norfolk Island, Esther walked to the top of a cliff for one last look at the spectacular view it offered. The sea was a deep, vibrant blue, the surrounding fields were lush and green, and the soft breeze was warm against her face. It really was quite a paradise, if a little lonely for a young woman of twenty-one. She looked forward to enjoying a wider social circle in Sydney, particularly as she knew that many of the officers of the New South Wales Corps had brought their wives out with them.

She was startled when Dr Wentworth suddenly appeared by her side. She took a step away, but he reached out to put his hand gently on her arm. He told her that she would do better to stay on Norfolk Island than to return to Sydney with Johnston. Esther looked at him questioningly.

Wentworth explained that Johnston would never marry her. He was bound to soon return to England and find himself a suitable wife, and Esther would be discarded; she must realise that she could never be accepted into his social circle. Wentworth was sure she would be happier if she chose to stay on the island.

Esther thanked him politely for his advice, but added that she could not agree with his opinion on the matter. Then she bobbed a curtsey and walked briskly back into the town.

✎ 30 May 1791 ✎

The Sydney that welcomed Esther and Johnston back was very different from the one they had left the year before. The cool green forest that had shadowed the banks of the stream was all but gone, except for a thin line of trees on either side that had been spared to protect the vital water from evaporation. And there was now a wooden picket fence running alongside the water, to stop wandering livestock from polluting it. The surrounding open woodland had been cleared and a bustling town filled the cove, with faded huts and neat brick cottages dotted along the edge of rough tracks that wound in all directions.

On the western side of the stream were officers' huts and a parade ground for the troops; there were storehouses, a bakehouse and the hospital; there was an observatory on the point, manned by Lieutenant William Dawes. On the eastern side was the stone Government House—still the only two-storey building in the settlement—where a touch of autumn colour decorated the oak trees, peach trees and grapevines that grew in its large garden. It overlooked neat houses belonging to the civil officers, and huts that had been built for the governor's servants and guard.

At the shoreline was a wooden wharf, a boatshed and a large, solid storehouse made of brick with a tiled roof, which was heavily guarded both day and night. Bennelong's cottage stood on the point. It had become a popular meeting place for the many natives who spent several days at a time in the town. Further east around the point, the government farm now lay barren, as all agricultural activity had been moved up the river to the more productive land around Rose Hill.

The two rivers, the Hawkesbury and the Nepean, had been found to be one and the same—flowing in a wide arc from far west of Botany Bay in the south, to empty into Broken Bay to the north—and more good farming land had been found along its banks.

⌒ 31 May 1791 ⌒

Esther couldn't wait to take Rosanna and Young George to visit Susannah Kable and find out all the latest Sydney gossip. Her first surprise was meeting Susannah's six-week-old baby boy, Enoch. But then Susannah told Esther what had happened to Mary Bryant after the *Waaksamheyd* had sailed.

Henry Kable had walked past the Bryants' hut the following morning and noticed that its door was open. He had peered inside and seen that it was eerily empty, and that a plank from its new wooden floor had been lifted and moved aside to reveal a large hole in the earth below—also empty.

Kable had then walked around to the wharf, where he noticed first that someone had spilled some rice on the path, and then that the governor's six-oared boat was missing from Bennelong's point. Kable had run all the way to Government House, and soon afterwards the colony became alive with gossip. It seemed that the Bryants had escaped!

Everyone had then started commenting that they had heard this and that during the previous few weeks, and it transpired that the Bryants had been planning their escape for months. Apparently Captain Smit had sold them a compass and some charts, and they had secretly bought food and muskets from some of the settlers. Fishing equipment had disappeared too, including a new net. According to what Kable had told Susannah, without the boat and that net—and it had to be said, Bryant himself—the colony would never be able to catch the required number of fish.

'What about Mary's children?' Esther asked with concern. Susannah replied that they must have taken the children with them. She added that Emanuel was only a few months old and Charlotte was such a busy little thing that she couldn't think it would be possible to care for her in an open boat. And where they had gone, nobody knew. There was nowhere *to* go.

Nevertheless, they had chosen their moment well. Bryant had only just refurbished the cutter, giving it a new mast, sail and oars, so it was probably more seaworthy than it had ever been. And there was also no ship left in the harbour to go after them.

Esther wondered aloud how four people could survive in such a small boat on the open ocean, but Susannah told her it was worse than that. Another seven convict men had escaped with them.

'So the boat is crammed full!' gasped Esther.

After a cup of tea, during which Susannah told Esther about the suffering of the convicts who had arrived on the *Surprize*, the *Scarborough* and the *Neptune*, their conversation moved on to the happier subject of the new army wives. Susannah said they had brought a much more civilised air to the place, particularly one accomplished lady called Elizabeth Macarthur. Susannah added with a smile that she thought Esther looked remarkably like her.

Mrs Macarthur's husband was a lieutenant in the New South Wales Corps. Susannah had heard that his father was only a draper, but she believed that Mrs Macarthur had the most cultivated manners in the colony—except of course for the chaplain's wife, but nobody ever saw her, and those two did not get along.

Susannah commented that the officers buzzed about Mrs Macarthur like bees. They were always visiting her with bunches of bush flowers, or a book they thought she might find amusing, or a piece of fruit they had grown in their gardens. The governor had even sent her some grapes from the vines he had purchased at the Cape. And when she was invited to dine at Government House, she was the only person in the whole colony who was not required to take her own bread.

Susannah also told Esther that Dr Worgan, who was returning to England on the *Waaksamheyd*, had given Mrs Macarthur the piano-forte he had brought out on the *Sirius*. Apparently, the Macarthurs' neighbours sometimes heard her practising it and reported that she had become quite proficient with 'God Save the King'.

Susannah poured her guest another cup of tea, then launched off again. Mrs Macarthur ran her household just as if she were living in polite society at home, and her little boy, Edward—although delicate in health—was always neatly dressed and well mannered.

Esther looked through the open doorway to see Rosanna and Harry cantering around the garden on their hobby horses, utterly barefoot. She wondered if perhaps she had let Rosanna run a little too free in Norfolk Island's agreeable climate. She resolved to pay more attention to her daughter's upbringing in future. While Susannah never expected the army wives to accept her into their social circle, Esther was very much looking forward to enjoying their company.

❧ 2 June 1791 ❧

Governor Phillip learned from Bennelong that the native name for the area of Rose Hill was Parramatta (the place where eels lie down), so in a diplomatic gesture he officially adopted the Indigenous name—although the brightly coloured parrots that had first been seen there continued to be called Rose Hillers (later rosellas). He told Johnston that the settlement had developed substantially during the last year, and that a small barge now regularly made the half-day journey there, taking supplies to and from Sydney.

Johnston was keen to see for himself how different Parramatta had become since he had taken the first convicts there. So he took Esther and the children on a visit up the river.

They arrived at a small wharf on the riverbank, which stood at one end of a road that was two hundred feet wide and a mile long. They followed the road up past some wooden barracks, a storehouse and thirty-two huts that squatted on either side of it. The huts were placed a hundred feet apart and were made from wattle and clay, with chimneys, thatched roofs and doors that, when open, made them look surprised. They comprised two rooms and were designed to house ten male convicts, although they had already each become home to fourteen.

Other huts in side streets housed female convicts and families, and they all had small, but flourishing, gardens. The town also had a barn, a granary, a bakehouse, a blacksmith and a basic hospital.

Parramatta was home to about five hundred and fifty people and it buzzed with activity. Esther and Johnston saw convicts busy clearing land, making bricks and roof tiles, building houses, making roads and chopping firewood. They also passed barrel-makers, shepherds, shoe-makers, tailors, bakers and nurses—everything a small town needed.

Johnston then wanted to inspect the newly built barracks, so he set off back along the main street while Esther and the children took a more leisurely stroll. Not long afterwards, Esther noticed a soldier and his wife watching her, and she recognised Elizabeth Macarthur from Susannah's description.

Susannah had been right—Elizabeth moved with uncommon grace. But so might any woman, Esther mused, who knew that every officer in the colony would jump at the chance to protect her from the slight-est harm. At twenty-four, Mrs Macarthur was just three years older than Esther. Her clothes fitted a figure kept in perfect shape by a corset, and her fashionable shoes were made of soft Moroccan leather. Esther was pleased to be able to make her acquaintance so soon.

As she and her children walked towards the couple, their two-year-old boy, Edward, trotted towards them, and Esther crouched down to greet him.

'Good morning, young sir,' she said. Elizabeth came nearer, and Esther stood up to bob a curtsey. 'You have a delightful little boy,' she added with a smile.

Elizabeth hesitated, then replied coolly, 'I do not believe we have been introduced.'

And before Esther could respond, Lieutenant Macarthur snatched his son away from her and hissed: 'How dare you address Mrs Macarthur in public! She cannot be expected to converse with women of your sort.'

He led his wife and child briskly away. Esther felt her face flush, and she looked around to see if anyone had witnessed the exchange. But everyone else was busy with their tasks.

⌒ 7 August 1791 ⌒

Rosanna ran in and out of the small cottage that was Esther and Johnston's temporary home, tickling Young George each time she dashed past him.

'Mind the furniture!' Esther called, as Rosanna bumped against Johnston's writing desk, causing it to wobble back against the wall. The seven-volume pile of *Annals of Agriculture and Other Useful Arts* toppled to the floor. They had been a parting gift to Johnston from his patron, the Duke of Northumberland.

Esther, battling the queasiness of early pregnancy, bent down to pick up the books. Beneath them she found a letter Johnston had been writing to Lieutenant Ralph Clark on Norfolk Island. As she put it back on the desk her eyes scanned its last paragraph: *I hope we shall soon see the* Gorgon *here to carry us to England, otherwise they must allow us field officers pay, for at present they ask a guinea a gallon for rum, and the same for a pound of tobacco and every thing else in proportion, but I hope we shall soon be in the Land of Plenty.*

Esther stood as still as a statue, staring down at the piece of paper. It seemed Dr Wentworth had been right, after all: Johnston had lied to her and was going home.

She felt devastated by everything those words meant. Quite apart from the pain of being tossed aside like a used rag, her mind reeled at the difficulties she would have to face, managing three children on her own.

◈ 25 August 1791 ◈

It was the end of winter. Gusty winds and glorious sunsets heralded the warmer weather to come. Four of the eleven ships that made up the Third Fleet to New South Wales had now arrived, bringing still more convicts but also more provisions. So full rations had at last been restored.

In the true spirit of spring, Barangaroo was heavily pregnant, and Bennelong proudly announced to Governor Phillip that she would do him the honour of giving birth in Government House. Phillip strongly protested, but Bennelong was determined. He saw great political advantage in his son—and he was sure it would be a son—having birth rights to Government House.

Phillip finally convinced him that the hospital would be a far more suitable place, and Bennelong was satisfied that at least his son would be born in the centre of the settlement. He asked for a British blanket in which to wrap his newborn child and Phillip readily gave him one.

Barangaroo, however, considered the hospital completely *unsuit-able*, contaminated as it was with the spirits of those who had recently died. When the time came, she did not submit herself to the care of the white doctors, nor take advantage of the shelter provided by her Sydney cottage. She did not even paddle across the harbour to be with her own clan. Instead, with her head still oozing blood from a beating Bennelong had given her that morning, she walked alone into the bush. Her newborn *daughter*, named Dilboong (bellbird), lay not on a British blanket but, according to native custom, on a soft bed of paperbark.

But Barangaroo was not a young mother, and she died soon after her daughter was born. Her body was cremated along with her fishing tackle, and her ashes were buried in the garden of Government House. The grieving Bennelong asked Phillip to find a British wet nurse for his baby daughter; but Dilboong also died a few months later, and was buried next to her mother. Bennelong was left all alone.

◇ 21 September 1791 ◇

The *Gorgon* brought Lieutenant King back from England to prepare to take up the post of Lieutenant-Governor on Norfolk Island. When he had stopped at the Cape of Good Hope on the way, he had purchased more supplies for the colony, including some invaluable cattle. But all three bulls had died on the voyage, and the colony was again left with no cattle to breed from until its one young bull calf grew up. King also brought more rabbits and pigeons to the colony—which must have seemed like a good idea at the time.

However, the *Gorgon* did not bring King back to Ann Inett, who had given birth to his second son, Sydney, while he had been away. Instead, King arrived with a wife—his charming but not very pretty cousin, Anna Josepha Coombe. And she was expecting their first child.

'Oh, Ann, I am so sorry,' Esther said when she heard the news. Ann replied that she supposed it was only to be expected. After all, he couldn't have someone like herself as his *wife*—First Lady of Norfolk Island, hosting vice-regal dinners and suchlike.

Ann looked out of the window and added that, apparently, the Kings had been married in St Martin-in-the-Fields in Trafalgar Square. Her voice trailed away. Esther could think of nothing to say.

Ann gave her head a little shake and turned back around. She said it was easy to think things were different in the colony, but when the men went back to England they were reminded of how it's all supposed to be.

She took a deep breath. Then she told Esther that King had promised to look after her. And the children. In fact, her children would have a life of privilege.

Ann gave a weak smile, but her mouth was trembling. She said that King was taking their son, Norfolk, to the island with him; his little brother, Sydney, would follow as soon as he was old enough. She turned to look out of the window again, adding that she wouldn't have the trouble of bringing them up on her own. She paused. She wouldn't have them at all.

Esther felt a wave of panic flood through her.

CHAPTER EIGHT

The Annandale Estate

❧ 31 October 1791 ☙

B y the end of the following month, the last of the eleven ships of the Third Fleet had arrived, bringing the total number of convicts in the colony to over two and a half thousand. While not treated as cruelly as those on the Second Fleet, many of the new arrivals were still too weak and emaciated to be able to work, adding yet another burden to the struggling settlement. So everyone's rations were reduced once again.

By now, some of the convicts had completed their sentences. They were known as emancipists. If they were male, Governor Phillip gave them a small grant of land, with convict assistance to clear it, grain to sow their first crop and eighteen months' provisions from the public store, to last them until they could grow enough food to feed themselves. Female emancipists received no land. They needed to either marry someone who owned land or find work which provided some associated housing.

❧ 12 November 1791 ☙

Since she had discovered that Johnston was returning to England on the *Gorgon*, Esther's emotions had ranged through disbelief, fear, self-pity and anger. She had been distant and aloof with Johnston, but he had attributed that to the fact that she was once more with child.

Now five months pregnant, she could barely contain the anger and the hurt she felt about his imminent abandonment of their relationship. She tried to calm her thoughts and work out what to do. However difficult it would be to care for three children alone in the colony, she was determined to prevent Johnston from taking any of them away from her.

She gradually concocted a plan: the night before the marines sailed back to England on the *Gorgon*, she would take four-year-old Rosanna and not-quite-two George into the bush and wait there until the ship had left. It would be summertime, and she was sure they would all be warm enough outdoors overnight. Johnston would have no choice but to leave for England on his own. Once the ship had gone, Esther would bring her children back into the town. She feared she had little chance of obtaining good employment with children to care for, but she was determined to keep them all together.

◇ 17 December 1791 ◇

When the day came, and before Johnston returned from his usual visit to Government House, Esther packed a basket with food and shepherded her two small children out of the house. She murmured a quiet goodbye to Johnston and the future she had thought they would have together.

She plodded along the dusty road and across the wooden bridge that spanned the stream. The water flowing beneath it was now only a muddy trickle. Large holding tanks had been cut into the sandstone on each side of the stream to collect and store the precious water that would otherwise run uselessly into the harbour, resulting in the name of the Tank Stream.

Esther and her children followed a track through the abandoned Farm Cove, which the native bush was attempting to reclaim. Out on the bright blue water of the harbour—which twinkled silver in the sunlight—she could see Colbee's wife, Daringa, fishing from her canoe, with her one-year-old daughter wedged firmly between her knees.

When they reached the trees on the other side, Rosanna skipped ahead while Young George toddled beside his mother. Not yet old enough to be 'breeched'—and so wear trousers—his little legs paddled beneath the bottom of his frock. The heat of the late afternoon filled the bush with heady fragrances. As they went, Rosanna pointed to plants and berries that Arabanoo had shown her, muttering to herself a mixture of English and the native words that always sprang to mind when she thought of him.

'Ivy, yes, boodjerree [good], boodjerree. Ah! Murrai [big] figs! Boodjerree, boodjerree.'

Esther snapped at her young daughter, telling her not to use such unsuitable words. Rosanna's bottom lip trembled and Esther suggested they stop for a rest. Rosanna sat upright on a large rock and crossed her ankles in the ladylike way her mother had taught her.

Then, all of a sudden, they heard the sound of cracking twigs and an emaciated white woman appeared from between the trees. Esther recognised her as the bullying convict, Ann Smith, who had escaped from the colony when they had first arrived, four years earlier. Ann's burnished skin was covered with scratches and scabs. She rushed at the basket of food and grabbed its handle. Esther shouted at her to go away, and tried to pull the basket from Ann's grasp. But, with the strength of desperation, Ann yanked it out of Esther's hands, causing Esther to lose her balance and fall heavily forward, hitting her head against the rock. Esther crumpled to the ground and lay still. Ann glanced at the two small children, hesitated for just a moment, then disappeared with the basket back into the bush.

Rosanna tried to wake her mother, but Esther didn't respond. The little girl looked anxiously around and saw Daringa down on the shoreline, just getting out of her canoe. Rosanna cupped her small hands to her mouth and called the way Arabanoo had taught her: 'Coo-ee! [Come here!] Coo-ee!'

In the fading early evening light Daringa looked towards the small girl.

'Weeree [bad]! Weeree!' Rosanna called. Daringa lifted her daughter onto her shoulders and scrambled across the rocky shore towards the tearful white child. Esther remained motionless on the ground.

Daringa spoke rapidly in her soothing, liquid-sounding language, but Rosanna could not understand her. Daringa undid the net bag she carried round her neck and took out a piece of oyster shell and some string made from entwined hairs. She made a small scratch on Esther's forehead with the shell, just enough to draw a little blood. Then she held one end of the string against Esther's forehead and rubbed the other end against her own bottom lip. She continued rubbing until her lip started to bleed. Then she nodded her head and began to sing, smiling reassuringly at Rosanna. She explained to the uncomprehending child that Esther's sickness would be drawn out along the string and she would soon be well. After a little while, Esther stirred and groaned.

'Mama!' shouted Rosanna, and smiled through her tears at the native woman with the bleeding lip whose conversation rippled over her head. Esther pulled herself up to sit against the rock, holding her head in her hands but Daringa motioned to her to stay still and rest for a while. After several minutes Daringa gently helped Esther to stand up. Then she slowly led the little group back past the old government farm until she could see firelight twinkling from the cooking fires down in the settlement.

Esther suddenly became aware of where they were.

'No!' she moaned.

But it was too late.

'There you are!' called Johnston, running up the hill towards them.

Daringa nodded and smiled at Rosanna, then she and her child melted into the shadows. Soon afterwards, Esther and her children were safely back in their own home. Johnston helped Esther into bed and then he sat on its edge. He stroked the back of his hand down the side of Esther's brown neck.

'What on earth were you doing out there, Hetty?' he asked.

Esther whispered that he was leaving them and going back to England.

'What? Of course I'm not!' Johnston replied. But she told him she had seen his letter to Lieutenant Clark. Johnston frowned, trying to recollect the words he had written. Then he explained that he had never intended to leave the colony himself. Why would he, when his family was in Sydney? He had only tried to convey in his letter his understanding of the other officer's feelings.

On the contrary, he added, Governor Phillip had offered him a promotion to the full captaincy of an extra new company in the New South Wales Corps. And thirty-seven marines had offered to stay and enlist on the condition that he be their commander. Of course, it would mean transferring from the marines to the army, but he would receive a generous bonus for doing so—equal to about ten months' salary.

Esther hadn't heard more than his first few words. Exhaustion had claimed her and she was fast asleep. Rosanna was too over-excited to sleep. She followed Johnston about the cottage, retelling the afternoon's drama again and again. Eventually, as the bustle of evening activity in the settlement quietened, she succumbed to his entreaties to go to bed, and fell asleep within minutes of his goodnight kiss.

Johnston took a candle over to Esther's sleeping body, slowly shaking his head at her notion of the natives being 'savages'. He was so grateful for Daringa's help that day.

However, Esther's ordeal was not over. Her unborn child had suffered extensively from her fall, and several weeks later Esther held the tiny, stillborn baby girl in her arms. She rocked to and fro, hugging her baby tight, and sobbing with grief.

◁ 20 June 1792 ▷

Governor Phillip had sent the *Atlantic* to Calcutta to buy more provisions and livestock, and now she sailed back into Sydney Harbour.

As well as the welcome supplies, the captain of the *Atlantic* brought news of the convicts who had escaped in the governor's boat two years earlier. And, for some days after they had heard the tale, Esther and Susannah could talk of little else.

For ten long weeks after they had slipped out of Sydney Harbour in the open boat, Mary Bryant and her fellow escapees had sailed and rowed over three thousand miles up the east coast of Australia. They had been drenched by rain, tossed by stormy seas, and sometimes had to bail for hours just to keep their small boat afloat. They had fished along the way and had pulled into shore now and then through raging surf to fill up their stores of fresh water and cabbage-tree palms.

Once, when they had stopped at an island between the mainland and the Great Barrier Reef, they had been able to feast on turtle eggs. But there was also a time when the winds had driven them out of sight of land for nearly three weeks, and they had been parched and starving before they had made it back to shore again.

Some of the natives they encountered along the way had been friendly, others hostile. In the Gulf of Carpentaria, after rounding Cape York, they had been attacked with bows and arrows and chased for miles by two large sailing canoes, each manned by thirty natives.

It had taken them four days to reach the other side of the gulf. They had continued along the top of Australia, and all the way across the Timor Sea, to finally tie up at the same wharf where Captain Bligh had moored his boat two years earlier. Through all those ten weeks, Mary had cared for her two small children in the wet and cramped conditions of the open boat.

The escapees had told the Dutch governor in Timor that they were survivors from the wreck of a whaling ship, and he had generously given them food and clothing. They had also, rather audaciously, charged some supplies to the account of the British Government. If William Bryant had remained sober, they may well have spent the rest of their lives in that tropical freedom but, in a drunken stupor, two months after their arrival, Bryant had boasted about their daring escape, and the following day they had all been imprisoned by the Dutch authorities.

They had then been handed over to Captain Edward Edwards, a ruthless man who had rounded up ten of the *Bounty*'s mutineers and was taking them back to England via Batavia.

◈ *8 December 1792* ◈

Of the forty sheep and goats that had been purchased in Calcutta, only nineteen had survived the voyage in the *Atlantic*. The one female buffalo that had been bought along with two males was so weak that, when she had tried to drink from a large pool in the stream, she had fallen into the water and drowned. That left the struggling colony with only male buffalos and only female adult European cattle—and they refused to breed together. Nevertheless, among the twenty-three cattle in total, there were some fine bull calves that were growing towards maturity.

Government farms now stretched across more than a thousand acres. There was also a rising number of free settlers in the colony. Some of these were emancipists; some were crew members from the *Sirius* who had decided to stay in Sydney; and some were marines who had accepted grants of land in New South Wales instead of returning to England.

From the government's flock of sheep, Governor Phillip gave them each one ewe, which they could mate with a government-owned ram, so they could begin raising stock as well as growing grain. Phillip also planned a well-designed town, with appropriately grand streets—each two hundred feet wide—arranged in an ordered pattern to allow the refreshing sea breezes to circulate around the buildings.

⟴ *11 December 1792* ⟿

Phillip had suffered pain from his kidney stones for many years. Recently, it had become so debilitating that he had been forced to request permission to return to England. He boarded the *Atlantic* to sail home. Esther and Johnston were part of the large crowd which gathered to wave him off.

Also standing on the deck, alongside the governor, were Bennelong and Yemmerrawanne, another young man from the Wangal clan who had become a favourite in Sydney. They were sailing to England to meet His Majesty King George III, the great chief of the white men.

The lieutenant-governor, and the commanding officer of the New South Wales Corps, Major Francis Grose, took over the administration of the colony. His easygoing attitude to the post could hardly have been more different from that of his predecessor.

The first thing Grose did was to charter the *Britannia* to sail to the Cape of Good Hope to buy cattle and extra provisions purely on behalf of the officers—beginning a trading enterprise that would overwhelm the following three governors of New South Wales.

Grose made three more fundamental changes to Phillip's management that would ensure his popularity among his men, but lead to trouble. At the second issue of rations after Phillip's departure, he ordered the convicts to receive less than everyone else, even though it was their manual labour that was required to build the colony and feed its people. Then he replaced all the civil officers with military ones.

Before the year ended, Grose also purchased more than seven thousand gallons of spirits from the master of the American trading ship, the *Hope*. He justified his decision to the Colonial Secretary by stating that the master would not sell him the beef, pork and flour required by the colony unless he also purchased the spirits. There had been little alcohol in the colony until that time, and the fiery liquid was soon sold to the officers who then traded it down through the social ranks to the convicts. Many convicts bartered their spare-time labour to obtain the mental escape it offered.

Before long, drunken colonists were staggering about the settlement, and most of the precious sheep Governor Phillip had given to the settlers had been sold for alcohol. If the sheep had not been bought by the officers to increase their own flocks, they would probably have been sold for meat and lost to the colony forever.

✎ *27 February 1793* ✎

In the oppressive heat of late summer, a year after she had given birth to her stillborn baby, Esther was heavily pregnant again. She stood next to Susannah in the town's small cemetery. They were both weeping. Susannah's two-year-old son, Enoch, had died. They watched as his little coffin was lowered into a pathetically small grave.

At the end of the sombre ceremony, a stone slab with an inscription was laid on top of the grave.

O cruel death that could not spare
A loving child that now lies here
Great loss to them he left behind
His eternal joy will find.

❧ 9 March 1793 ☙

Only ten days later, Esther felt almost guilty about the joy she felt
from the safe arrival of her second son, named Robert after Johnston's
younger brother. She and her family had only just moved into a new
home in the newly completed military barracks on the western side of
High Street. It was a comfortable home that had been converted from
quarters designed for two single officers.

Johnston was also given a fourteen-year lease on some land near
the Brickfields, between two creeks that flowed into Long Cove. Esther
pragmatically suggested they use it for raising pigs.

❧ 28 May 1793 ☙

While Governor Phillip had been able to give grants of land to
non-commissioned officers and marines, and also to emancipists and
free settlers, he had not been permitted to make grants of land to commissioned officers. British Army officers were expected to concentrate
on their military career, not become farmers or pastoralists.

However, because all productive farming land would increase the
likelihood of the settlement's survival, Phillip had requested permission to grant land to commissioned officers as well—another of the
ways he made New South Wales unique. Conveniently for Lieutenant-
Governor Grose, that permission now finally arrived from the Colonial
Office and Grose was able to grant his officers large parcels of land. As
well as increasing his popularity, it seemed sensible to him to encourage any farming efforts that would support the colony's survival, which
was still far from secure.

Twenty-nine-year-old Captain Johnston chose one hundred acres
about four miles from Sydney, on the southern side of the road to
Parramatta in the district of Petersham Hill. He called his property

Annandale, after the valley of the River Annan in Scotland, near where he had been born. Like all the other officers, Johnston was also allocated ten convicts to work his new land, plus another three to be domestic servants, all still fed and clothed by the government. So now Esther had staff to help with her many domestic tasks.

When the Colonial Secretary in London became aware of Grose's actions, he immediately instructed Grose to limit the officers to two convicts, for only two years. But Grose wrote back to England requesting clarification, hoping that a new governor would have been appointed by the time he received a reply.

Twenty-five-year-old Lieutenant John Macarthur chose a hundred acres of riverside land at Parramatta, which he called Elizabeth Farm as a tribute to his wife. Macarthur's land was next to the barracks at the edge of town and near James Ruse's successful farming enterprise (which John Harris, a doctor with the New South Wales Corps, had recently purchased from Ruse as part of Harris's farm).

Because his duties included allocating convict labour, Macarthur was able to ensure that the most diligent workers were sent to work on his own and his fellow officers' new properties. The officers were determined to see their own farms flourish, so they made sure their convict labourers were strictly supervised. As a result, *their* farms became far more productive than the government ones. Furthermore, the convicts themselves took pride in working on the superior private properties and worked industriously to maintain their positions.

Some of the emancipists began congregating along the Hawkesbury River. They enjoyed being so far away from authority, and the fertile flats proved to be some of the best land yet cultivated. However, their remoteness made the farms easy targets for raiding natives.

The farmers were forbidden by law to harm the natives, except in self-defence, but many of the ex-convicts retaliated for raids on their properties—and were attacked by natives in payback, creating a vicious cycle with unspeakable cruelties performed on both sides.

❧ 20 June 1793 ☙

By the time the *Britannia* returned to Sydney, the colony had food in the public store to last only ten more weeks. The voyage had once again taken a toll on the cattle aboard—of thirty-four cows only two survived the journey. Nevertheless, the officers now had plenty of other valuable supplies, including sugar, tobacco, flour and more spirits. They sold and bartered what they did not need themselves to a desperate market and made a handsome profit. Then they arranged for the ship to bring them horses from the Cape, when it next visited New South Wales, so they could ride around their properties as gentlemen should.

Few other settlers had any money, and so they were unable to buy goods directly from the ship—but the officers could draw bills of exchange on their own salaries as well as use the wages not yet paid to their soldiers to invest in provisions.

It had been a year since Esther and Susannah had heard via the *Atlantic* that Mary Bryant had been captured in Timor and was being taken to England via Batavia. The *Britannia* brought more news of the escapees, and Esther and Susannah were anxious to know every detail.

Captain Edwards had put all the convicts in handcuffs, and given them only just enough food to prevent their starvation. William Bryant and eighteen-month-old Emanuel had both died in Batavia. Edwards had then taken his remaining prisoners to the Cape of Good Hope. Three more of the convict escapees had died during that voyage.

Mary had been with the cruel Captain Edwards for six months when they had arrived at Table Bay at the Cape. The escapees had then been transferred to the *Gorgon*, which was on her way back to England with the returning New South Wales marines and their families. Only Mary, her daughter, Charlotte, and four other escapees had still been alive.

❧ 30 August 1793 ☙

Seven years after her trial at the Old Bailey, Esther completed her sentence and became a free woman. Although that meant she could leave Johnston's household and seek employment anywhere in the colony, and even return to England if she had the means, there was nowhere else she wanted to be. Her rejection by the army wives had surprised and hurt her, and most of the colony's 'exclusives' (the military officers, free settlers and civil servants) would still not accept her socially. Nevertheless, she now held her head a little higher when she walked around Sydney Cove.

To celebrate Esther's new status, Johnston presented her with a fashionable new dress that he had ordered from the *Britannia's* cargo and kept for the occasion. It looked bright and fresh among the drab convict garb and faded clothes worn by most of the other women in the colony.

It had a higher waist than was common and came with a new whalebone corset which supported Esther's bust, pulled back her shoulders and gave her torso a V shape. Elizabeth Macarthur would not be the only woman in Sydney with the defined figure of a lady.

❧ 8 January 1794 ❧

In the new year, it was time for Henry Kable to be rewarded for all his good work. Though still serving his sentence as a convict, he was promoted to Chief Constable of the Sydney Police and given a grant of thirty acres of land at Petersham Hill, about five miles southwest of Sydney. He named it Sunning Hill.

Sydney now had more than three hundred houses. Each one was surrounded by a neat picket fence, and the dusty roads were alive with people, dogs and the occasional horse.

During the six years since the Sydney settlement had begun, winding tracks had been worn between the temporary buildings. Now the grants of land given by Lieutenant-Governor Grose caused those tracks to become permanent streets, and Governor Phillip's well-ordered plan was forgotten. The area known as The Rocks on the western side of the cove remained the seedier part of town, with taverns and brothels ensuring a lively nightlife and plenty of work for Henry Kable and his constables.

One sunny morning, Esther and Johnston walked through the town on their way to the baker. Though it was a sweltering February day, Esther still wore her whalebone corset, as did all the well-dressed ladies in the colony. Rosanna and George ran along beside her, and one-year-old Robert sat on her hip, swivelling his head from side to side as he watched all the activity in the bustling street.

A rich aroma wafted out from the baker's house and Esther eagerly went inside to collect a steaming pie which sat on a rough plate of bark. Meanwhile, Johnston walked up the road to fetch the Kables from their nearby cottage. Susannah opened the door holding her six-month-old baby son, James. She smiled at Johnston and bobbed a quick curtsey.

As the two families walked up the road and over the bridge to join the track that wound around behind Farm Cove, Johnston asked Kable if he would consider acting as his agent to sell some goods he had arriving on the *Britannia*. He explained that it would not do for an officer in His Majesty's service to be involved in retail trade directly, but if he and Kable entered into a business partnership, he believed they could both profit from the enterprise. Johnston told Kable that Grose was returning to England and Captain William Paterson, the Commanding Officer of the New South Wales Corps, was taking over as lieutenant-governor.

The track led the picnickers past the pair of forest red gums that still stood on the ridge above Farm Cove, and all the way to a further rocky point where they could enjoy a fine view of the harbour. Esther settled herself on an outcrop of warm sandstone next to Susannah so she could tell her what she had heard about Nelly Kerwin, her friend from Newgate Prison.

Nelly's new husband had been killed by a falling tree on Norfolk Island, and soon afterwards poor Nelly had given birth to a stillborn baby. She had subsequently determined to leave the place and return to her children in England. So she had petitioned Lieutenant-Governor Grose, claiming her sentence had expired.

'But it cannot have done,' Susannah interrupted, glancing at the men who were standing out of earshot. 'Didn't you tell me she had been sent out for life?'

'Indeed I did,' continued Esther quietly, 'but no documents could be found to prove the case either way, so in the end he let her go!'

4 March 1795

On a crisp autumn day, the *Britannia* sailed back into Sydney Cove, bringing supplies for both the government and the officers, including forty-one good horses. Now the officers could ride around their properties, and their crops could benefit from the nutrient-rich manure their mounts produced.

7 September 1795

In spring, when Esther was pregnant again, the *Reliance* arrived with news of the final chapter of Mary Bryant's adventure. Esther and Susannah were sorry to learn that after Mary had left the Cape of Good Hope in the *Gorgon*, her little daughter Charlotte had died. Of the eleven escapees, only five were still alive when they finally reached England.

Mary had been taken to Newgate Prison. Meanwhile, the story of her hardship and heroic achievements had exploded in the London newspapers, causing a hugely sympathetic response from the public. Nearly a year later, and six weeks after her original sentence had expired, Mary had been granted an unconditional pardon and allowed to return to her family in Cornwall. She was still only in her twenties.

The *Reliance* also brought a new governor to Sydney. It was Captain Hunter, who had sailed back to England four years earlier after losing the *Sirius* at Norfolk Island. Now aged fifty-seven, he returned to Sydney with parts for a windmill, a town clock . . . and Bennelong.

When Bennelong had first arrived in England he had happily donned ruffled shirts and embroidered waistcoats. He had swum in the River Thames, listened to debates in the British Parliament and met King George III in his enormous palace. He had learned to box, to ice-skate and to smoke.

But he and Yemmerrawanne had not been able to maintain their happy disposition in the loud, grimy city, and they had pined for their homeland so much that they had both become ill. Young Yemmerrawanne had died from a chest infection in that foreign land and had been buried in the churchyard of St John's in Eltham. Bennelong had continued an unhappy existence until at last he had been able to step aboard another ship to take him home, two years after he had left its leafy shores.

As he finally sailed up Sydney Harbour, the stringent scent of eucalyptus reached his nostrils and revived him. By the time he landed at Sydney Cove, he was standing tall and proud, dressed immaculately in his British clothes and ready to hold forth among his people with stories of the far-off land that only he, out of them all, had visited.

However, while he had been away, the native people had stopped coming to his cottage on the point, and its bricks were being used for repairs at South Head. So Bennelong moved into Government House. He was no longer the merry Bennelong his native friends had known. His manner was haughty, and he asked them to wash and dress before visiting him, and to mind their manners while in his presence.

Bennelong was caught in a no-man's land between the two cultures that now inhabited New South Wales. He was keen to retain the prestige his clan gained from his association with Government House, and he fancied playing an important diplomatic role between the two cultures. But he was not European enough to feel at home in a house, and he missed the freedom of life beneath the stars. He disappeared for days on end, leaving his clothes carefully folded in Government House for his return. But happiness was not waiting for him among his own people either. Now in his thirties, he had unfamiliar habits and was no longer attractive to the native women.

Colbee and Daringa had recently welcomed a second child into their family. However, Daringa had died soon afterwards. Colbee had put his baby daughter into a grave with Daringa's body, placing a rock on her chest before burying her alive with her dead mother.

He explained to the British that he had had no choice because there was no one to breastfeed his baby girl.

Colbee had then taken a pretty new wife, Booreea. When the frustrated Bennelong forced his own attentions upon Booreea, Colbee was outraged at such a betrayal of trust. He lashed out, splitting Bennelong's top lip and breaking two of his teeth, which affected his speech and made Bennelong even more unattractive.

⌖ 30 September 1795 ⌖

Governor John Hunter was full of enthusiasm for his new post and keen to make a positive contribution after losing the *Sirius*, but it was not long before he realised how difficult his task was going to be.

The colony now had a European population of over three thousand, divided between settlements at Sydney, Parramatta and along the Hawkesbury River. Hunter reported to the Colonial Secretary that they were desperately short of salted meat, agricultural tools, shoes and blankets. He also pointed out that although the harvests now produced substantial quantities of grain, no barns had been built to store the bounty. He added that there were no clothes left in the government stores, and many of the people were nearly naked.

Hunter's appointment had also caused consternation among the military men. They had become used to their own commander acting as governor, and they resented a naval outsider telling them what to do. It didn't help that Hunter stood down the military magistrates and reinstated civilian ones to have control over the courts and the police.

Hunter had orders to reduce the number of convicts assigned to the officers but, when he travelled around the settlement and saw the pitiful state of the government farms compared with the bountiful private ones, he decided against withdrawing the convict labour after all. He doubted the government farms alone would be able to produce enough to feed all the convicts, and the current system appeared to be working well. At least the officers' farms were productive, and benefiting from them seemed preferable to remaining dependent on supplies from Britain. So the New South Wales Government, which had granted land to the officers for free, continued to pay for the food and clothing for convict labourers to clear and cultivate that land, and then paid the officers for the grain or meat it produced.

◈ 18 November 1795 ◈

In the midst of all his difficulties, Hunter received a particularly lucky break. Shortly after he arrived there were reports of some wild cattle in an area south-west of Sydney. He asked Johnston, his younger friend and fellow Scot, to join him to investigate the sightings. Unlike their early explorations with Governor Phillip, this time they had horses to carry their provisions.

Once more, as they left the activity of the town behind them, the peace of the surrounding bushland closed in. Flocks of rainbow-coloured lorikeets flew through the trees, decorating the drab landscape like bright confetti, and the tinkling, bell-like calls of the Rose Hillers reminded the men of the convent bells of Rio.

They travelled for many miles until the woods gave way to more open pasture, with lush grass cropped low and dotted with wide blue ponds that glistened like pools of mercury. Wild ducks and black swans floated on the water.

Suddenly, in the distance, Johnston and Hunter glimpsed an incredible sight . . . a herd of more than sixty cattle! They were all descended from the handful of animals that had escaped from the convict shepherd seven years earlier, and they were grazing contentedly on the rich grassland. Hunter decided to leave them where they were because they could be individually slaughtered if necessary, but were safe from the settlers, and the natives obviously had no interest in them. He named the area Cowpasture Plains.

◈ 7 January 1796 ◈

At the beginning of 1796 Johnston was given a fourteen-year lease of land on the harbour side of High Street. Esther supervised a team of convict workers who developed it into a productive vegetable garden.

From it, she was able to provide fresh vegetables for her family and their convict workers for many years.

The Annandale estate was also becoming productive. Wooden workers' huts had been built there so that Johnston's convicts could clear and farm the land, under the watchful eye of his trusted overseer, the convict Isaac Nichols.

∽ 18 January 1796 ∾

'We are off to Norfolk Island again, Hetty!' Johnston called out, returning from Government House. He walked into the bedroom where Esther had just finished breastfeeding her one-day-old baby daughter, Julia. Esther was aghast at the thought of having to move with a new baby all over again.

Johnston explained that Governor King was suffering so badly from gout that he was returning to England. Governor Hunter wanted Johnston to take over as lieutenant-governor on Norfolk Island. Esther looked down at her newborn daughter who was lying contentedly in her arms, her little lips pouting in her sleep. What about the fine house they had planned to start building at Annandale? Johnston said it would just have to wait.

'The *Reliance* sails in three days' time,' he explained, 'and Hunter wants me aboard.'

Though groggy from lack of sleep with her new baby, Esther thought hard about her situation over the following few hours. Then she proposed a plan to Johnston: she could stay in Sydney with the children to supervise the building of the house at Annandale and continue Johnston's trading business. She reminded him that the Macarthurs had already been living in their fine house for two years and, if she and Johnston both went to Norfolk Island, they might miss out on many valuable trading opportunities.

Johnston was not pleased with the thought of leaving Esther alone. But she reassured him that Mr Nichols would help her manage the properties and Mr Kable would ensure she didn't make any foolish purchases from the ships.

Johnston replied that at least he wanted to take Young George with him, to give him a taste of army life.

'But he is only six!' said Esther.

'Indeed, and he longs to work alongside me. Hunter is going to recommend him for an ensigncy when next he writes to the Duke of Portland.'

So Johnston took Young George to Norfolk Island and Esther remained in Sydney. She arranged for one of Johnston's horses to be broken to harness so that Isaac Nichols could hitch it to a cart and take her to Annandale Farm each week to inspect its progress.

Hunter did recommend George for an ensigncy, and the Colonial Secretary endorsed the recommendation, but Colonel Grose, now back in England, did not fancy the son of a convict becoming a commissioned officer in his regiment and opposed the appointment.

✑ 6 March 1796 ✑

'I have seen him!' Susannah told Esther excitedly, as she arrived for tea.

'Seen whom?' Esther asked.

'Dr D'Arcy Wentworth! He has returned to Sydney from Norfolk Island, and he has brought Miss Crowley and their three boys with him. He is as handsome as they say, do you not agree?'

Susannah added that she had heard that Wentworth had built up a substantial property on Norfolk Island by selling meat and produce from his farm. But Esther replied that she hadn't the slightest interest in Dr Wentworth's affairs.

Esther's maid interrupted their conversation to set down a box of luscious oranges.

'A token of friendship from Dr Wentworth, ma'am.'

CHAPTER NINE

Managing Alone

❧ 29 July 1796 ❧

After Captain Johnston had been back on Norfolk Island for six months, the shrapnel that had lodged in his leg during the American War of Independence began causing him so much pain that he had to retire from his duties as lieutenant-governor. He and Young George returned to Sydney on the *Francis*.

Esther was overjoyed to have them both home again. As soon as Johnston was able, she took him in the cart to show him the cleared site marked out for Annandale House. The building would face east across the shallow valley, overlooking Grose Farm towards Petersham Hill.

They imagined together what it would be like to live in their fine house, and Johnston suggested they send for some seedlings of Norfolk Island pine, so they could have a double row of the majestic trees along the sweeping curve of their driveway.

❧ 2 January 1797 ❧

It was now many years since the natives had sent their cleansing fires through the trees surrounding Sydney Cove, and the neglected forest was a tangle of accumulated litter. Each year, at the beginning of summer, soft, shiny, pink leaves would unfurl in clusters at the tips of the eucalypt branches, and nearly half of the old gum leaves in the forest would let go of their high branches and flutter to the ground, forming an oil-rich, combustible carpet. Then, in autumn, bark would peel away from the trees in long shreds that dangled from their trunks, ready to tempt any passing flame.

One blistering afternoon it came. The wind swung around to the north-west, bringing strong gusts of hot air from the inland deserts. As the heat built up, storm clouds formed on the far horizon and flashes of lightning sent down bolts of fire. One such strike burst into flame amid the mass of ready fuel . . . and set free a nascent fire.

Its flames danced through the bush, devouring the matted undergrowth and growing larger as they went. They were soon tall enough to lick the dangling firebrands of bark, which broke off and were carried by the strengthening wind far ahead of the fire front to spark new flames across the land.

The fires that the natives had traditionally created and had had under their control were obedient, but this one was a rampant delinquent. Starving and uncontrollable, it gorged on the built-up fuel and leapt from tree to tree, engulfing everything in its path.

For thousands of years the smell of bushfire had regularly filled the air, and the native animals now fled from it as they had always done: scurrying down bolt-holes, running ahead of the flames or flying above them. But this time they had little chance of escape. Searing flames were upon them in minutes; clean air was sucked away and the sky was filled with choking smoke. Before long, tiny burnt corpses were all that were left of countless forms of animal life that had covered every inch of the forest.

The cleared land around Parramatta saved the township from the full force of the blaze, but the wind drove thousands of burning embers ahead of the fire front and they rained down upon the town. The townsfolk ran to and fro, tossing buckets and bowls of water at the sparks that kept springing to life in their thatched roofs and stacks of hay.

John and Elizabeth Macarthur, and all their convict servants, fought to save the house at Elizabeth Farm, barely managing to extinguish each new spot fire before it became too large to contain.

In Sydney, Esther stopped to look up at the sky. The sun was veiled by grey smoke and had become a huge orange disc, imbuing everything with an ominous, monotone hue. She went on with her daily tasks as usual, unaware that settlers further west were fighting to save their homes.

Four-year-old Robert ran into the house, holding out his hand to show Esther the delicate piece of white ash that had floated out of the sky and onto his outstretched palm. He touched it with his finger and it mysteriously disappeared. Young George followed his brother inside, holding a whole charred leaf which he sniffed before satisfyingly snapping it in two. None of them understood the significance of what they were seeing.

As night fell, a plea for help from Parramatta reached Governor Hunter in Sydney and he ordered a convict chain gang to do everything they could to save the precious wheat crop. He promised that if they managed to hold back the flames, they would be freed from their chains.

As the fire spread east, Johnston and Nichols stayed alongside the farm workers at the Annandale estate to protect its buildings and harvest. When burning embers began falling on the buildings in Sydney, Susannah and Henry Kable beat out the flames that sprang up around their cottage, and Esther ran to and fro, using a water-soaked rag to help extinguish the small fires that kept appearing around her barracks home.

Still shackled together, the convicts at Parramatta fought the fire throughout the night, beating its leading edge with the only weapons they had: oil-rich eucalypt branches. Storm clouds that had been building behind the fire darkened the sky until at last huge, heavy drops of rain began to pelt onto the scorched earth. At first they just hissed against the flames, but gradually they became a deluge that finally extinguished the last golden remnants of flame. And the menace was gone.

When the sun rose in the morning the wheat still stood . . . and the convicts were freed from their iron shackles.

16 May 1797

Many of the larger properties in the colony now had at least some sheep grazing in their paddocks. They were mostly a small Bengal breed grown for their meat. But a chain of events had occurred that would change sheep-breeding in the colony forever, resulting in hundreds of millions of their small feet stamping across the fragile land.

The finest wool in the world came from Spanish Merino flocks which were forbidden from being exported. But as the Spanish Empire had crumbled, a few precious Merinos had been given to other European kings to win their allegiance.

Two rams and four ewes had been sent to the Dutch colony at the Cape of Good Hope. Two years later the commander there had been asked to return them to Holland, but he had cunningly only sent back the six original sheep and kept all their offspring. In 1795 the British had invaded the Cape and the commander had committed suicide.

Governor Hunter had since sent HMS *Reliance* and HMS *Supply* (not the First Fleet ship) to the Cape to buy more supplies for the Sydney colony. Captain Waterhouse of the *Reliance* had bought thirteen Merinos from the commander's widow, and Captain William Kent of the *Supply* (Hunter's nephew) had bought another thirteen.

And so the first Merinos now arrived in New South Wales—although only five rams and seven or eight ewes had survived the voyage. They were sold to several private landholders, including John Macarthur.

29 December 1797

Colbee had acted in a cowardly manner, bashing a young man who had stooped to pick up his shield during a fight. The young warrior had subsequently died and Colbee now had to face his punishment for breaking the warriors' code of conduct. He turned up outside the Sydney barracks to defend himself in the traditional manner.

Esther had given birth the day before to another fine son, named David. When she heard a commotion outside, she opened her door to discover its cause. She was astonished to see Colbee standing with only his shield for protection against an onslaught of spears. Though he was a skilled warrior, the force of so many impacts finally knocked him to the ground. He would have been killed if soldiers hadn't dashed out of the barracks and carried him inside. As it was, he was bleeding heavily from his wounds.

Bennelong—armed and naked—had stood by as an observer, but when he saw the soldiers blatantly interfere with native law, he was so outraged that he hurled his own spear directly towards them. Esther screamed as she watched the spear pierce one of the soldiers in the back and emerge through his belly. The other soldiers rushed towards Bennelong, but he was quickly led away, still boiling with rage, by the Provost Marshal.

The wounded soldier survived, and Bennelong disappeared from the colony. Other natives accustomed to staying in the town were now afraid to be seen, in case they were considered to be related to Bennelong and therefore might suffer revenge attacks from the soldiers. The bridges that so many had built between the two cultures were crumbling.

ᴥ 20 September 1798 ᴥ

Esther and Johnston were among the crowd who gave three cheers to Henry Kable as he threw open the door of his Ramping Horse Inn on High Street and announced that it was open for business. Governor Hunter had issued ten liquor licences in an attempt to gain some control over the sale of rum within the colony. Kable—having now completed his fourteen-year sentence—had jumped at the opportunity to develop another line of business.

As chief constable, he and his family now lived in a comfortable house next to the gaol, directly opposite Johnston's High Street property where Esther grew her vegetables. And Kable's prosperity continued to grow. He soon formed a partnership with another ex-convict, James Underwood, to build ships on the edge of the Tank Stream, just on the other side of Esther's garden.

‹⌐ 25 February 1799 ⌐›

Governor Hunter's task continued to prove difficult. He was up against the powerful officers of the New South Wales Corps, who were used to running things their own way. John Macarthur, in particular, was single-mindedly turning himself into a wealthy gentleman and vehemently resented anyone who restricted his progress. Less than a year after Hunter had arrived, Macarthur had sent a letter to the Colonial Secretary criticising Hunter's management of the colony. Hunter had also written to the Colonial Secretary, criticising Macarthur and refuting his accusations.

The Colonial Secretary had responded by reminding Hunter that he had so far been ineffectual in limiting the number of convicts allocated to officers and in preventing them from selling spirits. Further correspondence had travelled to and fro, until the Colonial Secretary finally wrote to Hunter with a string of accusations, including that Hunter bought large quantities of produce from the officers before he purchased anything from the smaller farms, which forced the settlers to accept lower prices elsewhere. In addition, the price of necessities in the colony had doubled, and spirits and other goods were bought by the officers from visiting ships and then sold by them to the settlers and convicts at up to double the price. He added in a postscript that Philip King had been appointed as lieutenant-governor to succeed Hunter if that became necessary.

‹⌐ 12 March 1799 ⌐›

Esther sat on her comfortable sofa with Rosanna who was nearly twelve. Her other children now included George (aged nine), Robert (six), Julia (three) and David (one). Captain Johnston leant against the mantelpiece while his old overseer, Isaac Nichols, stood by the window looking out to the bay. Nichols was now Superintendent of Public Works in Sydney and overseer of all the convict gangs, working under Johnston's direction.

However, all was not well. Nichols had been charged with receiving a sack of stolen tobacco but insisted he was innocent. Kable was

A witness giving evidence in one of the Old Bailey's courtrooms. (Thomas Rowlandson and Augustus Pugin, 1808)

Newgate Prison's imposing granite walls were designed to discourage law-breaking. (Thomas Medland, 1800)

Government House, Parramatta, where Esther's daughters were invited to stay.
(George Evans, 1805, ML SLNSW)

A later view of Annandale House nestled into its established gardens, creating an elegant family home. (J.C. Hoyte, c. 1855, ML SLNSW)

presumed to have been in cahoots with him and had been summoned as a witness.

'You must do something, Papa!' pleaded Rosanna. 'We cannot allow poor Mr Nichols to be treated this way.'

Johnston agreed. He offered to submit a glowing character reference to the court, and he assured Nichols that Governor Hunter would do the same. Did Nichols know of anyone who might hold a grudge against him?

Nichols replied that many of the other Corps officers were not well disposed towards him. When Governor Hunter had extended the government farms, Nichols had been ordered to stop assigning convicts to officers so they could work on the new government properties instead. The officers had taken a dim view of the arrangement, and Macarthur, in particular, had spoken his mind very freely.

Johnston told Nichols that the court would consist of three naval officers—Waterhouse, Kent and Flinders—plus three Corps officers and the new judge, Richard Dore.

Everyone wished Nichols luck for the trial, and Rosanna added that they would all be thinking of him.

⇜ 16 March 1799 ⇝

As soon as the trial was over, Matthew Flinders ran along the dusty road and hammered his fist on Johnston's door to tell him the verdict.

Guilty! And sentenced to fourteen years' transportation to Norfolk Island to work in a gaol-gang. Johnston and Esther were shocked. Flinders explained that the whole trial had been trumped up. The most disreputable rogues in the colony had been brought in to give outrageous hearsay evidence against Mr Nichols, and Macarthur himself had spoken against him. Waterhouse, Kent and Flinders were fully convinced of his innocence, but they had been outvoted four to three.

Johnston took the transcript of the trial to Governor Hunter, who concluded there was not the least proof for a conviction. He suspended the sentence, released Nichols and referred the case to England— where Nichols was later issued with an absolute pardon, although it took three years to arrive. The rift between Hunter and some of the Corps officers was growing wider.

Towards the end of the year, the building of Annandale House was completed. It was one of the first privately owned brick homes built in New South Wales and was visible from miles around. Like the Macarthurs' house at Elizabeth Farm, Annandale House was about seventy feet long and twenty wide. It had three main rooms: a large central hall with a parlour on one side and a bedroom on the other. Additional rooms were built along the back wall, and the kitchen was separate from the house as a precaution against fire—as was common throughout the colony. There were cool cellars beneath the main building, and a wide veranda that wrapped around the house to protect it from the summer's heat. The bricks had been made from clay found on the estate, and the fine woodwork was crafted from cedar cut from a nearby forest. A large bell with a clear, deep tone hung from the eaves of one of the outbuildings and was rung at six o'clock in the morning to begin each working day.

Esther was thrilled to become mistress of such a fine house, and she happily moved her family into their new home, planting a cutting of the red geranium by its front door. Now she could afford to light several candles each Friday evening before the Sabbath, but she was not able to observe other important Jewish days. The Jewish calendar is lunisolar and, as there was no organised Jewish community in the colony, Esther had no way of knowing when to observe Jewish New Year, Passover or Day of Atonement. Nevertheless, she taught her children as much about them as she could remember.

≈ 1 January 1800 ≈

It was a new century, and Sydney Cove had changed beyond recognition from the secluded bay it once was. Neat timber cottages and several brick and stone buildings clustered around the bay, intermingled with the now shabby original wattle-and-daub huts. Grand windmills graced the surrounding hilltops and there were a comforting fifty-six thousand bushels of wheat in the government stores. Even though its name had never been formally announced, Sydney was here to stay.

Dr Wentworth had established a country estate on land granted to him by Governor Hunter. It was two-thirds of the way along the Parramatta road from Sydney, and Wentworth called it Home Bush. He lived there with his convict mistress, Catherine Crowley, and their three children. He worked as assistant surgeon in the Parramatta Hospital, and the wealth he had accumulated on Norfolk Island—and the fact that he had an agent in England who could ship out articles for sale—also earned him a place in the officers' trading ring. His clothes reflected his success: his suit was finely cut, he carried a gold watch and he wore elegant rings on his fingers.

But rumours still circulated about his shady past, and the Corps officers were warned against associating with him. Nevertheless, he was undeniably good company and had spent Christmas Day with the lonely Governor Hunter at Government House.

◇ 6 January 1800 ◇

All Wentworth's wealth was of little value compared with what he was losing this day. Catherine Crowley had been only twenty-seven years old. So bright and cheerful. So eager to please him. Soon to be dust beneath the scorching earth.

He stood in the bright summer sunshine in the Parramatta churchyard, next to the three sons Catherine had borne him, as her coffin was slowly lowered into her grave. He bent down and picked up a handful of the hot, dusty soil and let it slip through his fingers onto the coffin below. Then he led his sons away.

◇ 11 January 1800 ◇

The new year blew in a different sort of convict. These were Irish rebels who, inspired by both the French Revolution and the new American republic, had risen up against England's sovereignty over their homeland.

During a battle at Vinegar Hill in Ireland's south-western county of Wexford, twenty thousand rebels—their hair cropped short to display their sympathy with the French—had been surrounded by half as many well-armed English troops. The troops had pelted the rebels with grapeshot and gunned them down with howitzers, then they had charged at them with razor-sharp sabres until no rebels had been left standing. Political sympathisers had been arrested and sentenced to transportation.

Now the *Minerva* brought the first exiles from the Battle of Vinegar Hill to New South Wales. They were political prisoners, not criminals. Their continuing resentment bubbled beneath the surface of their everyday activity.

Johnston's overseer at Annandale was now Thomas Biggers, an Irish convict who had arrived in the colony six years earlier. He told Johnston that he had heard that the Irish exiles were secretly planning a revolt.

Governor Hunter ordered the suspected ringleaders to be given an unbelievable five hundred lashes, inflicted over many weeks, as a deterrent against any further trouble. However, hundreds more rebels kept arriving on subsequent ships; whispered threats continued to be overheard, and an uneasy atmosphere pervaded the settlement.

◄ *6 March 1800* ►

Johnston had received another grant of nearly three hundred acres of land on the northern side of the Parramatta road, which meant his estate now stretched all the way to the harbour. It had quickly become like a small village, with servants' cottages, stables, storehouses, a dairy, a butcher, a baker, a mill, a blacksmith and even a barracks for a small detachment of soldiers to protect the property from native attacks.

Johnston had also been promoted to Brevet Major and, as well as Annandale, had grants of fertile land along the Georges River (which flows into Botany Bay), near where it meets Prospect Creek, beginning the development of the district of Banks Town. On one of the properties he built a farmhouse he called George's Hall. The other property became known as Johnston's Flat.

As autumn winds brought the first touches of chill to the air, Johnston stood behind Esther (heavily pregnant again) on the cool flagstones of their veranda at Annandale House. He wrapped his arms around her and gazed across his estate. He now controlled over six hundred acres of land. He could never have achieved anything like as much if he had stayed in England. He was well pleased with his decision to join the First Fleet.

But the winds of change that were swirling about the colony would soon blow him far from his comfortable home.

◇ *15 April 1800* ◇

Governor Hunter watched HMS *Speedy* sail up Sydney Harbour through his eyeglass. He was anxious to receive the dispatches she would be carrying—so many of his decisions were awaiting Colonial Office rulings. But the *Speedy* brought more than dispatches. She brought a long letter from the Colonial Secretary expressing his displeasure with Hunter's administration of the colony, the very end of which stated: *I am commanded to signify to you the King's pleasure to return to this kingdom by the first safe conveyance which offers itself after the arrival of Lieutenant-Governor King, who is authorised by His Majesty to take upon him the government of that settlement immediately on your departure from it.*

Just like that. All his plans and visions would come to an end as soon as Lieutenant-Governor Philip King arrived. King was twenty-one years younger than Hunter and had served under him on the *Sirius*. He had returned to England from Norfolk Island two years earlier due to ill-health and now it seemed he would be coming back to New South Wales as its new governor.

Hunter had not been able to prevent the officers from trading in spirits, nor stop them paying their convicts in rum, nor substantially reduce the number of convicts assigned to them. However, he *had* made some significant improvements to the settlement: stocks of cattle and sheep had increased; all the old buildings had been repaired and whitewashed; Sydney now had two stone windmills and a clock tower; the Government House at Parramatta had been enlarged; and two granaries had been built along the Hawkesbury River to store the harvests of grain.

Hunter looked up from the letter as his servant announced a visitor.

'Captain Macarthur to see you, sir.'

'Damn the man! Tell him . . .'

But Macarthur strode into Hunter's office with a wolfish smile. He said he wanted to be the first to acknowledge Hunter's efforts to improve the colony during his governorship and to wish him many pleasant years of retirement ahead in their fair homeland.

Retirement! How did Macarthur know about it? Hunter informed him that he remained governor until Lieutenant-Governor King arrived.

'Oh, but King is already here!' gloated Macarthur, adding that he had arrived on the *Speedy*.

'The devil he did!' said Hunter.

Macarthur had had his fun. As he walked out of the office, he left Hunter shaking his head at the thought that the Colonial Office had no idea of the complexity of administration in New South Wales. No idea at all.

Esther, who had just given birth to a daughter named Maria, was sorry to hear that Hunter would be leaving the colony, but Johnston told her that he would not be going for another few months, when the *Buffalo* was due to sail back to England. Until then, he would remain in his role as governor and continue living at Government House. King would have to wait his turn.

∾ 3 May 1800 ∾

Hunter's sudden sacking made many people nervous about their positions in the colony, and King made it clear that he would not tolerate any improper conduct.

'How can it be considered proper,' King demanded of Lieutenant-Colonel Paterson, 'that cattle belonging to the government roam about on land belonging to military officers? It is my understanding that Major Johnston has a great number which he *kindly suffers* to run on his private farm. You understand, sir, that we must trust to his honour to give up *all* that he so kindly takes care of when the time comes.'

Paterson reminded King that Johnston had been a marine and was a man of honour. The cattle were kept on his property for convenience, so as to be nearby the town when required for slaughter.

'Is there no government land to be had?' asked King.

'None that could restrict the animals' wanderings within certain boundaries, sir,' Paterson replied.

King promised to scrutinise all such arrangements as soon as he took office. Then he glared at Paterson and said that it was absolutely necessary to immediately prohibit any rum from being brought ashore, or there would be drastic consequences.

So, when Paterson learned that Johnston had recently given one of his sergeants rum as part of his pay, he decided to use Johnston, who carried the respect of his fellow officers, as an example to influence the others to change their ways.

Paterson told Johnston that he must immediately cease paying his men in rum. Johnston replied that the men were quite agreeable to the arrangement. But Paterson pointed out that Johnston valued the rum he paid to his sergeant at more than he paid for it himself. Johnston responded that that was because he had bought it wholesale. He had valued it in payment at still below its retail price and his sergeant could have sold it for a profit if he had so desired. And, if Johnston had paid him his full wages, he would only have spent part of it on rum anyway at the higher retail price.

Nevertheless, Paterson insisted that paying soldiers in rum was an abuse that would no longer be tolerated. Johnston replied that it was not within his power to immediately prevent it. It was an accepted method of payment and it would take some time to change such an established procedure. Paterson thumped his fist on his desk and spat out that they did not *have* time. He glanced quickly towards the open door before adding that all their actions were under scrutiny.

Johnston explained that a quantity of Corps funds was currently committed to trading purchases, but as soon as those sales were completed, he would see to it that all the officers made new arrangements. Paterson wiped a hand across his sweating brow and insisted again that the practice must stop immediately.

Johnston stood firm and told Paterson that if rum was not used as part of their wages, the men would be left underpaid. Paterson's face grew red with frustration.

'Confound it, man! Are you disobeying my orders?' Paterson heard a door being opened further down the corridor. He thought it might be King, and he panicked. He raised his voice: 'If you do not give me your word that from this very day no soldier will receive rum as wages, I shall have you *arrested*!'

Johnston argued that if he were to be arrested, then so too should all the other officers who had traded in rum—including Paterson himself. The sound of footsteps came closer. Paterson glanced again at the open doorway, and announced in a clear voice that Johnston was to consider himself under arrest from that very moment for contempt towards a commanding officer and for paying a soldier in rum.

A convict maid shuffled past his doorway . . . but the deed was done.

Johnston knew that many of the Corps officers who would be on the bench of a court martial held in the colony still held a grudge against him for supporting Isaac Nichols at his trial the previous year. So he asked Hunter to be allowed to return to England for his trial.

Esther, nursing her three-week-old baby Maria, was horrified by the thought of Johnston leaving her alone in the colony while he travelled all the way to England and back. But when the deposed Governor Hunter boarded the *Buffalo* to sail home to England, his trusted friend, Major George Johnston, followed him onto the ship.

✎ 21 October 1800 ✎

Esther waved valiantly as the *Buffalo* pulled away from the shore. But she was unable to speak. She bit her lip and tears ran down her cheeks. For, standing on the ship's deck next to Johnston, were also her two sons, ten-year-old George and seven-year-old Robert, and little Julia, who was just four and a half. They were all going away to school in England. Esther and Johnston believed that their children would benefit from receiving an English education, but Esther hoped vehemently that they would all return to live in New South Wales. She watched silently as half her family sailed out of sight, not knowing when she would see any of them again.

Susannah walked with Esther back up the hill, reassuring her that the children would receive a fine education in England. She also reminded Esther that the kindly Mr Hunter had promised to keep an eye on them there. He had already arranged for Robert to join the crew of the *Buffalo* during the voyage, to ease any homesickness he might feel.

But Esther could not help worrying. Not only was there a risk of the ship being caught up in the war with France before it reached England, but there was also a possibility that Johnston would feel differently about her once he returned to his familiar social circle.

⇜ *20 November 1800* ⇝

A month later, Esther visited Sydney Cove to inspect a consignment of tools she had just purchased from a visiting ship. Afterwards, she walked around to check her vegetable garden, then stopped for a cup of tea with Susannah Kable in the sunny gaol-house garden.

The *Diana*, a ship owned by Henry Kable and James Underwood, had just come into the harbour, to Susannah's great relief. It had been a gamble to buy the ship for a sealing venture in Bass Strait, but it had come back with a full cargo. Susannah explained to Esther the many benefits that would be obtained from the seals: their furs would be sold for cloaks and hats, their skins would make boots and shoes, and oil would be rendered from their bodies to be used in lamps. In fact, the venture promised to be so successful that Kable and Underwood were already planning to build another ship themselves.

Esther then asked about the Kables' store. Susannah said she loved working there, unpacking the new goods when they arrived, and knowing how pleased her customers would be to see them. She explained that dealing with the agents in England and the East made her feel like they were part of the real world and not just an isolated little colony in the middle of nowhere.

On her way home to Annandale House, Esther's thoughts dwelled on the fact that, compared to the sophistication of London, Sydney *was* just a small colony. She worried about Johnston being alone in London: a wealthy landowner, handsome, charming . . . and unmarried.

In fact, she had good reason to worry. At least one woman in England had already set her heart on becoming Johnston's wife.

In the midst of her thoughts, Esther had to pull her buggy up sharply when Dr Wentworth staggered onto the road. He clutched one of the buggy's wheels to steady himself and Esther could see that he was drunk. He was also unshaven and his clothes were dishevelled and splattered with mud. Esther had heard plenty of recent gossip about how, since Catherine Crowley's death, he had been drinking heavily and visiting disreputable women at all hours of the night.

Wentworth looked up at Esther through bleary eyes and told her that Governor King had all but ruined him with his stranglehold on trade. At that moment, John Macarthur happened to ride past. He glowered at the sight of Wentworth, drunk and filthy, conversing with the ex-convict woman. Curling his lip in disdain, he clicked his horse onward.

Esther felt sorry for the wreck of a man that the once-charming Wentworth had become. She told him that there was no knowing what he might yet achieve in the colony, and that Miss Crowley's sons deserved to have a father they could be proud of. He should do his best to be such a one.

He reached for her hand and lifted it to his lips, saying that her concern for his welfare meant the world to him. Then he staggered off into the crowds milling about the High Street market.

That evening, Esther sat at her desk in Annandale House, the only woman in the colony who was managing a large productive estate. She grew both wheat and corn, and there were more than a hundred and seventy government cattle agisted on her land. When she thought about what her future might hold, she rose from her desk and walked around in tight circles with her hands on her head. If she failed in her management of the estate; if the new Governor King ruled it unlawful for a woman to control such properties; if some fair lady in England won Johnston's heart while he was there; or worse still, if the *Buffalo* met with misfortune on the high seas and Johnston and her children all perished . . .

Before he left, Johnston had made a will to ensure that Esther would be provided for, in the event of his death. She would have a life interest in the Annandale estate, and all the household effects, plus any inheritance he received on the death of his mother. She would also be paid an annual income of fifty pounds.

Esther took a deep breath and looked out of the multi-paned window across the moonlit garden to the flock of sheep standing contentedly in a nearby field. Johnston had left everything he owned in her care. She just had to keep it safe for him until he returned. She was grateful that at least she had had the experience of managing his affairs while he had been away on Norfolk Island.

During the following months, Esther pored over the estate's accounts and studied the government sales. She called on the captains of visiting ships to discuss purchasing their cargo, and she listened carefully to the advice of her friend, Isaac Nichols, who was a frequent visitor to the house. She also consulted her overseer, Thomas Biggers. He was a burly Irishman who had been transported for life, and Esther never felt comfortable in his presence, but he had pleased Johnston by informing on the Irish exiles earlier in the year, so she had to work with him as best she could.

Esther was well aware of her dubious station as the mistress of Annandale. She had a dozen convicts working on her farm—one of the largest convict teams in the colony—and she went to great lengths to ensure they were all well cared for. She issued generous rations of meat, vegetables, fruit, sugar, tea, tobacco and bread, and she made sure they had sufficient clothing and comfortable housing.

At sunrise every morning, Biggers gave the convicts their tasks for the day, then he counted the stock and inspected the equipment, stables and fences. In the evening he counted the stock again. The gates of the property were closed at eight o'clock each evening and no one was allowed out after that time without Esther's permission. Biggers kept a record of everything that came into the farm and everything that was issued to the workers, and he presented his record book to Esther for review every Saturday night.

⌛ 5 August 1801 ⌛

A few months after Johnston had left, Esther faced her first major challenge. She had ordered some wheat to be delivered by boat to Sydney Cove, which she was going to sell to Dr Harris. Biggers had paid the boatman on delivery. But when Esther met Dr Harris at the Cove to complete the transaction, she saw that the wheat had been completely spoiled during the journey.

She was furious. Not only had she lost the value of the wheat, but the episode had also made her realise that she couldn't depend on Biggers to look after her interests. Dr Harris suggested that she needed to assert her authority as the manager of Annandale estate or others would take advantage of her, as the boatman had done. So she approached the court to demand that the boatman, Anthony Richardson, be ordered to refund the cost of transporting her wheat. She decided that for this purpose she should use what was most likely still her legal name, Esther Julian.

Dr Harris spared her the ordeal of facing the court herself by offering to give his testimony instead. The court found in her favour and Richardson was ordered to refund the seventeen pounds he had charged her for freight.

⌛ 13 September 1801 ⌛

After Hunter's departure, Philip King had finally been able to step into the role of governor. He had moved into Government House with his wife, Anna—the *first* First Lady of New South Wales—who now held the highest social rank of any woman in the colony.

Governor King had immediately begun ruffling military feathers by reducing the number of convicts allocated to the officers to only two each; he had also curtailed the importation of rum. When he then ordered a court to reconsider its judgment against a man found guilty of assaulting two officers (one of whom was Captain Macarthur), the court refused to obey, on the grounds that the governor was attempting to interfere with the process of justice.

Esther happened to meet with Henry Kable about a month after the failed court order to discuss the purchase of some cargo from a visiting ship. Kable told her that Macarthur had cut the governor from his social circle and expected all the other officers to do the same. But Lieutenant-Colonel Paterson, commander of the New South Wales Corps, had allowed his wife to continue her close friendship with Mrs King. Macarthur had been so furious with Paterson that he had threatened to make public the contents of a private letter that Mrs Paterson had written to Mrs Macarthur. Such a betrayal of his wife's confidence had been too much for a gentleman like Paterson to bear. He had challenged Macarthur to a duel.

༻ 14 September 1801 ༺

It had rained solidly for four days at Parramatta and the long grass was glistening as five men waded through it. The atmosphere was tense and few words were spoken. Enough had been said already.

Each duellist needed a 'second' to ensure the duel was conducted according to the established code of honour. Captain Piper acted as Macarthur's second and Captain Mackellar was second for Paterson. The fifth man standing in the damp grass was Dr Harris.

Macarthur and Paterson stood back to back, then each stepped out a distance of twelve paces before turning side-on to offer the narrowest target. The seconds tossed a coin to determine who would shoot first: Macarthur. A magpie's warble resounded through the trees, then all was silent again. Piper dropped a white handkerchief, Macarthur raised his pistol . . . and fired. The ball shot straight into the colonel's right shoulder, shattering its bone, and Paterson collapsed onto the grass.

'Hold your ground!' Mackellar called to Macarthur. Then he woodenly followed the code, in an effort to maintain his composure. 'Are you able to return fire, sir?' he asked Paterson.

'I think not,' offered Dr Harris, who had rushed over to tear open Paterson's bloody sleeve so he could examine the wound.

Paterson was taken to the hospital, but Dr Harris was not able to extract the bullet from the splintered bones of his shoulder. The colonel's life hung in the balance for several days while everyone waited to see whether he would live or die.

He lived. In the meantime, Governor King charged Macarthur with attempting to create dissension between himself and Paterson. When Macarthur demanded to be brought before a court martial to clear his name, Governor King granted his request by ordering him to stand trial in England. He argued that it would be impossible for a colonial court, which would largely comprise Macarthur's own colleagues, to reach an objective outcome. In his determination to rid Macarthur from the colony, King also wrote a long letter to the Colonial Office explaining in detail just how troublesome Macarthur had been.

15 November 1801

Macarthur took with him to England his nine-year-old daughter, Elizabeth, and seven-year-old son, John, so they could attend school there—his eldest son, Edward, had already left four years earlier, together with Norfolk King, both aged eight. Like Esther, Elizabeth Macarthur waved bravely from the shore as she watched the ship disappear down the harbour. She never saw her young son again.

8 April 1802

It took over a year for Macarthur to reach England. His ship lost its mast in a typhoon in the Arafura Sea, which necessitated a stop in Indonesia for repairs. Macarthur then travelled via India and St Helena before reaching his final destination. While he was travelling across the vast oceans, Johnston began sailing home in the *Buffalo*, the same ship that had taken him away to trial in England for part-paying his men in rum. In London, both the judge advocate general and the commander-in-chief had concluded that, without the accuser or any witnesses, a court martial in that country was impossible unless all the parties travelled to England, which in this instance was not considered worth the trouble.

They had felt, in any case, that Johnston would be acquitted of the charge due to a lack of evidence. As to the second charge, of expressing contempt towards his commanding officer, they had been inclined to think that his two-year enforced absence in travelling to England and back for the trial was punishment enough. They also believed that, if tried, he would receive no more than a reprimand. They had instructed Johnston to return to Sydney, where Governor King was ordered to release him from arrest so that he could immediately return to duty.

❧ 23 August 1802 ❧

It was Sunday afternoon, and Esther was singing nursery rhymes with two-year-old Maria when her overseer appeared at her door. Esther had asked Biggers—who had recently received a pardon—to see her after the Sunday service to explain why some cabbages she had requested him to deliver to Mr Jamieson, the Superintendent of Government Stock, had not arrived. During their conversation she also told him that she had not been pleased to hear that some of her farmhands had been complaining of being overworked, underfed and roughly treated.

Biggers glared at her and advised her to leave the management of the workers up to him. But Esther persisted in her attempt to impress upon him her desire to treat her workers fairly.

Biggers was incensed by her interference in his job. He had already been ridiculed by overseers on other properties for having to answer to a woman, and now she was criticising his methods. He grabbed her by the throat with his two hands and pushed her to the ground, shouting: 'You whore! I'm under no bond now and I'll do for you!'

CHAPTER TEN

Night Terrors

With Biggers' hands tightening around her throat, Esther tried to call out but struggled to take a breath. Maria began to wail. Biggers held Esther down with one hand still around her throat and began pulling up her skirts with the other. Esther scratched at his face and ripped his shirt in her efforts to get away. At that moment, her maid Mary Gilbert, wondering what was upsetting Maria, appeared in the doorway. She screamed at what she saw.

Biggers glanced up, then let go of Esther. He stood up, brushed himself down and stormed out of the room. Esther was still lying on the floor, shaking and gasping for breath, when Mary rushed over to help her to her feet.

The following day, Esther told Isaac Nichols what had happened. Nichols insisted that she prosecute Biggers for his behaviour, partly to protect herself from any further trouble from him but also to show everyone else that she was in control. Esther knew that this time she would need to attend the court herself, and Mary Gilbert agreed to appear as a witness.

When Esther stood up to face Judge Richard Atkins, all the fear and anxiety from the Old Bailey flooded back to her. But she summoned all her courage and struggled through to make her case.

As promised, Mary Gilbert appeared as her witness and explained what she had seen when she entered the room. Biggers was there too, but he sat composed on his seat while the court read out his elegantly worded defence, arguing that it was his duty to Major Johnston to prevent the cabbages from being harvested too early. He described how Esther had violently assaulted him for no reason and had torn the shirt from his back; that, in fact, *he* was the person who was assaulted and injured. Had he not defended himself, Esther would most certainly have deprived him of his life. Then he offered his torn shirt as evidence of her attack upon him.

Although it was clearly a case of he-said-she-said, the court decided that the prosecution had not been established for the purpose of obtaining any pecuniary damages, but merely for the protection of the plaintiff's person, so it found Biggers guilty. He was fined five shillings and ordered to pay a bond of fifty pounds himself and to find two other people who would pay twenty-five pounds each as a bond for him to: *keep the peace towards Esther Julian and all her family for one year from this day.*

Biggers shouted out that the Provost Marshal, Thomas Smyth, must have persuaded Mary Gilbert to give false evidence against him, which caused Smyth to swear and call Biggers a scoundrel.

Smyth subsequently sued Biggers for defamation. Biggers was ordered to pay fifty pounds damages to Smyth (two hundred times the fine ordered in Esther's case), and Smyth was fined five pounds for swearing in court and calling Biggers a scoundrel.

Esther's troubles with Biggers did not end there. Only a few days later she was in court again. Esther had accused Biggers of stealing some corn from her barn at George's River and he had immediately sued her for defamation.

Once again, he supplied an elegantly worded written defence in which he emphasised that he had been appointed by Major Johnston—a man towards whom he bore respect, veneration and esteem—and that Johnston's 'housekeeper', prompted by the most vindictive motives, had accused him of a crime which he didn't commit.

This time, Esther was brave enough in court to ask questions of the witnesses herself. And she made sure that she mentioned how Biggers had recently knocked her to the ground.

The court ruled in her favour and the defamation case was dismissed.

❧ 16 October 1802 ☙

Esther hurried to Sydney Cove as soon as she received Susannah's note telling her of the *Buffalo*'s arrival. Before she even alighted from the buggy she could see Johnston's tall figure standing on the deck. He had come back!

Esther had been so focused on managing the estate during his two-year absence that she had become quite used to being by herself. But now, seeing him waving to her, she realised just how worried and lonely she had been. And she felt ashamed for doubting that he would return.

During Johnston's absence, Esther had expanded their production of livestock and grain so successfully that, of all the recorded sales to the government over the following fifteen years, the ones made by Esther while Johnston was away, or just after he returned, were the largest.

She was relieved that he could once again take over responsibility for the estate, but she continued to assist him in its management and her name was often still recorded as the seller of their wheat and meat.

❧ 19 June 1803 ☙

One Sunday evening, eight months later, Esther was sitting in her parlour enjoying lively after-dinner conversation. Henry and Susannah

Kable, Isaac Nichols and Dr D'Arcy Wentworth had just been treated to a fine roast dinner at Annandale House.

Wentworth had pulled his life together, bought one of the finest houses in High Street, and employed three servants to take care of it. He had changed the names Catherine Crowley had chosen for his two younger sons: Dorset had become D'Arcy after himself, and Matthew had become John. But William had stayed William. And when they were twelve and nine, he had sent his two elder sons to school in England. He had ordered fine new clothes from his tailor in London and, with a new chaise and horses, he had begun to take his place among some of the prosperous Sydney land owners, if not among all those with unsullied pasts.

Lieutenant-Colonel Paterson had withdrawn ill, and Johnston had become Acting Commander of the New South Wales Corps. Now he complained to his friends that Governor King seemed to have no regard for army procedures although, he supposed, that was not very surprising as King was a navy man. Johnston added that he hoped His Excellency would soon be recalled and a new governor sent out.

Wentworth was in full agreement. He told his friends that Dr Balmain had been kind enough to send him a quarter-cask of Madeira from London but, as it was being rowed ashore, the landing permit was missing a signature and Governor King had seized the cask and referred the matter to a civil court. Then, when the court ruled his seizure had been unlawful, he overruled that decision and distributed Wentworth's Madeira to his own staff.

Nichols suggested that, in spite of his difficult behaviour, King had also achieved some good. There were fewer people living off the government store, the new government farm at Castle Hill was doing well, and he gave good jobs to emancipists. Even his decision to establish colonies in Van Diemen's Land seemed a wise one—there was no telling what the French might do, sniffing around with their 'scientific explorations'. They couldn't be trusted not to establish a French station in Bass Strait to harass passing British ships.

Esther leaned towards Susannah to tell her quietly that, apparently, it was now most awkward between Mrs King, Mrs Paterson and Mrs Macarthur. After being so friendly, the to-do between their husbands had put them in a very difficult situation, particularly as there were no other women of equal standing in the colony with whom they could converse.

'What are you up to these days, Kable?' Wentworth asked.

Henry Kable was no longer chief constable, but he still owned the store and the Ramping Horse tavern. He also had farms where he grew grain and raised cattle, sheep, goats and horses. He told Wentworth that he was currently establishing a coach service between Sydney, Parramatta and the Hawkesbury.

'And all Mr Kable can speak of is building more ships with Mr Underwood!' Susannah added proudly.

Wentworth mischievously remarked that he believed a friend of Johnston's had arrived recently on HMS *Glatton*. 'A Miss Bridget Edwards. I understand you made her acquaintance when last you were in England?' he said to Johnston.

Esther turned to Johnston with surprise, but he feigned disinterest in the woman who had followed him all the way to New South Wales in the continued hope of becoming his wife. He was relieved to be able to say that he understood Miss Edwards had formed an alliance with the ship's doctor during her voyage out and that she was going with him to the new settlement in Van Diemen's Land.

Susannah tactfully changed the subject by asking Wentworth about the two-storeyed house he had built in Parramatta, adding that Mr Kable had told her it was one of the finest in the colony. Wentworth returned the compliment by praising the three-storey mansion the Kables had acquired in Sydney.

After a pause in the conversation, Nichols said that he believed there were now more Irish convicts than soldiers in the colony, and that they kept trying to walk over the mountains in the hope of reaching China. Johnston agreed that was so, and added that their latest attempt had been a dreadful business. They had broken into farmhouses, stolen provisions, shot a manservant in the face and had had their way with a young girl, right in front of her mother. But Johnston reassured his guests that more than a hundred free men had been trained in arms to create a Loyal Association, in case of any further trouble from the Irish convicts.

◦ *4 March 1804* ◦

Esther and Johnston were sitting quietly on the cool veranda of Annandale House as the light faded in the west. They were watching a Spanish Merino ram from the King's flock at Kew together with three Teeswater ewes which Johnston's patron, the Duke of Northumberland, had sent out to him.

In Sydney, the ships at anchor swayed on the inky water as the Kables relaxed after a family dinner at home. Elizabeth Macarthur and her children were having supper with the Reverend Samuel Marsden and his family at his Parramatta residence.

It was a typical Sunday evening . . . except that two hundred Irish convicts at the Castle Hill government farm had just escaped. As the peace of the evening descended, one of them had deliberately set fire to his hut—a signal for the start of an organised rebellion. While the attention of the guards was focused on the burning building, hundreds of convicts poured out of their huts.

They planned to march to Parramatta and set fire to Elizabeth Farm, knowing that, with John Macarthur away in England, many of the soldiers from the garrison in town would rush to Elizabeth Macarthur's aid. Then the rebels would storm the garrison to steal weapons, and rendezvous at Constitution Hill with hundreds more convicts from Parramatta. They would travel together to the Hawkesbury, where their numbers would be boosted to more than a thousand by all the English convicts who would join them there. Then they would return to Parramatta to plant a symbolic tree of liberty in the grounds of Government House, and march on to Sydney, where they would commandeer all the ships, and sail away to freedom.

Everything began as planned. They quickly moved out into the surrounding countryside, attacked settlers who stood in their way, broke into farm buildings, stole whatever makeshift weapons they could find, and marched on through Prospect Hill and Toongabbie to gather more convicts to their cause. With the brutality of last year's rape still in their minds, women in their nightgowns fled with their children to cower in the darkening bush.

As the mob passed through Seven Hills, they dragged a farmer called William Joyce from his bed and took him hostage. But he managed to escape at Toongabbie, find a horse and gallop to Parramatta. He burst into the Marsdens' house with the news that the rebels were on their way. As Marsden and Elizabeth Macarthur dashed outside to see a distant glow of fire, the farmer galloped on towards the town.

The sound of beating drums called the sixty-five soldiers at Parramatta to arms and rallied the members of the Loyal Association. The signalling system to Sydney via the flagpole at Pendant Hills was of no use at night, so a messenger was sent on horseback to gallop to the governor and warn him of the uprising.

The Reverend Marsden feared the rebels might overcome the garrison so, at eleven o'clock, he bundled his own family, the Macarthurs and two other women with children into his small boat on the Parramatta River; then he clambered in himself and pushed off into the black water. They could hear the rebels shouting as they moved away from the shore. For four long hours they huddled together in the dark, as the boat drifted silently with the flow, past darkened farmhouses and banks of twisted mangroves, down the river towards Sydney.

At midnight, Johnston and Esther, who was seven months pregnant, were peacefully asleep at Annandale House when they were woken by a loud hammering on the front door. A trooper stood in the lamplight and breathlessly told Johnston that about five hundred armed convicts had broken out, that soldiers had begun marching from Sydney, and that Governor King was riding ahead of them on horseback and would arrive at any moment to give Johnston his orders.

Johnston, still in his nightclothes, ran down his long driveway to meet the governor. King ordered him to assume command of the soldiers and volunteers of the Loyal Association who were marching from Sydney towards Parramatta, then rode on ahead. Johnston rushed back to his house, shouting orders to have his horse saddled up, then threw on his uniform—sword swinging by his side—and thrust a pistol under his sash. He gave a second pistol to Esther and told her not to let *anyone* into the house until he returned. He kissed her on the forehead and slammed the front door behind him.

When the soldiers and men of the Loyal Association arrived, Johnston checked they all had good flints in their guns—which he ordered them to load. Then, to keep his horse fresh, he took it by the reins and walked beside his men, marching off down the dark, dusty road. The Parramatta road was hilly and the men had to march around large tree stumps which rose out of the gloom, and splash through two creeks that crossed the road, Duck River and Beckett's Creek.

The small boat carrying the Marsdens and Macarthurs reached Sydney Cove at three in the morning. After clambering out, the Marsdens took their guests to their Sydney house where Elizabeth thankfully settled her children into bed, then sat up nervously with the others waiting for news.

Meanwhile, at Annandale House, the male servants had all left to help Johnston defeat the rebels. Esther had dressed quickly and was sitting in her darkened parlour, holding the pistol. She had no idea what was happening in Sydney or Parramatta. After about an hour, she was startled by a pounding on her front door. She ran up behind the sleepy Mary Gilbert to stop her opening it, putting her finger to her lips. Esther still held the pistol in her shaking hand. The two women stood quietly in the hall and watched the doorhandle turn, but the bolt held fast and the door remained firmly closed. The pounding began again. Then it stopped, and they heard footsteps move around the side of the house. Esther followed the sound, pistol in hand.

She heard one of her precious glass windows shatter, and she stifled a scream. She pulled Mary back towards the room where her children were sleeping. When a large figure suddenly appeared in the hall, she closed her eyes . . . and pulled the trigger. A shot blasted through the darkened house.

'Hold your fire!' the figure called out.

'Dr Wentworth!' Esther exclaimed.

'Fortunately, I remain so,' he replied.

Esther demanded to know what he was doing, breaking into her house. Wentworth explained that battle was not his forte—it was best left to men like Johnston—and he had come to make sure that she was safe, knowing Johnston would have been called away. The governor had requisitioned all the horses, so he had walked all the way from town.

Esther's voice was shaking as she admitted that she was relieved to see him. Did he have any news of the rebels? No, Wentworth replied, but Sydney was in a state of uproar. HMS *Calcutta* was moored in the harbour with all its lanterns blazing. Her hundred and forty marines and sailors had come ashore to help defend the town. People were shouting and running about, and a roadblock had been put in place on the Parramatta road.

Mary brewed some tea and they all sat together, anxiously waiting for news.

❧ 5 March 1804 ❧

As the dawn's light tinged the eastern horizon, Johnston and his men reached Parramatta, where they were each given a spoonful of rum and half a loaf of bread. Then they walked on to Government House, where Governor King handed Johnston his hastily written orders. Johnston stared at the illegible scribble, and King snatched it back and read the orders aloud.

After he finished, Johnston waited expectantly. King continued: 'You may fire upon any person who flees when challenged. And, Johnston . . . do not let them reach the Hawkesbury.'

Thomas Anlezark, the governor's blue-coated trooper, mounted his horse and rode alongside Johnston.

Things had not gone to plan for the rebels: two groups had become lost on their way from Castle Hill; a misunderstanding over signals meant that Elizabeth Farm was never set alight; and the rebel messenger taking the final details of the plan to the Hawkesbury was arrested on the way, and so never arrived.

The remaining rebels met at Constitution Hill as planned, to reassess their position. The Parramatta garrison had now had time to fortify its defences, so they knew they were unlikely to be able to overpower it. They decided instead to go directly to the Hawkesbury to meet up with the hundreds more supporters they expected were waiting for them there.

The early autumn day was unexpectedly warm as Johnston led his men—who had marched all night—along the road to Toongabbie, where he learned there were about four hundred armed rebels gathered on Sugar Loaf Hill. He sent one group of men along the Hawkesbury road in a flanking manoeuvre, while he led the rest up the hill. However, by the time they reached its summit, the rebels had already moved on. Johnston continued until he and his men were about six miles past Toongabbie, where a farmer told them the rebels were only about another mile ahead.

As a ploy to buy time, Johnston sent the only other man on horseback, Trooper Anlezark, riding ahead, waving Johnston's white handkerchief as a symbol of truce. When Anlezark caught up with the rebels, they jeered at his suggestion of a surrender. They took the flint out of his pistol and sent him back to Johnston. Father James Dixon, the convict Catholic priest, was the next person Johnston sent to try to negotiate a solution. But he, too, was sent away by the rebels, who by then were only half a mile ahead of Johnston's men.

Johnston coolly asked Anlezark if he was prepared to face the rebels with him.

'I would follow you to hell, sir,' replied the trooper. Johnston told him to make sure he was armed.

It was now mid-morning, and the sun was shining in a cloudless sky as the two men, apparently unarmed, faced the angry mob. Johnston called out that he wished to speak with their captain. The crowd moved apart, opening a path. The rebels waited for Johnston to enter between their pistols, cutlasses, bayonets, pikes and pitchforks.

Johnston announced that their captain must have very little spirit if he would not come out and speak with him, considering Johnston was within pistol shot. Then Phillip Cunningham, a veteran of the Irish Battle of Vinegar Hill, and his deputy stepped forward from the crowd, swords in hand. They still refused to surrender, but agreed to wait while Johnston returned to his troops to bring back Father Dixon.

On his return Johnston said they must surely see the impropriety of their conduct. Cunningham replied there was no impropriety about it. They were asserting their natural right for freedom.

Johnston and Dixon both warned that there would be bloodshed if they did not come to their senses. However, if they surrendered now under the governor's terms, things would go easier for them.

'There will be no surrendering!' Cunningham retorted.

Johnston's horse, sensing the tension, snorted and stamped its hoof.

'What is it you want, Cunningham?' Johnston asked.

'Death or liberty!'

At that moment Johnston saw the red uniforms of his soldiers appear over the rise ahead and, instead of allowing the rebels to withdraw under the truce symbolised by his white handkerchief, he whipped his pistol from beneath his sash and clapped it to the deputy's head.

'As you wish, Cunningham!' he said. Then he growled at the deputy: 'Walk towards those soldiers or I shall blow your soul to hell!'

Trooper Anlezark took advantage of the moment and pulled out his own pistol (which had a new piece of flint). He held it against Cunningham's head, giving him the same choice. As soon as the two hostages had reached the soldiers, Johnston shouted the order to charge, and the eighty soldiers and volunteers ran towards the two hundred rebels, each firing at the other.

The soldiers were well trained: they formed alternating lines, each relentlessly advancing with an efficient technique of load-aim-fire, and then letting the line behind them move forward while they re-loaded their guns. And the volunteer settlers, who had seen their families terrorised and their farms ransacked, were now free to unleash their revenge. The surprised rebels were caught off guard, leaderless and unfamiliar with their stolen weapons.

In the melee, Quartermaster Thomas Laycock lashed at Cunningham with his sword, dropping him to the ground. Johnston was furious with such dishonourable conduct. He pointed his pistol towards his own soldiers and threatened to shoot anyone who killed a rebel in cold blood. The rebels, believing their leader was now dead, quickly lost heart and fled in all directions, followed by the soldiers who fanned out to chase them down.

When order at last prevailed, there were fifteen rebels dead, six wounded and twenty-six taken prisoner, but not one of Johnston's men was injured. The wounded Cunningham survived, but only until the following day when, under martial law, Johnston ordered him to be hanged without trial from the staircase of the general store at Green Hills.

⇜ 7 March 1804 ⇝

Johnston and his men marched most of the prisoners back to Parramatta. And the following day they walked wearily all the way back to Sydney, to an enthusiastic welcome from the townsfolk.

Eight men were sentenced to death for their part in the uprising (which became known as the Second Battle of Vinegar Hill). One's body was wrapped in chains to hang where he was executed on the track to Castle Hill, until his corpse rotted to a tangled mass of bones. Seven rebels were flogged and thirty-four were sent to work in the coalmines along the Coal River.

For the victors there were rewards. William Joyce, the farmer who had ridden to Parramatta to warn of the uprising, was given an extra grant of land adjoining his farm. Quartermaster Laycock, despite his behaviour, was granted five hundred acres, which he named Kingsgrove in honour of the governor. As a reward for Johnston, his son, Young George, who was still at school in England, received five hundred acres near George's Hall. Johnston himself was granted sixty acres adjoining that land, and another two thousand acres near Cabramatta, which he called King's Gift, making him the third-largest landholder in the colony after John Macarthur and the Reverend Samuel Marsden.

◆ 2 November 1804 ◆

Esther's two youngest daughters were spending the afternoon with Mrs Atkins, the judge's wife, who delighted in having four-year-old Maria to tea, and had offered to keep baby Isabella as well, because she had fallen asleep right in her arms. Esther was in the Kables' High Street store, looking at some fine black lace. Her hand reached out for it, but stopped before her fingers felt its touch. Her face flushed. The lace was exquisitely beautiful . . . but too painful a reminder of her past.

She cast her eye over the many other items that filled the shelves. Farming tools jostled for space amid the finest fashions from Bond Street, embroidered satin slippers, china jars of preserved ginger, colourful fabrics and painted paper parasols. Sydney's consumer society was well underway.

Susannah commented on the sad news about Isaac Nichols's wife, Mary, who had recently drowned. But then she turned to the more cheerful subject of Johnston's promotion to commanding officer of the New South Wales Corps and lieutenant-governor of the colony. She had heard that Lieutenant-Colonel Paterson was leaving to start a new settlement on the Tamar River in the north of Van Diemen's Land, to prevent the French from claiming it first.

As Esther browsed through the store, she told Susannah that their friend, Captain Piper, was now governor on Norfolk Island, and that Dr Wentworth seemed pleased with his own decision to return there. Wentworth had let his Sydney house to Captain Kent, but had taken his housekeeper, Miss Ainslie, with him. Susannah raised her eyebrows at that news.

Esther lowered her voice and moved closer to Susannah. She said she had heard that on Thursday evenings at the island barracks, some of the women who wished to ply their trade performed a dance of the mermaids for the men, completely naked above the waist and with a number painted on their backs, so that their admirers could engage their services afterwards.

'Good gracious!' replied Susannah.

⊲ 3 January 1805 ⊳

Esther thought constantly about her children in England. Like other young gentlemen, Young George and Bob would be learning English, Latin, Greek, modern languages, mathematics, science, history, geography, art and sport. She was delighted when they sent home plans they had drawn of Annandale Farm, because she hoped it meant that they were keen to return home and help manage the estate.

She and Johnston felt that Julia would benefit from staying in England for another couple of years, but they were eager for their two sons to come home. They asked Robert Campbell, a wealthy Sydney merchant who was travelling to England, to bring the boys back with him when he returned.

⊲ 18 February 1805 ⊳

Esther carefully untwisted the pieces of rag around which she had wrapped Rosanna's wet hair the night before, so that her seventeen-year-old daughter's hair hung in soft ringlets for her wedding day.

Rosanna was marrying Isaac Nichols. Though he was seventeen years older than her daughter, and it would be an Anglican wedding, Esther was happy that Rosanna was marrying a good man. She knew her daughter had always admired him, and following his wife's tragic death the previous year, their romance had blossomed.

Esther gently fluffed Rosanna's hair with her fingers, then stood back to look at her. Rosanna was wearing a fashionable high-waisted dress that gathered beneath her bust, just arrived from London. At that moment, Mary Gilbert came in with a posy of freshly picked flowers from the garden.

'You will be the prettiest bride this colony has ever seen, Miss Abrahams,' she said.

When everyone was ready, they climbed into Johnston's new open carriage, which Rosanna's sisters had bedecked with more fresh flowers. The two elegant white horses clip-clopped down the driveway, which was lined with small Norfolk Island pines, through the gates at the road to Parramatta, then along to the Female Orphan School in High Street where church services were held. Passers-by burst into applause as they arrived.

Susannah Kable and her daughter Diana had decorated the doorway with ribbons, and Esther's younger children ran alongside Rosanna as she walked towards it holding Johnston's arm. Inside, Isaac Nichols waited to become her husband.

When the marriage service was over, all the guests travelled to Annandale House for a grand wedding feast. The kitchen had never seen such commotion. Mary darted to and fro, issuing orders to the cook and adding final touches to platters of food before they were taken out to the guests on the veranda. As the afternoon's celebration wore on, a band struck up and the guests moved inside to dance.

The Reverend Samuel Marsden, who had performed the marriage service, did not approve of such frivolity. He remained outside with his wife, who occasionally looked wistfully through the open door at the twirling couples. Esther went out to talk to them. She said she believed Marsden planned to open a second orphan school at Parramatta.

'Quite so,' he replied. 'Education is the only way to liberate children from the shameful paths of their parents. Break their wills and allow them no play, that is my motto. For she who plays as a child . . .' and he looked directly at Esther, 'will play when she is a woman.'

'Indeed,' replied Esther, but there was a smile in her eye.

In England, the case against Macarthur had been ruled insufficient and he had been busy promoting his idea that New South Wales could supply valuable wool to the British clothing manufacturers. He had taken with him a box of the finest long-haired Merino fleeces from his flock at Elizabeth Farm.

Macarthur's timing could not have been better. The war with France had interrupted supplies from Spain, and British farmers were increasingly breeding sheep for meat rather than wool because of food shortages. Macarthur had appeared to offer a perfect solution: Britain would have a virtually unlimited supply of fine wool from one of its own colonies, and the export trade would make New South Wales more financially independent.

Macarthur had pointed out that all he needed was plenty of land and convict shepherds. He had been so convincing that the new Colonial Secretary, Lord Camden, had finally told him that, if he sold his army commission, he could have a new grant of five thousand acres of the best grazing land in New South Wales—the Cowpastures—plus thirty convict shepherds.

So, after an absence of four years, Macarthur arrived home to Sydney to be the colony's wealthiest man. He handed Governor King a letter from Lord Camden, outlining the allocation of land and convicts that were due to him.

King looked Macarthur straight in the eye, then offered him his hand. He knew his battle with Macarthur was over—and that Macarthur had won.

The following month Lord Castlereagh wrote to inform King that a new governor had been appointed to take over the administration of New South Wales.

๑ 13 June 1806 ๑

'Bella! Bella!'

Esther looked into one room after another, before finally crossing the courtyard to the kitchen.

'Mary, have you seen Bella?'

'No, ma'am, she ain't come in 'ere.'

'Jinny had her all morning but now she seems to have disappeared,' Esther said.

Esther's family was continuing to grow: George, Robert and Julia were still at school in England; David was eight, Maria six, and little Isabella was now two. Esther leaned heavily against the kitchen dresser. She was pregnant again and it would not be long before she gave birth.

'She's quick on them little legs,' said Mary as she wiped her sooty hands down her apron. 'I'll have a look around the courtyard and stables.'

'Thank you, Mary.'

Esther brushed her hand over her forehead. She wandered out of the kitchen and heard Mary in the stables calling Bella's name. Then she walked out of the courtyard, past the chickens pecking up the last of their morning grain, and towards a stack of old timber that had been piled up beneath a stand of gum trees. Suddenly, she heard Bella squeal from the other side of the trees.

Esther ran around the stack of timber to find Bella running up and down on the spot, screaming and holding out her hand. There was a black spider on her chubby finger. Esther brushed it off and picked up her small daughter.

'Thank goodness you are safe. There, there, stop your weeping, the spider has gone.'

But Bella's cries didn't subside. Jinny Grigg, the nursemaid, came running out from the laundry.

'Is she hurt?' she called.

'I think not. She may have been bitten by a tiny spider.'

Bella was crying and squirming so much that it was difficult for Esther to hold her. They walked back into the house where Esther tried to distract her daughter with games, but Bella didn't stop crying, and she vomited on the floor. Esther noticed her arm was wet with perspiration and she looked closely at her soft hand. It was turning pink and there was a tiny red mark on her finger.

Esther sat on the sofa and hugged her daughter close. Bella's small body was beginning to tremble, and it seemed to be growing rigid in Esther's arms.

'It was only a very small spider, Bella,' Esther said, rocking her to and fro. The room became blurred through her tears. 'Just a little black spider with a pretty red mark on its back.'

CHAPTER ELEVEN

The Trouble with Bligh

Isabella's funeral service was conducted by the Reverend Samuel Marsden in the garden of Annandale House, where her body was buried in a simple vault enclosed by a white picket fence.

Esther was still grieving when she gave birth the following month to another girl, named Blanche.

◇ *6 August 1806* ◇

Major Johnston was rowed out to the *Lady Madeline Sinclair* to escort the new governor ashore. It was Captain William Bligh of the Royal Navy—a short, stout bulldog of a man, with bright blue eyes and a pallid complexion. At fifty-one, he was nine years older than Johnston and had been recommended for the post by Sir Joseph Banks.

Bligh had been chosen because he had a reputation for being able to withstand intimidation—and the Colonial Office was increasingly concerned about the powerful influence that officers of the New South Wales Corps exerted over the colony's administration. Governor Bligh's major intentions were to prevent the officers dealing in rum and to abolish their monopoly of trade.

Everything began well enough. Bligh was welcomed with a written address of congratulations, signed by three prominent colonists on behalf of everyone else who mattered: George Johnston, for the military officers; Judge Atkins, for the civil officers; and John Macarthur, for the free settlers. However, soon afterwards Bligh received a petition from one hundred and thirty-five free settlers who were infuriated that Macarthur had taken it upon himself to represent them—particularly as he had recently withheld selling his sheep in order to drive up the price of mutton. And then Bligh received another petition from an extra two hundred and forty-four Hawkesbury settlers who were equally incensed that Macarthur had welcomed Bligh on their behalf.

Not long afterwards, Johnston told Esther that Bligh treated all the officers very civilly and, if he continued as he had begun, Johnston expected they would all get on very well.

But that's not quite how it turned out. Bligh was yet another naval-officer-turned-governor, who was used to a crew trained to obey his every command, not a community of seven thousand, largely free, people. The colonists came from a wide variety of social and economic backgrounds, and now included many entrepreneurial ex-convicts. The colony needed a governor with strong diplomatic skills who could foster its growing economy. Bligh had many good qualities, but diplomacy wasn't one of them—instead, he had an explosive temper and a knack for upsetting people.

He began, as Hunter and King had been before him, full of enthusiasm to carry out his orders. However, Bligh's manner was far more confronting than that of either of his predecessors. A man who always liked to be in control, he regularly interfered in the work of the civil and military officers, making arbitrary decisions and unleashing a vitriolic tirade whenever his actions were questioned, and sometimes even when they were not.

⟢ 15 September 1806 ⟣

As soon as Esther and Johnston heard that Robert Campbell had returned to Sydney, they hurried down to the cove to welcome their two boys home from England. The daylight was fading before Campbell finally came ashore—alone.

He explained that the boys had never turned up to travel with him, and he had no idea of the reason why. Esther and Johnston could do nothing but wait until an explanatory letter could arrive by another ship from their contacts in England. At last a short note arrived from (ex-governor) Hunter, explaining that everyone had thought the boys should remain in England a while longer, to give them the opportunity to be introduced to the Duke of Northumberland.

Esther's heart ached with disappointment, but she quickly came up with a plan. Johnston had already arranged with the Reverend Marsden and his wife to bring Julia back with them when they travelled to England the following year, so now he could ask them to bring the boys back with them as well. Esther was not fond of Marsden, but at least she knew her children would be safe with him.

The only problem was, that by the time the Marsdens reached England, arrangements might already have been made there to send the boys home with someone else—and Esther worried about who might be entrusted with their care.

⟡ 17 September 1806 ⟡

Bligh had been in Sydney for little over a month when Macarthur spoke to him about his plans for developing a wool industry.

Bligh blustered at once: 'Are you to have such flocks of sheep as no man ever heard of before? No, sir! You have five thousand acres of land in the finest situation in this country by making false representations respecting your wool. But by God, you shan't keep it!'

'That land was granted to me by the Secretary of State, sir,' Macarthur countered.

'Damn the Secretary of State!' said Bligh.

It was early morning, and the two men were standing in the garden of Government House at Parramatta while on a social visit to the Kings, who had not yet left the colony. When they walked back into the house to have breakfast with their hosts, Bligh accosted King with such violent and insulting language that the ex-governor was reduced to tears. Nevertheless, Macarthur was determined to convince Bligh of the importance of his sheep so, after breakfast, he suggested they visit Elizabeth Farm to inspect his flock.

When they arrived, Macarthur mentioned again that the Secretary of State had been very supportive of his enterprise.

'What do I care for him?' Bligh retorted. 'He commands in England and I command here!'

28 January 1807

While Esther was waiting for her children to come home, her thirteen-year-old son Robert had decided to join the Royal Navy.

The kindly Hunter wrote him a letter full of friendly advice: *Be sure Bobby to take good care of your clothes and remember that if you are careless you will soon lose on board ship all you have; without good clothes you can never appear clean, and without cleanliness you will never be respected but despised . . . If you should discover at any time a disposition amongst any of your shipmates to card playing or any sort of gambling, never join in such amusements; your time can at all times be better employed in reading, writing, drawing, etc.*

10 February 1807

At last the Marsdens sailed for England! And Esther could look forward to her children coming home with them. She still had no idea when that might be—only that it would be many months away. In the meantime, she could look forward to welcoming her first grandchild, as Rosanna was expecting a baby.

10 April 1807

It was late in the evening when Esther received the news that Rosanna had gone into labour. She hurried into Sydney Town, remembering so vividly the night she had assisted Susannah with the birth of Diana. But this time it was a little boy who entered the world, named Isaac after his father.

Esther, at thirty-seven, couldn't quite believe that she was now a grandmother, but she smiled all the way home.

John and Gregory Blaxland were the first truly wealthy free settlers to emigrate to New South Wales. They were friends of Sir Joseph Banks, who had suggested the idea to them. They had been further encouraged by the Colonial Office, which had promised free passage for their families, their servants and all their luggage and equipment, plus grants of thousands of acres of land, and dozens of convict workers each, who would be fed and clothed by the government for eighteen months.

In exchange, the Blaxland brothers had agreed to invest thousands of pounds of capital into the colony's economy. They were both skilled and experienced gentlemen-farmers from Kent, and they looked forward to a prosperous future in New South Wales.

They had brought with them from England their wives and children, servants, farm managers, cattle, sheep, sheepdogs, a swarm of bees, cases of seed, books, pens, paper, medicine and ploughs. They had also brought tools for shoemakers, saddlers, carpenters, blacksmiths, coopers and wheelwrights. The Blaxland brothers meant business.

Now their two fine carriages turned off the Parramatta road and into the driveway of Annandale House. They rattled along the track flanked by the growing Norfolk Island pines, and pulled up in front of the tall white columns that supported the veranda of the house.

Over a welcoming lunch, John Blaxland explained to Johnston that they were disappointed to have found Governor Bligh less than obliging. Blaxland had been guaranteed eight thousand acres, but had received only just over one thousand, and only twenty-three of the eighty convicts he had been promised.

Governor Bligh had argued that although Blaxland had invested six thousand pounds of capital, he had not put it all into agriculture. The fact that he had also bought a butcher shop and a whaling vessel seemed of no consequence to Bligh, although Blaxland was of the opinion that they would contribute just as handsomely to the colony's economy.

Blaxland's wife, Harriet, added that the governor had seemed to be deliberately trying to provoke them with the first three convicts he had sent: a one-eyed, one-armed old man, a sixty-year-old asthmatic and an idiot.

'And yet the governor has *eighty* men working to beautify his gardens at Government House,' she added.

'And what about his own farm!' snorted John's brother, Gregory. 'He takes animals heavy with young from the government flock to graze upon his land. Then, after they have given birth, he returns them, keeping the offspring for himself, with no alteration to the records of government stock.'

Gregory's wife, Elizabeth, explained that they had given up everything they had in England to start a new life in New South Wales, and the British Government had given them every encouragement. But now they found that its promises were not being kept by the Governor of New South Wales.

After lunch, Esther took the two Mrs Blaxlands for a stroll around her garden, though its winter blooms could not compete with the richly coloured gowns worn by her two visitors.

At first, Esther sensed an awkwardness between herself and the Blaxland wives. But, after some time, Elizabeth Blaxland asked if Esther knew why the governor had not brought his wife out to the colony. Esther explained that she was apparently terrified of the sea. Bligh had therefore insisted that his son-in-law, John Putland, be appointed as his aide-de-camp, so that his daughter Mary could accompany him as First Lady.

Esther then explained what the commotion had been about at church the previous Sunday. She described how Mary Putland had chosen to wear a particularly daring dress to the service. When she had entered the church on the arm of Governor Bligh, who was in full naval uniform, the strong light behind them had made her gossamer-thin dress virtually transparent. As she was wearing no petticoats, everyone could clearly see her lacy pantaloons. Some of the soldiers had begun lasciviously chuckling and, when Mary realised she was the cause of their attention, she did the only sensible thing and fainted. As she was carried from the church, Governor Bligh angrily demanded an apology from Johnston and his 'whole ill-mannered Corps'.

Harriet and Elizabeth could not repress their smiles and chuckles at Esther's tale, and the three women were soon chatting happily together.

⌘ 7 July 1807 ⌘

Dr Wentworth had sent his third son, John, to join William and D'Arcy at school in England. Then, in April, he had returned from Norfolk Island to New South Wales to take up duties as assistant surgeon at the hospital at Parramatta.

One morning, the local chief constable turned up at Wentworth's house, under orders from Governor Bligh, to accuse him of using convalescing convicts from the hospital to work for him. Wentworth agreed that there were indeed five patients who were performing light duties for him while they recuperated, in order to keep their minds occupied. The chief constable then rounded up the patients and sent them to work on the government farm instead.

However, two of the patients were clearly still in need of treatment—one had an ulcerated leg and the other an open wound on his arm—and the overseer at the government farm promptly sent them back to the hospital. As they had been removed on the governor's orders, Wentworth refused to readmit them until Bligh explained why he had taken them away. Bligh responded by arresting Wentworth for contempt.

⌘ 21 July 1807 ⌘

Esther thought the whole dispute had got quite out of hand. She was dismayed when she learned that Wentworth had been found guilty, and that it was Johnston's unhappy duty to publicly reprimand him in front of the troops.

Wentworth submitted quietly to the reprimand and returned to his work at the hospital. But two days later, Bligh suspended him from his duties and stopped his salary, refusing to give any explanation. Judge Atkins pointed out to Bligh that, as Wentworth had submitted to the sentence of the court, the governor had no legal right to penalise him any further.

'The law, sir!' replied Bligh. 'Damn the law: my will is the law, and woe unto the man that dares to disobey it!'

When Lord Castlereagh at the Colonial Office learned of the incident, he wrote to Bligh: *Your suspension of Mr Wentworth on such a charge, and your concealing from him the nature of it, and your declining to bring him to trial in the colony, is not reconcilable with the principles of British justice.*

❧ 20 August 1807 ❧

Bligh's reputation was going from bad to worse.

'You will never believe what has happened!' spluttered Kable as he marched into his large Sydney home.

Kable told Susannah that, because of the governor's new orders to prevent smuggling, cargo was no longer allowed to be transferred between ships at anchor in the harbour, but must be loaded into boats and brought ashore, which attracted a wharfage cost. Kable, Underwood and their business partner, Simeon Lord, had requested permission to transfer some cargo to the *Sydney Cove* because the casks were too large to be carried by any of their boats and would be damaged by being taken ashore and back out again. The governor had never replied to their written request. Kable had now just been informed that Bligh had laid charges against the three men.

'Whatever for?' asked Susannah.

'Insolence, I gather, just for making the request!'

Susannah said that was ridiculous, and she was sure they would never be found guilty. But Bligh's magistrates did find all three men guilty. Kable and the others were each fined a hundred pounds and sentenced to one month's imprisonment for their audacity to question the governor's orders.

⌘ 12 December 1807 ⌘

A few months later, Sergeant-Major Thomas Whittle knocked on the door of Major Johnston's office.

'What is it, Whittle?' Johnston put down his pen.

Whittle explained that Governor Bligh had hammered on the door of his house in Spring Row early that morning and told Whittle that he had to pull his house down. The governor wanted to reclaim the land it was on. Whittle had told Bligh that he had a lease given to him by Governor King, but Bligh shouted that both the land and the house belonged to himself and that Whittle was to have the house pulled down at once. Whittle told Johnston the house was worth six hundred pounds to him, and he asked where his wife and six children were supposed to go.

Johnston sighed. He placed the tips of his fingers together, then leaned down until his nose touched his forefingers. After a moment, he looked up. He said that he was not prepared to let the governor terrorise his men in their own homes. A man's property was too sacred to be taken away merely at the whim of a governor. If His Excellency wanted to reclaim government land, then he should wait until the leases came up for renewal. He told Whittle to sign the lease over to him. Whittle could stay in his house as long as he liked. If Bligh wanted it down, he would have to come to Johnston about it.

Esther told Susannah all about the dramas when they next met. She was pleased to be able to add that Whittle's house was still standing, although five others had been demolished on the governor's order. Then she told Susannah that Bligh had since declared that Dr Thomas Jamison's lease near the boatsheds was required for government boats; Garnham Blaxcell's leased land was needed for the government timber yard; Dr Harris's lease was detrimental to the parade ground; John Macarthur's lease was required for a church; and Major Johnston's vegetable garden should be used instead by the gaol opposite.

Johnston walked out of the burning summer sun and into Kable's Ramping Horse inn. Kable was there, and they shared a jug of porter. Johnston said he thought Bligh had now managed to offend every class of citizen in the colony. Except for the Hawkesbury farmers, Kable reminded him—they had sung Bligh's praises ever since he had given them assistance after a devastating flood.

As for the Corps, Johnston continued, Bligh had discarded the carefully designed roster for officers to sit as magistrates, and instead appointed whichever ones he wanted at the time, with no regard for their military duties. He moved troops from one duty to another, without any reference to Johnston, their commanding officer. And the soldiers assigned to Bligh's bodyguard could not withstand his constant bullying and kept asking Johnston to transfer them to another post. Johnston told Kable that he had written to the Duke of York, commander of the British Army, to complain of Bligh's treatment of his men.

He paused to take a welcome gulp of porter. Then he told Kable that when he had tried to visit Bligh at Government House to discuss the roster issue, the governor had not even let him speak—he had just dismissed him from his presence.

Kable said all Bligh's new regulations were certainly making it difficult for businesses to thrive. He had stopped issuing grants of land, which made it impossible for the necessary expansion of food-producing enterprises. Johnston nodded and remarked that John Blaxland had written to Joseph Banks with a long list of complaints about Bligh.

The talk turned to Macarthur, whose schooner, the *Parramatta*, had been impounded when she came in the previous month until he paid a fine, because a convict had escaped on her outward journey. Bligh had refused to hear Macarthur's appeal so, instead of paying the fine, Macarthur had surrendered the ship—and would claim compensation from his insurers. He had told the crew that he would cease paying them immediately. Judge Atkins had issued a summons for Macarthur to face trial, but had refused to reveal what the charges were.

Johnston told Kable that Macarthur had called for payment of a bill of exchange for twenty-six pounds that Atkins had given him fourteen years ago. Atkins had disputed the amount of interest, so Macarthur had told Bligh he must have another judge to sit at his trial because Atkins had a conflict of interest. The governor had refused.

'A tangled web indeed!' said Kable.

Macarthur's trial was due to be held in two days' time.

'God knows where all this will end,' sighed Johnston.

∾ 24 January 1808 ∾

The Corps' troubles with Governor Bligh were put aside while they celebrated twenty years since the colony's foundation with a regimental dinner. There was plenty of good food and wine, innumerable toasts, and several officers danced a jig. Nevertheless, Johnston was mindful that they should keep their heads, with Macarthur's trial due the following day. He took a bottle away from one inebriated officer, and stopped the music at ten o'clock.

The officers wandered out, patting each other on the back before heading home in various directions. Johnston clambered into his buggy and flicked the reins to set off along the dark Parramatta road. The moon had not yet risen, and the buggy tumbled about as its wheels jumped over rocks and slid into ruts. When the driveway to Annandale House came into view, the horse sensed the proximity of home and broke into a canter, pulling the bouncing buggy behind it as it rounded the bend.

'Steady on!' Johnston called, as he pulled back on the reins, but the right wheel slipped into a ditch and the buggy crashed onto its side, throwing Johnston heavily onto a rocky outcrop.

Battered and bruised, he managed to right the buggy and lead the pony up the long driveway, where his waiting groom rushed out to meet him.

'Are you injured, sir?' the groom asked.

'I shall live,' Johnston muttered, and he limped thankfully through his front door.

‿ *25 January 1808* ‿

The courtroom was abuzz. Sitting at its head was the ageing Judge Atkins, his face tinged pink and his eyes bleary. With him on the bench were six officers of the Corps, including Captain Kemp, Lieutenant Lawson and Lieutenant Laycock (who had faced the Irish rebels with Johnston). Many settlers had also crammed into the courtroom to witness Macarthur's trial.

Before Atkins could be sworn in, Macarthur spoke up about his objection to Atkins being involved. He said that, considering the disagreements between them, and the fact that it was Atkins who had committed Macarthur for trial, it hardly seemed fair that he be allowed to sit in judgement.

Macarthur paused dramatically, to ensure he had the attention of everyone in the courtroom. Then he turned to address the six officers who made up the court.

'You have the eyes of an anxious public upon you,' he said, 'trembling for the safety of their property, their liberty and their lives. To you has fallen the lot of deciding a point which perhaps involves the happiness or misery of millions yet unborn.'

'Hear! Hear!' the crowd cheered.

But Atkins responded, wagging his finger at Macarthur: 'I shall commit you to gaol for contempt of court, sir!'

Captain Kemp leapt to his feet. 'You commit, sir? No sir, I shall commit you!'

The room erupted with cheers and Atkins stormed out, waving his arms at the gathered crowd and declaring: 'You can all go home, there can be no legal court without me!'

The officer magistrates sent a message to Bligh, asking him to appoint another judge. Bligh refused, and sent a note to Johnston, requesting his assistance. The six officers, having been sworn in, considered themselves a legitimate court and released Macarthur on bail until the following morning.

Esther and Johnston were unaware of the day's courtroom drama as they sat quietly at Annandale House in the late afternoon. Esther was watching birds flit across the wide lawn outside her window. It was her favourite hour—the peaceful interlude after the busyness of the day, before she dressed for dinner.

But Johnston had not been busy that day. His right arm was cosseted in a black silk sling, his face was discoloured with reddened bruises, and he winced with pain when he leaned forward to allow Esther to place another cushion behind his back. Dr Harris had visited him earlier in the day to bleed him, so that his injured right arm might heal the faster. There was a sudden knock at the front door.

'No visitors, Het,' said Johnston. Esther returned after a minute with a note from the governor's secretary. 'What the devil now?' asked Johnston.

His Excellency, under particular public circumstances which have occurred, desires me to request you will see him without delay.

Johnston called in the trooper who had delivered the note.

'Look here,' Johnston said, indicating his sling, 'send my compliments to the governor, but tell him that I am unable to pen a reply to his request and I am too injured to travel to Sydney. As you can see, I am incapacitated.'

'Yes, sir!' The trooper saluted and disappeared.

'I cannot think what trouble Bligh has caused this time,' Johnston said to Esther, 'but whatever it is, it can wait till the morrow.'

❧ 26 January 1808 ❧

Esther heard Johnston call out in alarm. She rushed into the room to find him sitting in his chair, the bruises on his face now sickeningly blue, waving a letter he had just received from Governor Bligh.

'Six of my officers have been charged with treason!' he said.

Dr Harris was there again and Johnston turned to him. 'You say His Excellency has arrested Macarthur again?'

'The town is in an uproar, I tell you,' Harris responded. 'The people are shocked that the governor would arrest Macarthur again, without address to a court. I should not be surprised if there is a riot before too long.'

'Good God, why cannot these men be content with a peaceful existence?' asked Johnston. 'If those officers are imprisoned, I shall be left with only two to command four hundred soldiers!' That thought brought him quickly to his feet, but he sat down again heavily, wincing at the jarring it caused to his arm.

'You know the punishment for treason,' the doctor pointed out.

Of course Johnston knew. Hanging.

But surely it would not come to that. Surely not even Bligh would order officers, who held commissions from His Majesty, to be put to death. But then, in his dealings with Macarthur, the governor *had* shown that he had no qualms about imprisoning an officer along with common felons. And the regiment simply could not function if six of its officers were imprisoned. Johnston stood up again more carefully, limped into the hall and disappeared into his bedroom.

A moment later he reappeared, one arm tangled in a jacket and holding his boots under the other. Esther rushed over to help him.

'I require the carriage,' he told her.

'I have already called for it,' she replied.

'I cannot allow the Corps to be rendered ineffective,' he said, to no one in particular. 'This is a colony of convicts, for God's sake!' Stalling for time, he sent a note to Bligh, then kissed Esther on the forehead and headed for the door.

Esther implored him to sort out the problem quickly, completely unaware that the events of the moment would propel them both into history. She reminded him that David and Maria had been practising a poem to recite to him that evening.

Shortly afterwards, the carriage was jolting towards Sydney, carrying Dr Harris and Johnston—resplendent in his scarlet uniform—to the doctor's handsome residence, Ultimo House, where the officers were waiting for them.

Lieutenant Laycock was the first to meet them. His voice was shaky.

'Bligh is charging us with treason, sir.'

'So I understand,' replied Johnston.

'And he has arrested Macarthur again,' added another.

Johnston nodded.

'There's talk that Macarthur's life is in danger—the gaoler has given him a cutlass for protection,' said a third.

'Don't be absurd!' Johnston retorted.

Sergeant-Major Whittle added that the soldiers were wild about the situation. They had threatened to pull the gaol down if the six officers were arrested. Whittle had sent word to de-commission the canon at Government House, just in case. Johnston, bruised and aching, found it hard to believe that events had already escalated to such a point. It was now five o'clock in the afternoon.

'Very well. Whittle, go ahead to the barracks and prepare the men for parade,' Johnston ordered, confident that at least he could restore order among his own men.

But when he arrived, hundreds of civilians were also tumbling into the parade ground, and he was soon surrounded by a volatile crowd.

'Down with Bligh!' they chanted. 'Down with Bligh!'

Johnston called for everyone to calm down and announced that he would visit the governor at once.

'You cannot do that!' someone called out. 'You know what he's like—he might arrest you and confine you to Government House, and then where shall we be?' The crowd roared in agreement.

Johnston looked around for someone sensible to fill him in on the situation. He caught sight of Henry Kable who, along with Dr Wentworth and the Blaxland brothers, was pushing towards him through the crowd. Johnston made his way through the jostling throng to meet them.

Kable said he was relieved to see him. There was much rash talk going on, but he knew the people would listen to Johnston.

'What are they saying?' asked Johnston.

'That Bligh has gone too far,' said John Blaxland.

'They are after his neck,' added his brother.

'You must get Macarthur out, sir,' interrupted Whittle, who had followed him through the crowd. 'The court released him on bail—the governor had no right to arrest him again.'

'Vinegar Hill!' someone shouted from the crowd. '*John*ston! *John*ston!'

Johnston agreed that Macarthur should not have been arrested. He led his companions towards the relative sanctuary of his office, and a dozen more followed them into it. Johnston worked his right arm free from its sling. He gritted his teeth against the pain and wrote out an order for Macarthur's release on bail. He signed it as lieutenant-governor—a role he was formally entitled to only if Bligh was absent or incapacitated. The order was rushed away to the gaol while Johnston considered his next move. People in the crowd outside were still shouting his name. Others were baying for Bligh's blood.

'You might need to make a move to protect the governor's life,' suggested Wentworth.

'What move?' Johnston asked.

'Arrest the governor,' several people said at once.

'The governor's or the people's blood could be on your hands if you do not,' said Gregory Blaxland.

Johnston repeated the words, shaking his head: '*Arrest* the governor.'

That really would be an act of treason.

CHAPTER TWELVE

First Lady

≈ 26 January 1808 ≈

Macarthur strode into Johnston's office.

'God's curse, Macarthur,' said Johnston, 'these fellows are advising me to arrest Bligh!'

Macarthur agreed that it seemed the only thing left to do.

'And take over command myself?' asked Johnston.

'There is no one better,' replied Macarthur.

'Hear! Hear!' came a chorus of voices.

Johnston took a deep breath and held his bruised face in his free hand. He told the assembled men that the last thing he wanted was the governorship. The wealthy emancipist merchant Simeon Lord said that was precisely why he was the best man for the role. Everyone knew that he had never aspired to the position, so they would know he was acting only out of necessity.

Macarthur suggested it might be wise for Johnston to show that he had the support of the people, so he took a sheet of paper and wrote: *The present alarming state of this colony, in which every man's property, liberty and life are endangered, induces us most earnestly to implore you instantly to place Governor Bligh under an arrest, and to assume the command of the colony. We pledge ourselves, at a moment of less agitation, to come forward to support the measure with our fortunes and our lives.*

Over the next few days over one hundred and fifty people signed the petition.

Meanwhile, Johnston took another piece of paper and dipped his pen in ink. He shifted a little in his chair, trying to find a comfortable position for his injured arm.

Sir—I am called upon to execute a most painful duty. You are charged by the respectable inhabitants of crimes that render you unfit to exercise the supreme authority another moment in this colony; and in that charge all the officers under my command have joined. I therefore require you, in His Majesty's sacred name, to resign your authority, and to submit to the arrest which I hereby place you under, by the advice of my officers, and by the advice of every respectable inhabitant in the town of Sydney.

When he had finished writing, Johnston looked in turn at each of the officers and friends who surrounded his desk.

'I pray this day ends without bloodshed.' He took another deep breath. Then he slammed the flat of his left hand onto the desk. 'Very well! Let us do what must be done!' He stood up, reeled slightly, and walked out onto the parade ground.

It was twenty years to the day since Johnston had first stepped ashore at Sydney Cove. Now, in the early evening light at the end of another summer's day, he prepared to arrest the colony's governor. He ordered the four hundred red-coated soldiers to take up arms and fall in. The troops fixed bayonets to their muskets and the officers drew their swords. Johnston took his place at the head of the column.

The band burst into the rousing 'British Grenadiers' and the armed regiment, with its flag flying in the warm breeze, marched out of the parade ground. They turned left into High Street and, as they went, hundreds of people poured out of their houses to watch the spectacle or even walk alongside them.

The soldiers swung right and marched across the now solidly built brick bridge over the Tank Stream, past Simeon Lord's impressive four-storey residence, then up the hill towards Government House. Excited children danced alongside them.

Inside Government House, Bligh had been enjoying a glass of port after an early dinner with friends when news reached him of Macarthur's release from gaol. He had gone upstairs to put on his uniform and now heard the stirring music from the band wafting towards him.

When he looked out of the window, he saw the regiment marching out of the sunset towards him. He dashed into his office to snatch some papers; some he tore up, others he stuffed into his shirt.

The guards at the gates to Government House fell back as their colleagues approached, revealing the Corps' sole opposition: Governor Bligh's daughter. The recently widowed Mary Putland came running down the path towards them. She ignored the bristling bayonets and beat at the soldiers with her parasol.

'Rebels! Traitors!' she screamed, as they cowered beneath her attack. 'How dare you come here like this! I shall not let you murder my father!'

'Do not be alarmed, Mrs Putland!' Johnston said, as he walked towards her in defiance of her parasol. 'I assure you, no one is being threatened.' He motioned for the troops to surround the house. 'I apologise if we have upset you. We have merely come to formally deliver a letter to your father.' He put his hand on her raised parasol and slowly pushed it down until its tip touched the ground. 'You must allow us to pass,' he said gently.

John Palmer, the commissary, had come out of the front door to see what was going on. When he saw the troops, he ran back inside and slammed the door. It was opened again by some of the soldiers, who had entered the house through the back door.

The governor's dinner guests were still in the dining room, but Bligh was nowhere to be found. In the diminishing light, the soldiers searched the house, the gardens and the outbuildings, without success—until, after about an hour, one of them saw the edge of a bedcover move in an upstairs servant's room.

He bent down and ran his musket along the floor beneath the bed. It passed unhindered. Then he ran it back the other way . . . and this time it struck an obstacle.

When he crouched down to look under the bed, he saw the governor, supporting himself on his hands with his feet braced against the back legs of the bed, and his back arched up off the floor.

'The game is up, sir,' the soldier said. Then he called out: 'He's in here, boys!'

Bligh was hauled out and brought down to face the soldiers. His face was flushed and damp with perspiration, his uniform covered in feathers and fluff. When he reached the bottom of the stairs, his daughter flung her arms around him and he patted her reassuringly on the shoulder.

'There is no cause for alarm, Your Excellency,' Johnston said, handing him the letter. Bligh read it slowly. Johnston suggested that they speak privately in an adjoining room, where he carefully explained that he required Bligh to resign his authority and submit to arrest.

Bligh stood in silence.

Johnston assured him there was no threat to his personal safety. He would merely be placed under house arrest, and his every personal need would be attended to.

Bligh nodded in resignation and they shook hands.

It was after nine in the evening before everyone finally went home. Johnston posted five soldiers outside Government House, then publicly declared martial law.

The townsfolk rejoiced!

Bligh could hear the happy shouts from his upstairs window, and he could see lighted windows all around the town. Kable's tavern, like all the others, was filled to overflowing with celebrating colonists. Children played in the dusty streets, their parents too jubilant to care about bedtimes. The only casualty of the rebellion had been Lieutenant Laycock, who was injured when he fell through a manhole in Government House while searching for Bligh.

When Johnston arrived back at the barracks, the soldiers began chanting: 'No tyranny! Johnston for ever!' But Johnston and the other leaders of what would become known as the 'Rum Rebellion' gathered more quietly. They spent the evening going through Bligh's papers and questioning his supporters.

Johnston took a moment to write a note on a tiny piece of paper to Esther. *Bligh arrested. All is well. Must stay.* He folded it over and over, then walked out to a pigeon house behind the barracks, where he took out a pigeon and tied the note carefully around its leg. Then he walked to the back fence and threw the bird into the air, watching it wheel about and fly off into the darkening sky towards Annandale House.

When Esther read his note, she sighed. More trouble with Bligh! She did not realise that, as Johnston was now the lieutenant-governor, she had been thrust into the role of First Lady, the highest female social rank in the land.

⤙ 27 January 1808 ⤚

The following day, Johnston issued a public proclamation stating that peace had been established and that he had withdrawn martial law. He also noted that he had appointed magistrates and other public officers from among the most respectable officers and colonists which, he hoped, would secure the impartial administration of justice.

He declared that, in future, no man would have just cause to complain of violence, injustice or oppression; and that no free man would be unlawfully taken, imprisoned, or deprived of his house, land or liberty.

He praised the colonists. *Words cannot too strongly convey my approbation of the behaviour of the whole body of the people on the late memorable event. By their manly, firm, and orderly conduct they have shown themselves deserving of that protection which I have felt it was my duty to give them, and which I doubt not they will continue to merit.*

He also praised the military men. *Soldiers! Your conduct has endeared you to every well-disposed inhabitant in this settlement. Persevere in the same honourable path and you will establish the credit of the New South Wales Corps on a basis not to be shaken.*

On the same day, the officers and settlers presented Johnston with a letter with eighty-three signatures. They offered their *most grateful thanks for your manly and honourable interposition to rescue us from a situation which had threatened the destruction of all which men can hold dear. We hail you, Sir, as the protector of our property, liberty, lives and reputation . . .*

The celebrations continued. Bonfires were burned at street corners, sheep were roasted on spits, and many public displays of support appeared for the rebel government.

➴ 28 January 1808 ➶

When Esther accompanied Johnston to the town the following evening, she saw for herself how grateful the residents were, and she was proud of Johnston's role in saving the colony from such a tyrant.

A makeshift sign declared: *Success to Major George Johnston, may he live forever! Our deliverer and the suppressor of tyrants.* A poster showed Johnston crushing a snake with his foot and stabbing it with his sword. There was even an effigy of Bligh burning in a bonfire, while people cheered and the military band played a tune called 'Silly Old Man'.

However, when Johnston noticed another bonfire on the church hill, near the grave of Lieutenant Putland—the late husband of Bligh's daughter—he jogged up the street towards it.

'Have some respect, man!' he called out to Sergeant-Major Whittle. 'Find another place for your fire.'

➴ 2 February 1808 ➶

While the townsfolk celebrated, Macarthur's trial was formally continued. The officers, unsurprisingly, found him innocent. They even triumphantly carried him around the town on a chair to celebrate his acquittal. Wentworth's suspension from duty without explanation also came before the court, which acquitted him and restored him to his position as assistant surgeon.

Meanwhile, Johnston wrote to Lieutenant-Colonel Paterson at Port Dalrymple on the northern coast of Van Diemen's Land to tell him what had happened, and he began gathering evidence to send with a dispatch to the Colonial Office.

Johnston administered the affairs of the colony as conservatively, and with as much stability, as he could manage, but it was a complex business. He moved into the grand two-storey commandant's residence in High Street so that he could be nearer to all the government officers. Then he appointed Macarthur to the new, but unpaid, position of Secretary to the Colony, to help him with the administration. Johnston also announced that most of Bligh's orders would remain in force, including those regarding the importation of spirits.

Esther stayed out of the way at Annandale House and was not involved in the affairs of the administration. However, when Johnston came back home at the end of each week, she listened attentively as he talked about the difficulties he faced. He told her that he did not know why anyone would choose to be governor. He explained that he and Macarthur were doing their best to keep the colony stable, but some people expected them to hand out government land or stores to anyone they chose—and became most annoyed when they did not. Even their friends, the Blaxlands, insisted that Johnston deal personally with all their affairs. He had explained to them that he was not in a position to make all the grants they expected, and that they must wait until a new governor was appointed.

In the end, Johnston made twelve grants of land, all of them subject to confirmation by the next appointed governor. One was to Young George, and another was to his new aide-de-camp, Lieutenant William Lawson.

Johnston decided to barter three hundred government cattle in exchange for the grain required for the stores that year. He explained to Esther that, by doing so, he would not need to draw on any treasury bills. He knew that cattle owned by private individuals increased in number far more quickly than those in the government herds, so he felt his decision would also help the colony to become more independent.

'What will happen to Governor Bligh?' Esther asked.

Johnston had offered him passage back to England, but Bligh had refused every ship Johnston had nominated, insisting on HMS *Porpoise*.

However, Johnston was reluctant to allow him onto a Royal Navy ship, on which he would be the highest-ranking officer and therefore able to take command. In any case, the *Porpoise* was not currently in port. Johnston had sent her to Van Diemen's Land to collect Lieutenant-Colonel Paterson who, as the senior officer, could then take over the colony's administration.

But Paterson was reluctant to become involved in the situation. As Lieutenant-Colonel Joseph Foveaux was due to return soon from England to resume command of Norfolk Island, Paterson decided to wait where he was, in the hope that Foveaux would take over administration of the colony instead. So Johnston had to continue his burdensome role as lieutenant-governor.

⊶ *3 May 1808* ⊷

On one of his visits home, Johnston told Esther that King George III's seventieth birthday the following month demanded a suitable celebration. But Bligh was still living under house arrest in Government House. Esther suggested that Johnston host a ball in his Sydney commandant's residence, and Johnston approved of the idea.

'Perhaps Mrs Kable could find you a new gown that would be suitable for the occasion,' Johnston offered.

'But I myself would not attend the ball, surely,' Esther replied.

'Of course you must. Such an occasion requires a hostess.'

'But my position is not . . . conventional.'

'It is conventional enough for Sydney.'

The reality of Esther's new position had suddenly become clear to her, and it filled her with dread. How would the townsfolk respond? Would she be able to conduct herself to their satisfaction?

The first step was to look the part. Susannah delighted in producing a magnificent gown that had just arrived from Paris. It was of blue silk trimmed with gold beading and handmade lace, and it had a short, embroidered muslin train. She also offered a jewelled feather for Esther to wear in her hair.

Once Esther had the dress, she began to feel more confident, although her emotions still swung wildly between excitement and trepidation.

A few days before the ball, Esther sent her servants to clean and polish every inch of the commandant's house. She even allowed Mary to stay there, to begin the preparations for a magnificent feast.

Although she tried to remain optimistic, Esther (now aged thirty-eight) was nevertheless relieved to hear, two days before the ball, that Elizabeth Macarthur had just given birth to her ninth child, keeping all the Macarthurs at home.

❧ 4 June 1808 ☙

On the day of the King's birthday, Esther worked nonstop, overseeing the final arrangements for the ball. She festooned the commandant's house with flowers and greenery, and placed dozens of candles throughout its various rooms. After finally dressing for dinner, she walked down the grand staircase to where Johnston was waiting, her head held high and her eyes sparkling. Johnston smiled and nodded his approval. Then he bent to kiss her hand.

'You look magnificent, my dear Hetty,' he said.

Esther responded with a beaming smile and a small curtsey. Johnston offered her his arm and they walked to the front door to greet their first guests. Esther took a deep breath. Would anyone dare to slight her while Johnston, their hero, was by her side?

Dr Wentworth had made sure he was the first in line. He kissed Esther's hand with a flourishing bow and loudly exclaimed that she was the most elegant First Lady who had ever graced the colony. When the next couple stepped up, Esther's heart was pounding. The gentleman bowed to kiss her hand and his wife gave her a polite curtsey. As each new guest arrived, the men kissed Esther's hand and the women curtseyed. Esther's heart began to slow down and she finally followed the last of her guests inside.

There, she heard many of the women openly express their admiration for her work. The dining table was crowned with a magnificent candelabra which cast a dancing light over the feast: legs of lamb that had been slowly roasted over flames until they dripped with sweet stickiness; rare roast beef, carved wafer thin; honey-glazed suckling pig; spicy curried fowl; succulent roast duck and boiled turkey. Around the edges of the table were plates of fresh, plump oysters, pale green cabbage and golden carrots; waiting on the mahogany sideboard were apple tarts, glistening jellies and richly decorated cakes.

The weather was fine, the atmosphere was jubilant and Esther relaxed into her role. She conversed with her guests, she confidently introduced those she thought might share similar interests, she danced with Johnston and Wentworth, and she discovered—to her delight—that the other colonists did indeed accept her as their First Lady.

If only Elizabeth Macarthur could have been here, after all.

✎ 28 July 1808 ✎

Six months after the rebellion, Lieutenant-Colonel Joseph Foveaux, a superior officer to Johnston, arrived back in the colony. Bligh hoped that Foveaux would reinstate him as governor, so he sent three messengers to the ship to ask Foveaux to meet with him at his earliest convenience. But, when they arrived on board, they found that Johnston and Macarthur were already there, and in the middle of deep conversation with him.

Foveaux had only intended to call in to Sydney to check on his property, named Surry Hills, on his way to Norfolk Island. He was shocked to find Bligh under arrest and Major Johnston in command. When Johnston explained what had happened, Foveaux felt compelled to stay in Sydney and take over the administration until he could get Paterson back from Port Dalrymple. Johnston thankfully retired from the role.

Esther had enjoyed her position as First Lady, but she was nonetheless relieved to return her focus to her family—particularly as the ship that bore Foveaux had also brought Young George, now a fine gentleman of eighteen.

Foveaux relieved Macarthur of his position as Secretary to the Colony, but he left the rest of the rebel government in place. He didn't want to become too involved himself, so he kept Bligh under house arrest at Government House, although he allowed William Kent— Acting Naval Captain of the *Porpoise* following Putland's death—to visit him.

ᵔ 4 August 1808 ᵔ

'Poor Kent had no idea what he was in for,' Johnston told Esther. 'Bligh's rank is superior, so, as soon as Kent arrived at his house, Bligh began abusing him for not reinstating him as governor—as though Kent could have any hand in it! Bligh told Kent that, if he knew his duty, as soon as the guns were aboard the *Porpoise* he should face them towards the town and batter Sydney until the people delivered the government back to Bligh.'

'He knows no bounds of reason!' said Esther.

'Kent told him that he did not believe his duty led him to sacrifice so many innocent lives,' continued Johnston. 'But Bligh just flew into another rage, telling Kent he would make him repent.'

ᵔ 9 January 1809 ᵔ

A year after the rebellion, Lieutenant-Colonel Paterson finally returned on the *Porpoise*. Bligh tried to get an order to Captain Kent to arrest Paterson and keep him a prisoner on the ship, but Johnston's aide-de-camp, Lieutenant Lawson, reached the ship first and immediately took Paterson to meet Johnston instead.

When Paterson took over as lieutenant-governor, he also decided not to reinstate Bligh, but to leave the administration as it was, until the whole situation could be reviewed in England.

ᵔ 19 January 1809 ᵔ

Meanwhile, Foveaux had asked Macarthur to repay five hundred pounds which appeared to be missing from the time Macarthur had been Secretary of the Colony. Macarthur was outraged at the insinuation that he had mismanaged the colony's finances, and replied to Foveaux's request by challenging him to a duel. Then he asked Johnston to be his second.

The duel was fought on the Annandale estate and Macarthur won the toss to shoot first. He stood ten paces from the portly Foveaux and took the first shot. He missed.

'It is your shot, sir,' Johnston called out.

'I shall not return fire,' answered Foveaux. 'To tell the truth, I have no idea what any of this is about. All I can say is that it is disagreeable to have to account in this manner for a request I made as part of my duty as lieutenant-governor.'

'Very well,' said Johnston. 'I say, Macarthur, as honour has been satisfied, will you end the matter there?' Macarthur nodded silently and Johnston continued, 'Then I suggest we all retire for some refreshment.'

Macarthur was later obliged to pay the financial discrepancy.

⤳ 24 January 1809 ⤵

Even locked away in Government House, Bligh could still make life difficult for Paterson, now the lieutenant-governor. A new captain for the *Porpoise* had arrived in Sydney. However, Bligh pulled rank and ordered the captain to refuse Paterson's request to use his ship to transfer convicts from Norfolk Island to Hobart.

Paterson could not allow such interference in his administration, so he sent Johnston to tell Bligh in person that if he did not withdraw his order, he would be removed from Government House and imprisoned in the officers' barracks until he left for England.

Standing in the drawing room at Government House, it was the first time the two men had seen each other since the rebellion a year earlier. Characteristically, Bligh refused to withdraw his order, so Johnston took him under guard to the barracks. Bligh's daughter, Mary Putland, ran alongside the chaise and took Bligh's arm as he walked into the two-room barrack. But, once inside, she fainted onto the sofa.

4 February 1809

Johnston was keen to travel to England to personally explain the situation that had precipitated his action and to seek a court martial, which he hoped would vindicate his conduct. By this time, unaware of the rebellion, the Colonial Office had promoted him to brevet lieutenant-colonel. Now he prepared to travel to England on the *Admiral Gambier*.

Esther was suddenly busy packing his trunks, repairing his clothes and gathering together all the bits and pieces she thought he might need for a long sea voyage and another stay—who knew how long?—in England.

Johnston would take with him, as witnesses for his case: John Macarthur, Dr Thomas Jamison, Dr John Harris and the commissary clerk, David Mann. Macarthur would take two of his sons, William and James, to follow their older brothers to school in England. Johnston and Esther had both found it too distressing to have their children on the other side of the world. So, although their son David was now old enough to go to school in England, they had decided to keep him in Sydney, where he would continue being educated by his governess.

23 February 1809

Before Johnston left, Esther was able to enjoy one more happy event. The lieutenant-governor, William Paterson, hosted the largest ball that had ever been seen in the colony. It was held in the upper apartments of the newly built military barracks.

Esther attended as Johnston's partner. The rooms glittered with candlelight and music reverberated through the building as the full band of the New South Wales Corps played dozens of country dances. At midnight, Esther and the other guests retired to the supper room to enjoy a luscious feast.

29 February 1809

Bligh had negotiated with Paterson to let him sail to England as a free man on HMS *Porpoise*, accompanied by his daughter. Paterson had drawn up an agreement that stated that Bligh could take anyone else he wished, as a witness to his cause (provided their absence would not unduly affect the colony), on the following conditions: that he not impede the *Porpoise's* journey in any way; that he proceed directly to England; and that he not interfere in any way with the government of the colony . . . *to the strict and unequivocal observance of which Governor Bligh hereby solemnly pledges his honour as an officer and a gentleman.*

Both Bligh and Paterson had signed the agreement, and Bligh finally boarded the *Porpoise* with his daughter, his secretary and his domestic servants. The ship sailed away from Sydney Cove and towards the Sydney Heads . . . but she did not proceed to England.

Bligh had no intention of leaving New South Wales. He fully expected that anyone in authority sent out from England would immediately reinstate him as governor. He took over command of the ship and dropped anchor just inside the heads. There he waited, delivering a handwritten proclamation to the captain of each new ship that entered the harbour, declaring a state of rebellious anarchy existed in the colony.

The *Admiral Gambier* was ready to sail to England with Johnston and Macarthur, but her captain feared the armed *Porpoise* would fire upon her as she passed—and that Bligh would then arrest Johnston and Macarthur—so he delayed their departure, hoping that Bligh would sail on to England.

⌖ *19 March 1809* ⌖

Bligh did finally give up waiting. The *Porpoise* put on sail and disappeared out through the heads. But she still did not sail towards England. Instead, Bligh sailed down to the new settlement of Hobart in Van Diemen's Land.

Colonel David Collins, who had been Sydney's first judge advocate, had been sent by Governor King, with four hundred colonists, to establish a settlement at Port Phillip, so that the southern part of the continent of New Holland could be claimed for Britain before the French had a chance to do so. However, that settlement had been abandoned after a few months and Collins had moved everyone to Hobart, establishing a colony there instead, where he was now the lieutenant-governor.

At first, Collins received Bligh very respectfully. He even gave up a suite of rooms in Hobart's Government House for Bligh's daughter, Mary Putland, while Bligh remained on the *Porpoise*. However, it did not take long for Bligh's personality to alienate Collins, particularly after Bligh ordered Collins's son to be flogged for insubordination. Collins wrote later: *God knows I never had any malice in my heart until I came into contact with this detestable brute.*

When Paterson, in Sydney, learned of Bligh's treachery, he wrote to Collins about how Bligh had violated his word of honour, and he forbade Collins to have any communications with Bligh or to supply any provisions to the *Porpoise*.

Bligh already had enough provisions on board to last a voyage to England, but he also threatened to fire on every ship that visited Hobart if it did not come alongside the *Porpoise* so that he could gather news from Sydney and commandeer even more supplies.

◈ *29 March 1809* ◈

It was the day of Johnston's departure. Esther brushed a speck of dust from his uniform as he finished dressing.

'You have made a note to buy shoes for the children while in England, have you not?' she said.

'Hetty . . .'

'Make sure they are sturdy—with the way they gallop about here, it is no use purchasing flimsy ones,' she continued, as she straightened his jacket but avoided his eyes. 'I have cut out the shape of their feet so that you can be sure of their sizes.'

Johnston caught her arm and held it.

'Esther!'

She stopped talking and stared at the floor. Her tears dropped silently onto her shoes. She knew the punishment for mutiny was death. Johnston brought her hand up to his lips and kissed her fingers.

'My darling Hetty. All will be well.' He lifted her chin and kissed her. 'I shall sort out this mess and return before you know it.'

The *Sydney Gazette* reported his departure: *Lieutenant Colonel Johnston embarked at 10 in the morning, and received military honours; the populace taking leave of this much esteemed officer with reiterated bursts of acclamation.*

∽ 31 July 1809 ∾

Alone again.

Esther sat at her desk in Annandale House. The building was considerably larger than it had been. Its main rooms now consisted of a hall, dining room, large parlour, small parlour, two bedrooms, a powdering room, two kitchen offices and two maid's rooms. It also had a loft with a small dormer window.

Esther looked out across the sweeping fields to the bush far beyond. The sky was a vivid blue above the olive-green trees, but the air outside was frosty. She gathered her wrap more closely around her shoulders and asked her maid to put another log on the fire, just for the comfort of seeing the bright flames blaze up around it. It had been a cold winter. Johnston had been gone for four months, and Esther had worked tirelessly to manage the large estate.

It was a far greater task than it had been the last time Johnston was away. She now had to manage multiple properties with hundreds of cattle, sheep, goats and pigs, plus a stud farm of thirty-five horses. She employed twenty-eight convict workers and dozens of free labourers. At least she had Young George to help her this time. He loved the outdoor life and seemed to have a natural affinity for the large, cumbersome beasts that lumbered across the land in place of the small, agile animals that used to hop about it so lightly. But he would also soon be responsible for one of her troubles.

Meanwhile, on the other side of the world, his younger brother, Robert, was proving his worth in the Royal Navy. Esther didn't yet know it, but in January Bob had helped to evacuate Macarthur's nineteen-year-old son, Edward, and many other British soldiers from a battle at Corunna in Spain, after Napoleon had tried to trap them on the peninsula.

Every day, Esther met with her new overseer to discuss the day's work. The valuable cattle were counted every morning and evening, the fences inspected, the sheep sheared, their fleeces cleaned and packed, the goats moved between pastures, the pigs fed, and all Johnston's beloved horses groomed and exercised. The services of the magnificent thoroughbred stallion, Northumberland, were also in high demand. Esther had learned to sow her wheat in March and to harvest it in November, then to set fire to the stubble and plant corn in its place.

Once a month, she rode out to her distant farms along the Georges River to meet with their overseers and inspect the stock. Then she would send an estimate of the beef and mutton that she would be able to sell to the government stores the following month. She soon became one of the government's largest suppliers.

As well as raising sheep for meat, Esther also had a growing flock that she was selectively breeding for the quality of their wool. They were descendants of the first Merino and Teeswater longwool sheep that Johnston had received from England a few years earlier, and they were contributing to the evolution of the large hybrid which would become known as the Australian Merino.

Everything that was received onto the estates was recorded: food, tools, timber, grain, clothing and rum. Everything that was allocated to the workers was also carefully noted in the account books. Esther could not afford to let anything she did come into question.

She knew her situation was tenuous. If Johnston did not return— and she dared not dwell on that possibility—she would have no formal standing in the colony. Even if he were permitted to return, he might well have to forfeit all his property. She hardly dared to think about the possible consequences of Johnston's actions. For a quiet man, he had lived a disturbingly dramatic life. Sometimes Esther's worries would almost overwhelm her, but she continued to work hard with the task at hand.

She now re-read the application on her desk. It was for a grant of five hundred acres of land along the Georges River near Banks Town, adjoining the northern boundary of land that Johnston already owned, and close to a grant at Salt Pan Creek, for which the farmer James Ruse was applying. But this application was for herself—a safeguard, just in case. She even used her maiden name again, Esther Julian, to make sure everything was legally correct. Young George also applied for an extra hundred acres of his own. If Johnston did not return, or all his properties were taken away, at least there would be other places where Esther and her family could live.

The thought of ever having to leave Annandale House filled her with dread. She had worked so hard to make it a beautiful home. There was fine furniture in every room: dining tables, armchairs, bookcases, bureaus, side tables, desks, looking-glasses, beds, chests of drawers and washstands. The main parlour even had a thermometer, a barometer and a telescope.

Outside, Esther had designed sandy paths that wound around the gardens, paths that she could walk on soon after the summer downpours she had learned to respect. The paths threaded between perennial garden borders and the still youthful, and now bare, English oaks and elms, which would soon don cloaks of soft green for spring. Golden daffodils were already nodding their heads beneath their boughs. In summer, she could visit her orchard to pluck ripe, warm fruits bursting with flavour from the trees she had planted there— cherries, peaches, pears, oranges, figs and apricots. She could pick large bunches of juicy grapes from her vineyard and arrange them on the silver platter that sat on the sideboard in her dining room. And she could offer her guests wine that had been made from her earlier harvests.

She had even grown to admire the mighty eucalypts that remained in pockets on her property. The green leaves of a nearby forest red gum hung willow-like from their high branches, and Esther knew they would soon be tinged with the bronzed pink of new growth in spring. Even now, a pair of New Holland honeyeaters were feeding on the nectar offered by its winter blossoms, and a ringtail possum lay sleeping in one of its hollows.

But Esther knew her future at Annandale was inextricably linked to Johnston's. One day a ship would sail up the harbour with news of his fate. Until that day arrived, she would work tirelessly to preserve her livelihood and her home.

She opened her stock register once more. The winter had been not only cold, but dry; so dry, that the grass underfoot had turned brown and crisp. Esther had lost some of the cattle on her outlying farms. A few had died of starvation and others had been poached by bushrangers—convicts who had escaped and now eked out a living by stealing and scavenging from the edge of the colony. Esther had placed ads in the *Sydney Gazette* warning that she would take action against trespassers.

Meanwhile, in Parramatta, Elizabeth Macarthur was looking out of her own window. With Macarthur in England, she was also managing a productive property. She saw that the sky was darkening, bringing heavy clouds and rumbling thunder.

At last there would be rain, she thought.

⌒ 1 August 1809 ⌒

It rained in Parramatta, soaking into the thirsty farmlands and filling up the wells. It rained in Sydney Town, washing the dusty houses and muddying the streets. It rained at Annandale House, hammering on the roof and soaking into the dry gardens. It rained along the Hawkesbury, it rained at Castle Hill, and it rained at Banks Town. It rained every day and it rained every night. The long winter's drought was broken.

At Parramatta, Elizabeth Macarthur instructed her overseer to fence off a paddock that had turned to mud beneath the hundreds of pounding hooves of her sheep. In Sydney, Susannah Kable hung her wet washing in front of her kitchen fire. At Annandale House, Esther spoke soothingly to the restless horses which had been kept inside their stables for days on end.

And still the pelting rain fell from the sky. Elizabeth brought her sheep away from the river. Susannah spread straw over the muddy entrance to her Sydney store. And Esther moved her cattle away from Johnston's Creek.

∽ 7 August 1809 ∽

The Blue Mountains, as they were already known, became drenched, and water cascaded down their sides onto the already sodden Sydney plain. The rivers swelled as the tumbling water made its way determinedly to the sea. Higher and higher up the riverbanks it rose, rushing faster and faster as it was pushed by the weight behind—until the banks could no longer hold the roaring water and it burst over the top and flooded across the fields, sweeping away everything in its path.

Esther worked in the pouring rain alongside Young George and all their farmhands to make sure her precious cattle were safe. When she could see that the others could complete the job, she called to her son through the windy squall.

'George! We must see to the sheep by the river.'

Although Esther was soaked and shivering with cold, she and Young George set off in a buggy along the rough, muddy track that wound through the thick bush to the Georges River. As the water came into sight, she could hear desperate bleating and saw that all the sheep were penned in stockyards by the river which were now flooded with water.

'No!' cried Esther. 'Why was I not told that they were all still penned!'

She and Young George jumped down from the gig and ran across the squelching ground. They waded through the rushing water to reach the struggling sheep and try to lift them over the rails to safety. But their winter fleeces were sodden, making them extremely heavy. As Esther and Young George clung to each panicked animal, the raging current wrenched it out of their hands, over the far-side rails and away down the roaring river.

CHAPTER THIRTEEN

Mrs Johnston

Esther sat at her desk, holding her head in her hands. The rain had stopped at last, but all five hundred sheep at the Georges River had drowned, including the hundred and fifty she had bought after Johnston had left. It was a heavy blow.

Though she felt her loss keenly, she knew it did not compare with the calamity facing other families along the rivers. She called in her overseer to check that he had complied with the requisition order from the governor for all available boats. They were being rowed about the flooded plains to rescue families still clinging to rooftops, and to deliver fresh water and food to other houses that were completely cut off by the floodwaters.

Everyone felt the effects of the disaster. Lives, crops and livestock had been lost, houses swept away and farmers left in debt with no crops to sell. Prices soared. No one was allowed to export any bread, flour or wheat, and bakers were forbidden from baking any cakes, biscuits or pastries, because all the flour was needed to make bread for those many colonists who were now destitute.

◇ *12 September 1809* ◇

The following month Esther had another crisis on her hands. Rosetta Marsh, a successful female trader, sent her dark bay mare to

204

Annandale to be mated with Johnston's large thoroughbred stallion, Northumberland. Esther asked Young George and her groom, James Hooper, to manage the task.

The following day, she received an angry note from Rosetta telling her that Rosetta's mare had died during the night. Apparently, when Northumberland had mounted her, he had mistakenly entered her rectum, causing it to rupture. Rosetta was furious and told Esther that she would be taking her to court for negligence.

Esther was devastated that such a tragic error had occurred at Annandale. The last thing she needed was to appear incompetent. She questioned Young George about it, but he said that neither he nor Hooper had realised anything was amiss at the time. Nevertheless, Esther told him that, as he had been present when the accident had occurred, he should represent her in court when the case came up.

← 23 October 1809 →

It was always an exciting moment when mail arrived from England. Any colonists expecting a letter or parcel would visit the captain of each arriving ship, in the hope of collecting their mail. However, the ships' captains usually had no idea who the recipients were, and they often gave letters and parcels to the wrong people. So Lieutenant-Governor Paterson had appointed Rosanna's husband, Isaac Nichols, as the colony's first postmaster.

Soon afterwards, Esther visited Rosanna's large Sydney house to play with her grandchildren—Rosanna had given birth to another son four weeks earlier, named George in honour of Johnston.

As Esther picked up her baby grandson, she asked: 'And how do you like being married to a postmaster?'

Rosanna replied that it was most agreeable. Mr Nichols still continued in his role as Superintendent of Public Works, *and* as Assistant to the Naval Officer, but now he also boarded every new ship to collect the mail for everyone in the colony. He would place a list of addressees on the wall outside his house, and also put a notice in the *Sydney Gazette*; then everyone would come to collect their items.

Rosanna was pleased that her husband's positions kept him in the colony and she liked to think that he was gaining the respect of the free settlers.

Rosanna's maid brought in some tea and poured it into two fine china cups, while Rosanna and Esther talked about the recent marriage of Susannah Kable's daughter Diana, to William Gaudry. They had been the first couple to be married in the newly built St Philip's Church, and Henry Kable had given them two horses and seven cattle as a wedding present.

⊱ 28 December 1809 ⊰

The Sydney settlement of more than ten thousand people now spread not only to the Nepean River in the west and the Georges River to the south, but also to Newcastle in the north. The native people around Sydney Cove had given up their traditional life—their sacred places had been vandalised and their social and spiritual foundations had collapsed. There were a few who accepted the white men's ways and lived in the town, but many more clung to the fringes of the settlement, and their old life, living a culturally sterile existence that was periodically numbed by rum.

Bennelong had taken Boorong, the girl adopted by the Reverend Richard Johnson, as his third wife. He had discarded the British way of living and had become an elder of the Kissing Point tribe, who had been forced from their traditional land at Parramatta. He held the respected position of one who could knock out teeth during initiation ceremonies, but he was no longer admired by the white settlers. He craved their rum, but when he could get it he became a menacing drunk. If he dined at Government House, he was now directed to eat at the servants' table.

⊱ 31 December 1809 ⊰

Each new governor of New South Wales had done his best to guide the young colony along a steady path. But when the settlement turned twenty-one, a governor arrived who, like Arthur Phillip, had such vision for its future that the effect of his decisions would be evident for hundreds of years.

After the difficulties that had continually arisen between the naval governors and the military officers, the British Colonial Office had finally sent a military man to govern the colony. And he had brought with him a new regiment of soldiers to replace the troublesome New South Wales Corps.

Fifteen guns were fired from HMS *Dromedary*, and were answered by the battery at Dawes Point, as forty-seven-year-old Governor Lachlan Macquarie and his young wife, Elizabeth (thirty-one), both Scottish, landed at Sydney Cove. The new regiment formed a guard of honour all the way from the shore to Government House, the fresh troops resplendent in their bright new uniforms.

Governor King had extended Government House, and it had since been freshly painted. That morning, it had been filled with fresh flowers by Elizabeth Paterson, the lieutenant-governor's wife, a fellow Scot, to welcome the new First Lady.

ᴄ◦ 1 January 1810 ◦ᴄ

Macquarie arrived with orders to reinstate Bligh for twenty-four hours, so that Bligh could formally hand over the governorship to him. However, Bligh was still on the *Porpoise* in Hobart. So Macquarie arranged for the King's commission, appointing himself as the new Governor of New South Wales, to be read out in front of the two military regiments: the old New South Wales Corps and the new 73rd Regiment.

On the same day, Macquarie issued a public proclamation announcing the necessity of his immediately taking upon himself the role of command. It also explained that he was *compelled publicly to announce His Majesty's high displeasure and disapprobation of the mutinous and outrageous conduct displayed in the forcible and unwarrantable removal of his late representative, William Bligh.*

(Macquarie had been given orders to arrest Johnston on his arrival in New South Wales but, when he had stopped at Rio de Janeiro on his voyage out, he had been relieved to learn that Johnston had just departed it on his way to England.)

So Macquarie got on with his job as governor. He recalled the New South Wales Corps and installed his new regiment. He also made it clear that he intended to reward any citizens, whatever their social status, if they conducted themselves well: *the honest, sober and industrious inhabitant, whether free settler or convict, will ever find in me a friend and protector.*

He was as good as his word.

16 January 1810

Sydney society was in a frenzy of celebration. Anyone of note visited Government House to pay their respects to the new governor and his wife. Lavish dinners were hurriedly organised, houses were decorated, bonfires burned and bands played. There was even a fireworks display, which the governor and his lady watched from their veranda at Government House.

17 January 1810

In Hobart, Bligh had learned that the Colonial Office had declared Johnston's rebellion to be a mutiny, and also that Lachlan Macquarie had taken over as the new Governor of New South Wales. He hurriedly sailed back to Sydney, arriving only two weeks into Macquarie's tenure.

At first, Bligh and Macquarie were very polite to each other. Bligh acknowledged that he needed to return to England to participate in Johnston's trial, but he soon began irritating the new governor. Macquarie wrote to his brother that Bligh was *a most disagreeable person to have any dealings or public business to transact with.*

27 February 1810

Three years after they had left, the Marsdens finally returned to Sydney, and Esther hurried down to the cove in the hope of seeing Julia at last . . . but she was not with them.

Esther's heart sank once again. It had been more than nine years since she had seen her daughter. The enormous distance between them seemed almost too great to bear. She could only hope now that one day Johnston would be able to bring Julia home.

Governor Macquarie wasted no time putting into place practices that would influence the development of a new, unique social structure. He and Elizabeth were hardly settled into their new home before they invited the fifty-eight convicts and overseers who worked at Government House to a dinner to celebrate St Patrick's Day.

The workers, dressed in their best clothes, filed into Government House and stood around awkwardly, while Macquarie and Elizabeth moved among them, chatting informally. However, it wasn't long before the workers began to relax and, when a band started playing popular songs, everyone merrily joined in with the singing.

Aghast at the stories of prolonged floggings that had been ordered by the previous naval governors, Macquarie limited all floggings to fifty lashes, introducing time spent in gaol gangs as an alternative punishment. He also announced that he wanted to remove *the scandalous and pernicious custom so generally and shamelessly adopted throughout this territory, of persons of different sexes cohabiting and living together, unsanctioned by the legal ties of matrimony.*

Apart from her association with the rebellious Johnston, it was obvious to Esther that her social position did not meet with the new governor's approval. But could she ever marry Johnston? She really didn't know whether her secret marriage to Abrahams had been legitimate. Nelly had probably been right, and it had all been just a ruse to seduce her. She certainly hadn't been married in an Anglican ceremony. And dozens of convicts who had been legally married in England had decided they had no hope of ever being reunited with their spouses, so they had conveniently forgotten about them and had married again in New South Wales.

The day arrived for the court case against Esther for the neglect of Rosetta Marsh's mare. As instructed, Young George appeared on Esther's behalf and pleaded not guilty. He told the court that he had worked as a groom for ten years in England and had never experienced such an accident. Another of Esther's servants told the court that he had been standing only about twenty yards from the event and had not seen anything unusual.

Nevertheless, Esther was found guilty of negligence and ordered to pay eighty pounds to Rosetta, plus all the court costs. Esther felt ashamed by the whole episode, but Susannah reminded her that she had not been to blame and that under her management the Annandale estate had become one of the finest sheep and cattle properties in New South Wales.

Bligh would be returning to England in HMS *Porpoise*, in convoy with two other ships that were taking members of the old New South Wales Corps back home. But before they sailed, the naval officers of the *Porpoise* held a lavish ball aboard the ship for all the colony's civil, military and naval officers and their ladies. Esther knew that, even though Macarthur had been instrumental in the rebellion against Bligh, Elizabeth Macarthur would be at the ball—she was universally admired. But Esther also knew that no invitation would arrive for herself.

In town that morning, she heard the band practising their tunes, and saw bright decorations being strung across the ship. The quarter-deck was covered with an awning, and sideboards were being fitted between the gunports to be laden with food and wine. Esther was back home alone in Annandale House before the hundred guests arrived for the ball that evening—the ladies all dressed in their finest gowns. They danced till eleven when they stopped for supper, before resuming dancing till three in the morning.

❧ 10 April 1810 ❧

The following day, Esther felt brighter than most of the other ladies when she joined the many hundreds of colonists who walked alongside the old New South Wales Corps as they marched down the hill to the government wharf, where they tumbled into boats to be rowed out to the ships. As they pulled away from the shore, they exchanged mighty cheers with the colonists who had grown so used to seeing them around the town.

Esther returned to Annandale with a heavy heart. Another link with Johnston had been broken.

❧ 4 May 1810 ❧

At long last, Bligh was ready to sail to England. He and his widowed daughter, Mary Putland, moved all their belongings onto the ship that would take them home. However, Bligh's delaying tactics had had consequences he could not have foreseen.

A few days before they sailed, Maurice O'Connell—the commanding officer of the new 73rd Regiment and the lieutenant-governor—asked Bligh for his daughter's hand in marriage. Bligh flatly refused to give his permission. But then he learned that Mary had encouraged O'Connell's affections, that she had already accepted his proposal, that the governor had promised to give the couple some land as a wedding present, and that Mrs Macquarie had offered to hold the wedding reception at Government House. Clearly outnumbered, Bligh reluctantly consented to the match.

❧ 8 May 1810 ❧

A few days later, he gloomily gave his daughter away, and the wedding party walked to Government House for a hastily organised celebration. Governor Macquarie kept his promise and presented the newlyweds with a grant of land they named Riverston Farm. Then, at last, Bligh left for England.

The King's birthday rolled around again, but this time it was Elizabeth Macquarie's task to arrange a suitable celebration on the public holiday. Esther took her children into town to join in the festivities and they waved with the rest of the crowd as the 73rd Regiment, commanded by O'Connell, paraded past them.

Later, when the lawn in front of Government House was thrown open to the public, Esther and her children followed the crowds across it to listen to the new regimental band play its stirring music. Esther smiled with appreciation at Elizabeth Macquarie's decoration of the whole length of the Government House veranda. It was festooned with greenery and whole orange branches, interspersed with glowing lanterns, which gave it the appearance of a luminous orange grove.

Five months later, the inhabitants of Sydney gathered to watch the colony's first organised horse races, at what became known as Hyde Park. Governor Macquarie had declared three days of public holiday so that all the colonists—convicts, labourers, farmers, merchants, officials, army and navy personnel—could socialise together.

Wentworth gave Young George's hand a hearty shake and congratulated him on convincing Esther to come along on the last day of the races. Then he lifted Esther's gloved fingers to his lips. She bobbed a curtsey.

'Have you entered Northumberland in the races?' Wentworth asked Young George.

'Certainly not! Can you imagine what Father would say if I injured his beloved stallion?'

'William is going to give Gig another turn around the track,' said Wentworth.

'Then I wager today's race will be a contest between your Gig and Mr Underwood's mare,' said Young George. At that moment, he saw his friend in the crowd. 'There is William now—please excuse me, sir.'

'Of course,' said Wentworth. Young George bowed and moved away. Wentworth shouted after him: 'Tell him I have some money riding on him!'

Wentworth's nineteen-year-old son, William, had only recently returned from his schooling in England. He was a stocky, broad-shouldered young man with a shock of unkempt red hair.

The regimental band began playing as Esther turned to Wentworth. She asked if he knew that Governor Macquarie had requested the return of all the titles for land grants that had been issued since Bligh was deposed, so that he could review them all and decide for himself if they were worthy.

Wentworth said that he did, and that Macquarie had also granted nearly all of them again.

'Well, he has not granted mine—or Young George's,' replied Esther.

Wentworth said he thought that was perhaps because Macquarie wanted to await the outcome of Johnston's trial before he sanctioned their grants. He added that Esther was managing Johnston's estate so capably—providing the government with a substantial proportion of its supply of beef and mutton—that Macquarie was sure to confirm her grants.

He told her that all his own grants had been confirmed. He had also been appointed as the colony's principal surgeon *and* a magistrate—much to the dismay of some of the more conventional gentry, and therefore to Wentworth's particular delight. What's more, Macquarie had also entrusted him with the position of Treasurer of the Police Fund, which Wentworth considered rather a coup.

Then Wentworth told Esther that Macquarie had been widowed by his first wife, and that he and the present Mrs Macquarie had lost their infant daughter before they left England.

'Are you trying to make me feel sorry for the man?' asked Esther.

'I am trying to help you to understand him. Did you know that he and Johnston served together in America? Apparently, they were quite close friends at the time.'

'How did you discover that?' asked Esther.

Wentworth explained that he had recently dined at Government House, along with young Dr William Redfern. Then he hesitated—at that dinner, Macquarie had told him that he believed Johnston would be executed for his mutinous actions against Bligh. Wentworth kept that information to himself.

Instead, he gave a chuckle, telling Esther that John Macarthur was sure to be infuriated that the governor had been inviting emancipists like Dr Redfern to his table.

They stood in silence for a while, until Esther said she had seen a notice that a Mr Mackneal had put in the *Gazette*, describing how his young wife had deserted both her husband and her infant son.

'The man is an imbecile,' said Wentworth.

'And his wife is just seventeen,' said Esther. 'She *is* residing with you, then?'

'Ann looks after me when I am in Sydney or Parramatta.'

'And Maria Ainslie "looks after you" at Home Bush?'

'She does, indeed.'

'Really, Dr Wentworth! Ann is younger than your own son. And what about the governor's disapproval of unmarried couples?'

'Must I be *completely* devoid of female company?'

Just then, the crowd surged towards the small picket fence that ran around the one-mile track, to watch the beginning of the next race. The horses snorted and stamped their hooves at the starting line. The crack of a pistol resounded through the air—and they were off!

'Go, my boy!' Wentworth shouted to his son, waving his fist in the air.

William sat firmly astride his mount, his red hair flopping up and down, as Gig galloped along the raceway. After one lap, a faster black gelding was a nose in front. William slapped his riding crop against Gig's rump and round they went again. The crowd cheered as Gig slowly edged forward. By the time the horses had rounded the final bend and crossed the finish line, Gig was in front by a head.

'Bravo!' shouted Wentworth.

30 October 1810

Encouraged by Wentworth's praise of her abilities, Esther requested confirmation of her land grant from Governor Macquarie. She mentioned her large family, and her intention to settle in New South Wales. She also said that she had a considerable number of cattle, for which she needed grazing land. She hoped that Macquarie would take her case into his *kind and generous consideration* and she gratefully acknowledged his *generosity and goodness*.

After reading it through, Macquarie dipped his pen in ink and wrote *Inadmissible!* Nevertheless, Esther continued to use the land for some of her stock to graze on while she waited to know Johnston's ultimate fate.

4 November 1810

In England, nothing could be decided about Johnston's case until Bligh had arrived. So Johnston had to bide his time, while the whole country was preoccupied with the war with Napoleon and fears of a British revolution. He lived in Leicester Square, only two blocks from the drapery shop in Coventry Street from which Esther had stolen the lace. Julia was still at school in Hackney, but Bob visited his father when he came home on leave from the Royal Navy. Nevertheless, as the interminable months passed slowly by, Johnston's spirits plummeted.

He worried about the outcome of his trial and, if he escaped with his life, how he would be able to pay the hundreds of pounds of his legal expenses. None of the people who had pledged *to support the measure with our fortunes and our lives* had actually delivered any financial assistance.

He tried to remain positive by making notes in the worn leather notebook he had brought from Annandale House of useful items he could take back to Sydney—if indeed he ever had the chance. They included glass to replace broken windows, paint, casks of nails, brass locks, fire grates and irons, brass hat knobs, sheets of lead for gutters, hemp linen, box plants for hedges and a light carriage.

Then he turned the page and wrote a new heading: *Building castles in the air*. Underneath it he listed some ideas for improvements he would like to make to the Annandale estate. They included creating a new vineyard near Johnston's Creek and building a gatehouse on the Parramatta road. Then he noted down some items that he could buy in England to sell at a profit in the colony, such as wine, brandy, sugar and rum.

When the New South Wales Corps finally arrived back in England, Johnston was ordered to resume his command at Horsham Barracks in Kent, while he waited for his court martial to begin.

His patron and former commander, the Duke of Northumberland, showed his support for Johnston by writing to his member of Parliament. *It appears to me that Johnston could not possibly act otherwise than as he did; the urgent necessity of the case justified fully, in my opinion, the violence, if you have to call it so, of Johnston's procedure. Nothing else could have saved the colony, and even Governor Bligh's life . . . Johnston, instead of censure, deserves the thanks of administration, and ought to be amply rewarded for his firm and determined conduct.*

But, still, Johnston had to wait, eagerly reading letters from Annandale and copies of the *Sydney Gazette* which Esther sent to him. Meanwhile, Esther continued to competently manage the large estate.

➤ *30 March 1811* ➤

Sydney's dusty tracks were widened and straightened, and given signposts displaying new names which honoured King George; the royal dukes of Kent, Clarence and York; the previous governors Phillip, Hunter, King and Bligh (whose street was the shortest); the late Prime Minister Pitt; the Colonial Secretary, Lord Castlereagh; Macquarie himself and his wife Elizabeth.

Then Macquarie wisely moved the villages that had sprung up along the Hawkesbury River to higher ground, to protect them from the ravaging floods. He named the new towns Windsor, Richmond, Pitt Town, Wilberforce, Castlereagh and Liverpool. The roads radiating out from Sydney were improved, including one which branched off Parramatta Road a couple of miles from Annandale House, along which Esther could now comfortably drive her buggy all the way to George's Hall.

Macquarie also reorganised Sydney's police system by creating five separate districts, each allocated six constables supervised by a chief constable. And whom did he appoint as the Superintendent of Police to manage the whole operation? Dr Wentworth. What a surprising place Sydney was!

Wentworth's Sydney house was at the edge of The Rocks, near the wharf and warehouses, and not far from Isaac Nichols's Jolly Sailor Inn. It was a central location and Esther sometimes visited him there when she was in town.

On one of her visits, they discussed the sad news that James Kable, Susannah's eldest son, had been killed by pirates. He had died eighteen months earlier, but the news had only just reached Sydney.

'James did so love the sea,' said Esther, 'and no one could have prevented him from going to Canton. He was doing what he loved most. But seventeen!' She shook her head. 'It is much too young an age to die.'

Susannah and Henry Kable had retreated to their Windsor property where they owned a store and brewery. Of their eleven children, two had died and seven were still living at home.

∽ 7 May 1811 ∾

Johnston's court martial finally began, three years after the events that had precipitated it. There were twenty-three witnesses for the prosecution and nineteen for the defence. The court consisted of the judge advocate general and fifteen military officers.

Each side took six days to present its case. Among those who spoke in Johnston's defence was Vice-Admiral (and ex-governor) John Hunter, who described Johnston as 'a most zealous active officer . . . as perfect as any man I ever knew'.

Arthur Phillip also praised him: *This officer whose activity and zeal for the promotion of the public service was ever conspicuous, from the experience I had of his indefatigable attention to the various and fatiguing duties I had occasion to be so much engaged in . . . It gives me particular pleasure to have this opportunity of offering . . . my personal testimony to his merits as an officer in any or every situation.*

↤ *18 November 1811* ↦

Esther was visiting her new baby grandson, six-week-old Charles Nichols, when Rosanna handed her a copy of *The Times* which had just arrived by ship. Esther shook with apprehension as she tried to focus on the report of Johnston's trial. Her whole future depended on what she would read. Her eyes settled on the words: *Lieutenant Colonel Johnston is guilty of the act of mutiny . . . sentence him to be cashiered.*

Esther crushed the paper to her chest and sobbed with relief. Johnston had lost his military rank, his income and his honour . . . but he was alive and free to come home!

↤ *2 April 1812* ↦

As for Macarthur, he became somewhat stuck. Bligh had accused him of being the leading promoter and instigator of the mutiny against him, so Macquarie had received an order to arrest Macarthur if he returned to the colony. Despite the whole situation having been investigated during Johnston's trial, that order still stood. So Macarthur dared not return to New South Wales until he could get the order cancelled.

His return was later authorised, on the condition that he recognise his 'impropriety of conduct'. But he would never admit that he had acted dishonourably, and he refused to accept the authorisation until those words were withdrawn. He became depressed and would languish in England for another five years, all the time lobbying the British Government to change its instruction—and leaving his wife, Elizabeth, to manage his properties.

↤ *26 November 1812* ↦

Twenty-four years after the colony had been established, it finally received some money to circulate. The British Government had sent ten thousand pounds worth of Spanish dollars to be used as currency.

To make the coins go further, the pragmatic Governor Macquarie asked a convicted forger to cut out their centres and re-stamp them. That meant that the holey dollars (the outer rings) could retain their value of five shillings and the dumps (the centres) could be used to represent fifteen pence. It also meant that the coins would be useless anywhere else, so they would stay within the colony.

∽ 2 January 1813 ∽

After their troubles with Bligh, the settlers of New South Wales were greatly appreciative of their new governor. They placed a public announcement in the *Sydney Gazette*: *We cannot sufficiently appreciate the blessings we enjoy under your administration, nor can language convey to Your Excellency the high and grateful sense we entertain of the integrity that dictated, of the wisdom that planned, and of the vigour that carried into effect such various regulations, so truly calculated to contribute to our comfort, happiness, and future prosperity.*

∽ 3 January 1813 ∽

Bennelong, who had been Governor Phillip's friend and had acted as cultural ambassador between the British settlers and the Indigenous people, died in an orchard on the Parramatta River that belonged to the brewer, James Squire. His body was buried among the orange trees. His Wangal kinsfolk displayed their grief by staging a large ritualised battle.

Nanbaree—a Gadigal man and Dr White's adopted son, who died several years later—asked to be buried in the same grave as Bennelong as a mark of his great respect for the Wangal warrior.

∽ 30 March 1813 ∽

Esther's own comfort, happiness and future prosperity were realised when Johnston and seventeen-year-old Julia finally returned home. Esther had not seen her daughter since she had been four years old.

Johnston was laden with goods and comforts for the family: clothes, shoes, bolts of cloth, table linen, paper, ink, tools, wines, books and magazines. He had also borrowed money from both his agent and

Macarthur to buy a commercial cargo which he could now sell in the colony. The Colonial Office had requested that Governor Macquarie treat Johnston like any ordinary settler, and had even paid for his passage home.

Esther was relieved and jubilant to have all her family (except for Bob) back together again. She could hardly believe that, after four long years, Johnston was once again standing beside her, ready to take over responsibility for the large estate which had become such a thriving enterprise under her management.

⇔ 14 April 1813 ⇔

To celebrate Johnston's return, he and Esther hosted a ball for their friends at Annandale House. Among the many guests were Johnston's aide-de-camp Lieutenant William Lawson, John and Gregory Blaxland, D'Arcy Wentworth and his son William.

John Blaxland asked Wentworth how the governor was able to pay for such an expensive building as the Sydney Hospital, which was under construction at the time. Wentworth replied that the governor was not paying for it, Wentworth and his partners were. They had agreed to do so in return for being permitted to import forty-five thousand gallons of rum over three years.

'Good Lord!' said Blaxland. 'And the Governor has agreed to that?'

'He has indeed,' replied Wentworth. 'And we have the free labour of twenty convicts as well. The colony desperately needs a hospital and the Colonial Office is already criticising the governor's expenditure so, by this means, he gets a new hospital at no cost.' (Despite the fact that he had been given specific instructions to prevent trade in spirits, Macquarie paid for the construction of several fine buildings by granting permission to the builders to import rum.)

Wentworth then asked Blaxland if he and his brother had ever received the full grants of land they had been promised. Not as much as they had expected, Blaxland replied. He told Wentworth he had ended up with some swampy land south of the Parramatta River, which he had named Newington after an estate in Kent. He had drained it and made salt pans for salting the meat from his cattle. He had also built a comfortable home there, where his wife, Harriet, had created a charming garden. However, because there was not enough land left near the colony to raise his cattle, he had had to buy another eight thousand acres in the Coal River valley.

Blaxland went on to explain that his brother, Gregory, had bought an estate called Brush Farm and had then been given a grant of four thousand acres along South Creek, not far from William Wentworth's place at Vermont. With their dairy in town and their slaughterhouse at Cockle Bay, Blaxland believed they could expand substantially, if only they had more grazing land. They were at a loss to see how the growing colony would be able to graze enough cattle to support it, if better pastureland was not discovered soon. Gregory was all for exploring a way west across the mountains in the hope of finding promising pastureland on the other side, but so many had tried to cross them before, and none had been successful.

At that moment, Gregory Blaxland was telling the younger Wentworth the same thing.

'How do you plan to find a way across?' asked William Wentworth.

'I want to follow the ridges rather than the valleys,' answered Gregory, 'as George Caley did further north. He managed to get quite a distance.'

'But he now declares it an impossible task, I believe,' said William.

'Well, I should like to try it myself,' countered Gregory. He told William that he would start by crossing the river near his place at South Creek. North and south of there had proven fruitless, but a kangaroo shooter had shown him a way up one of the lower ridges. Then he would keep between the streams that empty to the left and right.

'You really are serious about the venture,' said William. 'Imagine the glory if you were to succeed! The thrill of being the first one to see what lies on the other side—I should give anything for that.'

'You can join the quest if you wish. I have already discussed it with His Excellency, and he suggested I also take Lieutenant Lawson, who is apparently an accomplished bushman with surveying experience, which could prove useful.'

"'Tis done, sir! I shall join your party.'

◆ *11 May 1813* ◆

And so it was that Gregory Blaxland (thirty-four), William Lawson (thirty-eight) and William Wentworth (twenty-two) walked off into legend.

The romantic William Wentworth had recently been paying Julia Johnston much attention, but she had politely rejected his advances. Nevertheless, on the day the explorers departed, he sent her a poem.

No more, no more can night impart,
One hour to cheer my drooping heart,
Or e'er again the peace renew,
Its constant beat is still for you.
My restless soul still far will flee,
And, sighing, roam in search of thee.

The explorers set off, as Gregory had planned, from his farm at South Creek. It was late autumn, with a heavy dew, and they took with them four servants, four packhorses and five dogs.

Like all those who had tried before, they found the going very difficult. The undergrowth was so thick that it tore their clothes and scratched the flanks of their horses. Deep, rocky gullies fell away from either side of the ridges, and there was so little water on the higher parts that, at the end of each exhausting day, they often had to clamber down cliffs to find enough water to keep going.

They discovered the best way to make progress was to leave the horses and some of the men at each campsite, then cut and blaze a path through the thick scrub, before retracing their steps to the campsite for the night. In the morning, they would move all the gear, men and horses to the point they had reached the previous day, before beginning to hack a path through the next section. That meant they had to walk over each section three times. Nevertheless, they slowly made progress through the eerie emptiness of the mountain bushland.

One day, near what would become Linden, the ridge on which they were travelling narrowed, with deep precipices on either side and a cliff rising to block their way. Fortunately, they managed to discover a small opening through which they could pass.

On the twelfth day, they reached the top of the third and highest ridge. They continued past a sturdy tree near what would later be named Katoomba, into which Lawson carved his initials, before they pushed on across the mountains towards a place Macquarie later named Black-Heath. On the eighteenth day, they reached the edge of Mount York, where they discovered another pass in the rocks and began to descend the other side of the mountains. It was so steep that they had to unload the horses and carry everything themselves, digging a trench into the side of the mountain by hand to give the nervous horses a footing.

The climate on this side of the mountains was quite different, and thick frosts covered the ground each morning. The men realised, with joy, that what they had thought was poor, sandy ground seen from a distance was in fact lush grassland which the frosts had turned brown.

◇ 1 June 1813 ◇

They wandered through open meadows threaded with gurgling streams until—twenty-one days out from Blaxland's farm—they finally climbed a hill shaped like a sugar loaf, and looked across a vast expanse of grassland.

The cattleman among the three could see its enormous agricultural potential, remarking that it was the best-watered country of any he had seen in the colony and that there was enough land to support the colony's cattle for thirty years or more.

The soldier considered it would make a safe retreat if the French ever invaded Sydney, as so few men would be required to defend the mountain pass.

And the poet raised his arms to the sky. *The boundless champaign burst upon our sight, Till, nearer seen, the beauteous landscape grew, Op'ning like Canaan on rapt Israel's view.*

And then they turned for home.

ᕮ 1 November 1813 ᕭ

Macquarie's military background had allowed him no sympathy for mutinous behaviour and he had expected to dislike Johnston when next they met again. However, after he had discovered more about the lead-up to the rebellion—and had made Bligh's acquaintance himself—he had been prepared to withhold judgement of his old friend and fellow Scot.

His patience was rewarded, and he was pleased to be reminded that, far from having a rebellious nature, Johnston was every bit a gentleman: quiet, uncomplicated and immune to the drive for power. They renewed their friendship and Macquarie restored the grants of land to Esther and George that he had previously revoked.

ᕮ 13 November 1813 ᕭ

Six months after the mountains were crossed, Governor Macquarie sent his surveyor, George Evans, to confirm the discoveries that had been made by Blaxland's party, and to explore what lay beyond the sugarloaf hill. Evans took five men and travelled a hundred miles further than Blaxland, Lawson and Wentworth had reached.

He was delighted with what he found: long, thick grass, abundant game, rivers so full of fish they would bite as soon as a line was dropped into the water. It was the finest country he had ever seen, with enough feed for increasing stocks of cattle for a hundred years.

ᕮ 28 March 1814 ᕭ

Following the death of her first baby, Elizabeth Macquarie had suffered the heartache and disappointment of seven miscarriages. But now she had carried her ninth pregnancy to full term.

While thirty-eight people attended a dinner at Government House—to farewell Bligh's daughter and son-in-law, who were returning to England—Elizabeth lay in an adjoining room, engulfed in the throes of childbirth. Just before midnight, Dr Redfern called out that a healthy baby boy had been born. Macquarie rushed in to see Elizabeth and their new baby. Then he sat with them for a couple of hours, before sleeping in his wife's dressing room for the night.

⟷ 7 May 1814 ⟷

Bligh had turned Farm Cove, which adjoined the Public Domain, into the Governor's Garden—and declared it out of bounds to everyone else. It had since been landscaped into pleasant walks among Norfolk Island pines and exotic trees from faraway lands.

Governor Macquarie had subsequently ordered the removal of any remaining tree stumps, so the whole area down to the sandy beach was now smooth grassland. The pair of forest red gums still stood on their ridge, and a few native families lived amid the surrounding shrubbery in what would become Sydney's Royal Botanic Garden.

Elizabeth Macquarie so enjoyed walking through the gardens to admire the view from the point of the far headland that convicts had been employed to carve a seat for her there, named Mrs Macquarie's Chair.

The governor would not know for many months if Britain happened to be at war with a visiting ship's country of origin, so each ship was required to anchor in Neutral Bay, which was safely out of gunshot of Sydney and too far away for convicts to reach by swimming. From her seat on the warm Sydney sandstone, and cooled by refreshing sea breezes, Elizabeth could watch all the foreign ships lying at anchor.

⟷ 18 July 1814 ⟷

Before any farmers could move to the fine land on the other side of the Blue Mountains, a road had to be built across them. The man who undertook this enormous task was former military officer and magistrate

William Cox. Cox had bought Brush Farm from John Macarthur and sold it later to D'Arcy Wentworth, who sold it to Gregory Blaxland.

Cox hand-picked a gang of thirty burly convicts who were promised their freedom at the end of the task, and they were guarded by six soldiers. Using only pickaxes, crowbars, grubbing hoes, block and tackle, and gunpowder, they worked through the misty rain and icy frosts of winter.

They levelled the road, cut into rock shelves and spanned twelve deep gorges with log-built bridges. In an astonishing feat, they completed one hundred and one miles in six months to the day—and gained their freedom.

∞ 12 November 1814 ∞

Esther had lived with Johnston for twenty-six years, borne him eight children and in his absence had managed his properties for a total of six years. In the spring of 1814, aged forty-five and using her legal name, Esther Julian, she finally became his bride in a Christian marriage ceremony. Governor Macquarie had granted them a special licence which allowed them to be married outside a place of Christian worship and without requiring the banns to be read aloud on the three Sundays before the wedding.

Under a gloriously blue sky, Esther and Johnston drove in the fine carriage Johnston had brought back from England to Rosanna and Isaac Nichols's home at Concord, where they exchanged their vows before the stocky figure of the Reverend Samuel Marsden. Rosanna and Nichols were the legal witnesses, and the family celebrated afterwards with a sumptuous wedding feast.

John Macarthur was still in England, but the day after Esther's marriage, Elizabeth Macarthur called on her to present her with a jewellery box as a wedding gift. Esther's hands trembled slightly as she looked at the beautiful box in her hands and thought about what it meant to receive it. She softly bit her bottom lip and looked up. Elizabeth was full of smiles.

Wentworth later congratulated Esther on her marriage, admitting that he had hoped for a different outcome. Esther suggested that he marry one of his housekeepers, Marie or Ann. She reminded him that the governor would prefer him to be married.

'I cannot see the point in marrying now,' he replied.

And he never did.

◅ 25 December 1814 ▻

It was Christmas Day—Esther's first Christmas as Mrs Johnston. She had long ago embraced this very Christian tradition to please her family. Although the day was sweltering, the family dined on traditional roast goose and plum pudding. There were toasts to the King, the colony, the newlyweds, and to twenty-one-year-old Robert's safe return from fighting with the Royal Navy.

When the feast was over, everyone sat on the veranda, replete and content, while the young children played in the garden. Esther indulged in the maternal delight of watching her own children, unobserved. Rosanna was sitting next to her husband, Isaac Nichols. Esther found it hard to believe that her eldest daughter was now twenty-seven, with three fine sons of her own—two of whom would soon go off to school in England.

Young George was talking to Nichols. Earlier in the year, Governor Macquarie had appointed the twenty-four-year-old as a government clerk, declaring him to be an *honest, honourable, active, vigilant and zealous young man, entirely devoted to his duty, which he executes highly to my satisfaction.*

David (seventeen), Maria (fourteen) and Blanche (eight) were playing skittles on the garden path. As 'currency' children—those born in New South Wales, and distinct from 'sterling', who had been born in England—they had grown up with many friends in the colony.

Esther smiled as eighteen-year-old Julia walked onto the veranda, carrying a large Christmas cake which she carefully placed onto a small table. How ever would they manage to fit in any more food?

Mary Gilbert had followed Julia out, to deliver a note to Esther. It was from Elizabeth Macquarie, inviting Julia, Maria and Blanche to stay with her at Government House, Parramatta, for the first week of the new year. Not having any daughters of her own, Elizabeth always enjoyed their girlish company.

Esther smiled again. How her circumstances had changed since she had lain on the hard, grimy floor of Newgate Prison, a poorly educated, pregnant sixteen-year-old convict. Since then, she had survived a long, harsh sea voyage with a small baby, experienced extended periods of hunger and suffered years of separation from her partner and children. While women her age in England had been reclining on their sofas reading Jane Austen's romantic novels, Esther had been administering one of New South Wales's largest agricultural properties. At the same time she had managed to raise her children to be welcomed into the colony's highest society. Even more gratifying, she had won the respect and friendship of the colony's most important people.

Esther looked again at the invitation. It occurred to her that her own life reflected that of the colony itself: a remarkable transformation from an inferior convict beginning, through drama and hardship, to finally achieving a position of respect.

As Mark Twain wrote, decades later:

Australian history is almost always picturesque; indeed, it is so curious and strange, that it is itself the chiefest novelty the country has to offer, and so it pushes the other novelties into second and third place. It does not read like history, but like the most beautiful lies. And all of a fresh sort, no moldy old stale ones. It is full of surprises, and adventures, and incongruities, and contradictions, and incredibilities; but they are all true, they all happened.

Epilogue

Esther enjoyed several years of comfort and prosperity before her life became challenging once more.

Young George

After Young George had worked in the Commissary Department for three years, Governor Macquarie gave him another grant of six hundred acres adjoining King's Gift, which he named Lockwood after a Scottish castle belonging to the Johnston clan. Young George built a home for himself there.

Governor Macquarie then appointed him Superintendent of Government Flocks and Herds, giving him the job of rounding up the government's herd of over a thousand wild cattle which roamed through the Cowpastures district. Many others had tried to capture them, without success. But Young George had an affinity with cattle and he came up with a creative plan. He introduced some tame cows to mingle with the wild ones, and built winged yards into which he could gently direct them. Along with his new position, he was given another grant of land at Bankstown between Esther's block and the Georges River.

On 11 February 1820, Young George fell from his horse during a wild race with one of the Macarthur boys at Camden Park. He was kicked in the chest and severely injured. Johnston sent for a doctor and rushed to his son's side at the Macarthurs' cottage. Governor Macquarie soon heard the news and sent a ship's doctor to assist. He also wrote to Johnston of his hope for George's recovery, adding that as each day went by both he and Elizabeth never failed to ask about Young George from every one they saw.

But the situation was hopeless. George's body spluttered with life for a few more days before it succumbed to his injuries and his life petered out altogether. He was thirty years old. His body was taken back to Annandale House and laid to rest in the family vault.

The *Sydney Gazette* reported: *This last tribute to the memory of Mr Johnston was numerously attended by almost every person of rank or consideration in the colony, amongst whom were His Excellency the Governor and his staff . . . it has seldom been our lot to record an event that has been so universally felt and deplored.*

John Macarthur wrote to Johnston that Young George's death had *inexpressibly disturbed us all, for he was a most deserving young person.* Governor Macquarie also wrote a letter of sympathy, saying that he considered Young George to have been an honour to his family and *one of the brightest ornaments* of Australia. He grieved for his young friend: *for such I truly considered him—for his equal, I never expect to meet again in New South Wales.*

The following month, Macquarie invited the whole Johnston family to spend the day at Government House in Sydney and he directed Francis Greenway, the government architect, to design and build a new family vault to house the remains of Young George and his baby sister Isabella.

George Johnston

In 1817 Governor Macquarie granted Johnston another fifteen hundred acres northwest of the Macquarie Rivulet in the Illawarra district, which Johnston named Macquarie Gift. He used it to grow the country's first clover from seed sent out by his patron, the Duke of Northumberland. Johnston continued to improve his properties, including extending

Annandale House and building two grand two-storey buildings on his Lower George Street leasehold—opposite the gaol, where Esther's large vegetable garden had been.

However, his health had been declining for ten years before the shock of Young George's death in 1820 took its toll. Two years later Johnston was returning home along Parramatta Road with his youngest daughter, Blanche, when two men jumped out from behind a tree. The horse swerved violently, which overturned the gig and tossed Johnston and Blanche down an embankment. The men stole all their valuables before disappearing into the bush.

That incident seemed to exacerbate his ailments and he died less than a year later, on 3 January 1823, aged fifty-eight. The Reverend Samuel Marsden conducted his funeral service at Annandale House and his remains were interred in the family vault. At the family's request, Marsden consecrated the vault, making it the first private consecrated burial ground in the colony.

Johnston's will divided his large quantity of livestock equally between Esther and his five surviving children. It also bequeathed the Annandale estate to Esther while she was alive, after which it was to go to Robert, who also received some grants along the Georges River. Johnston left to David his three grants at George's Hall, plus Esther's six-hundred-acre farm at Banks Town (which had become his property when Esther married him) and portions of two other properties. Julia, Maria and Blanche shared the George Street lease, King's Gift, Macquarie Gift and three other properties.

In 1989 there was a pleasing historical echo when one of Johnston's descendants, Rear Admiral Sir David Martin, legitimately became the Governor of New South Wales.

Johnston Street, Johnston Lane and Johnstons Creek in Annandale, and Johnstons Bay are all named after George Johnston.

Esther

Esther's son, George, had died in 1820; her husband in 1823. Her daughter, Maria, moved to India in 1825 where she—and both her small children—died in 1827. It seems that Esther found solace for her grief in alcohol, which sometimes caused her to behave erratically.

Johnston's will had left the Annandale estate to Esther for her lifetime, to be inherited by Robert upon her death. Robert was now the head of the family, but was not able to control his major property. This situation became a source of conflict.

Esther lived at Annandale with Robert, Julia and Blanche, but by 1825 she was accusing Robert of violence towards her, and decided to leave for England. She advertised Annandale House, including all its furniture, for lease. Robert was furious at the prospect of having to vacate his own home for strangers, and he convinced Esther not to go.

However, four years later, Esther (then aged sixty and often staying with Rosanna) could bear her situation no longer and this time decided to mortgage Annandale House and return to England.

Nine days later, Robert attempted to have her declared insane and therefore unfit to manage the estate, so that he would be able to take control. He engaged his friend William Wentworth, now a barrister, to represent him in the resulting commission of inquiry in the New South Wales Supreme Court. Esther engaged a Jewish lawyer, David Poole, and his assistant Mr Stephen. The hearing was reported in the *Australian* newspaper (not related to today's publication).

Mr Stephen observed that Esther's efforts and good judgement had made it possible for her to accumulate an extensive property and that *a wish to wrest that property from her appeared now to be the motive which influenced the parties instituting the present enquiry.*

He further declared *that the eccentric habits of this lady, even admitting them to have been heightened by the occasional practice of drinking too freely, presented no grounds for pronouncing her insane.*

The Johnston's family doctor described Esther as eccentric, with a hasty temper and an abrupt mode of expressing herself, but couldn't say whether someone suffering from *mental anxiety, occasioned by supposed oppression, or ill treatment would have a similar effect.*

He had seen Esther driving *most furiously through the streets* and deemed *such behaviour to be an act of madness*. He admitted that she might *be very capable of managing her house and farming concerns* because she was *at times lucid and perfectly composed*. Nevertheless, he was of the opinion that her *extravagant behaviour* was the result of *mental imbecility*.

Mr Stephen then prepared to cross-examine the ten witnesses whom Robert had brought in to speak against Esther (many of them probably his servants), but the *Commissioners were of opinion, that such a course would occupy considerable time to no purpose*. Mr Stephen said that he also had forty witnesses to speak in Esther's favour; however, the commissioners saw no need for them to do so, considering all the previous witnesses had been unanimous in their views.

The jury foreman asked Esther directly what had caused her described behaviour, and she replied that she had suffered a series of violent and oppressive acts until she could bear it no longer and decided to leave the colony.

She had become friends with Jacob Isaacs, and his Jewish wife, who owned a pub in Petersham. Isaacs gave evidence that during the previous five years Esther had often come to his house, craving protection and showing him her bruises from being kicked. He then described a violent confrontation which he had witnessed himself. He admitted that *she does take a glass, so do we all*. But he considered her *a woman fully capable of minding her own affairs, or of managing those of any other person*.

Esther's grandson, Charles Nichols, said that she was always an industrious woman and had frequently complained to him about Robert's violent treatment of her, but that he had *every reason to doubt the truth* of what she had said, and he avoided her company.

William Wentworth pressed the court for a decision. The jury retired for a hour before finding that Esther was *not of sound mind, nor capable of managing her affairs*. However, the court did not transfer the ownership of the Annandale estate to Robert. Instead, it appointed both Robert and his brother David as trustees, to administer the property until Esther's death.

After the inquiry, Esther went to live with her son David, first at his property called Lockwood (which adjoined King's Gift), and later at George's Hall where she stayed until she died on 26 August 1846. Her death certificate recorded her age as seventy-five. Her body was laid to rest, in accordance with George Johnston's instructions, beside him at Annandale. Their remains were later moved to a family vault at Waverley Cemetery. Annandale House was demolished in 1905.

A pavilion was built and dedicated to Esther in 2002. It stands next to Johnstons Creek, where it flows into Rozelle Bay, on land that was once part of the Annandale estate.

Rosanna

Rosanna and Isaac Nichols prospered in the colony. They owned large farming properties, they built ships and they entertained many of Sydney's most important residents at their Bachelor Balls and Foundation Day dinners. They had three sons together before Nichols died on 8 November 1819 at the age of forty-nine.

The following year, Rosanna married a farmer named James Stuart (or Stewart). Her half-sister Blanche Johnston acted as witness. After Rosanna's second marriage, her children sometimes lived with Esther at Annandale House. Rosanna died (before Esther) in 1837, also aged forty-nine.

Rosanna's second son, George Nichols, became the first Australian-born solicitor, and also editor and part-owner of the *Australian* newspaper, which had been founded by his friend William Wentworth. In 1841 Nichols appointed the Honorary Secretary of the Sydney Synagogue as his personal assistant. He was later elected to the New South Wales Legislative Assembly, where he argued successfully for the government to make equal provision for public worship by Jews as by Christians, since they contributed equally to the revenue of the colony. He was a brilliant orator and sometimes mentioned in his speeches that he was the grandson of Esther Abrahams. He became the colony's first auditor-general before his death in 1857.

Robert

Napoleon was defeated at Waterloo in 1815, after which Lieutenant Robert Johnston (then twenty-four) came home to New South Wales. Governor Macquarie sent him off on a voyage of discovery (during which Robert named the River Clyde) and also on an exploration to discover the source of the Warragamba River. He married in 1831 and had nine children. In 1865 Robert was promoted to the rank of commander in the Royal Navy. He died in 1882 at the age of eighty-nine.

Julia

Julia never married, but after Robert's wedding in 1831 she left Annandale House and went to live with Blanche's family. She died in 1879, aged eighty-two.

David

The day after the death of Young George in 1820, Governor Macquarie appointed David Superintendent of the Government Flocks and Herds, and he later became a successful grazier. He seems to have had a close relationship with Esther, who lived the last part of her life with him at George's Hall.

In 1836 David married Selina Willey and the wedding reception was held at his sister Blanche's home. The following year he built a new house at George's Hall, further up the hill from the flood-prone original one, which he called The Homestead. It was a large, single-storey home with a wide veranda. It still stands today, in Lionel Street.

When he and Selina had a daughter in 1838, they named her Esther. She was followed by another six children. David died at Annandale House in 1866, aged sixty-nine.

Maria

Maria married Captain Thomas Brotheridge in 1824 and gave birth to a son, named George, the following year. They moved to India in 1825 and two years later had a daughter who died after only a few hours of life. Maria herself died a week later, and her little boy died the same year, on his way back to New South Wales with his father. Captain Brotheridge died a few months later at Annandale House.

Blanche

Blanche married Captain George Weston, of the East India Company, in 1829. They went to India as newlyweds—where Weston became a judge—before returning to New South Wales, where they built an Indian bungalow on King's Gift, which they renamed Horsley after Weston's birthplace in Surrey. Blanche had eight children and died in 1904, aged ninety-eight, outliving all her siblings.

Lachlan Macquarie

Macquarie did his best to help the native people who had been displaced by the British settlement. He gave them grants of land at Georges Head (Mosman), with huts to live in, clothes to wear, tools, food and a fishing boat. He also established a school to teach their children scripture and give them skills which would enable them to work within the settlements. He hoped that they would marry each other and be granted farms along the Richmond Road at Blacks Town (Blacktown). Any native farmers who settled there would be given free food, clothes, tools and seed for six months.

Despite these initiatives, attacks on the fringes of the colony became more sophisticated, involving bands of up to sixty warriors, who had now learned how to use guns. The farming families became too fearful to remain on their isolated properties. Like governors before him, Macquarie felt compelled to act.

In April 1816 he sent out three detachments of soldiers to the camps of known hostile warriors. With no success after two weeks, one of the detachments heard the cry of a child and they charged through the scrub towards it, firing their guns and driving the native people over the edge of a cliff to their death in the Cataract River. Reprisal attacks by natives followed, including two hundred sheep being driven over a cliff.

As a consequence, Macquarie banned all armed natives from coming within a mile of any farm or town, but as native men always carried their spears, this resulted in another period of banishment. Over time, some of the outlawed native warriors were killed or exiled and Macquarie declared an amnesty for the rest of them, if they gave themselves up at an annual feast. The war on the Cumberland Plain finally came to an end.

Nearly one hundred and eighty people attended the next 'General Friendly Meeting of the Natives' at the Parramatta marketplace where the children from the native school, including Bennelong's four-year-old son Dicky, showed off their reading skills.

Two years later, three hundred natives came from as far away as the other side of the Blue Mountains to attend Macquarie's annual feast. And when the yearly school examinations were held for the hundred white children and twenty Native Institution students, Macquarie was delighted to announce that the main academic prize had been won by Maria Lock from the native school (who later married Dicky).

In 1817 Macquarie proposed the establishment of a colonial bank. Wentworth, together with his son John, Dr Redfern, Dr Harris, Mrs Macquarie, Mrs Campbell and forty-two others, took shares in the Bank of New South Wales.

The continent that contained New South Wales was known as New Holland. But after Matthew Flinders had circumnavigated it, he had suggested the name 'Australia'. In December 1817 Macquarie recommended to the Colonial Office that the name 'Australia' be officially adopted.

Macquarie commissioned many impressive buildings designed by Francis Greenway, including Hyde Park Barracks, the Government Stables (now the Sydney Conservatorium of Music) and St James's Church in Sydney, St John's Church in Parramatta, and the courthouse and St Matthew's Church in Windsor. Many people in England thought it was preposterous that he should commission such grand buildings at Botany Bay—which is what they still called the colony, even thirty years after it had moved to Port Jackson.

The Colonial Office also worried that transportation to New South Wales was becoming less of a deterrent to criminals in Britain—emancipists were doing too well. And it received a stream of letters from Sydney's 'exclusives' criticising Macquarie's habit of welcoming emancipists into colonial society. But they could not hold back the current of change that now formed such an integral part of the colony. What might have stemmed the tide in the old country was flushed away in this land of opportunity. And Macquarie did all he could to keep the floodgates open.

After eight years as governor, Macquarie tendered his resignation, which was not initially accepted. Instead, an inquiry into the colony's affairs was ordered, with John Bigge as its commissioner. Bigge arrived in September 1819, taking Macquarie by surprise. The following year, Macquarie's resignation was accepted and he returned to Scotland.

When Bigge's report was published, it criticised Macquarie's administration, including his acceptance of emancipists and his lavish building program. Nevertheless, Australian society had already begun its relentless shift towards a more egalitarian one than the British society from which it had come.

Macquarie died in 1824 and his coffin was followed up London's Regent Street by forty coaches, including the Duke of Wellington's.

D'Arcy Wentworth

Wentworth's Sydney Hospital was finally completed in 1816 but he found its management took up too much of his time, now that he was by far the largest landholder in New South Wales. So he appointed Dr Redfern to take his place there.

By 1818 Wentworth was of a certain age. He wanted to retire to his country estate, Home Bush, but he also wanted to continue enjoying the pleasures that Ann Mackneal's youth (being still only twenty-five) afforded him. The problem was, forty-three-year-old Maria Ainslie (herself thirteen years younger than Wentworth) was the mistress who had always 'looked after him' at Home Bush. Ann lived between his two townhouses in Sydney and Parramatta.

Wentworth announced his intention to move Maria out of the way to Sydney and install Ann and their four young children at Home Bush. His son John was furious. He considered Maria his second mother and was appalled that she should be replaced by his father's younger mistress. His brother William felt the same way and saw Ann as an opportunist: *a woman, who for the single sake of ameliorating her condition (for my father has long been past the prime of life, when he could have been expected to inspire love) has abandoned her child, her husband, who has, in fact, burst asunder alike the ties of nature as of society and stigmatised herself by the violation of every duty.*

Past his prime or not, Wentworth moved Ann into Home Bush and sent Maria to Sydney. John refused to speak to Ann or to live under the same roof, so he left his father's house and went to sea. Wentworth never saw him again, for he died of yellow fever a year later, at the age of twenty-four, and was buried at sea.

Wentworth fathered eleven children, three with Catherine Crowley and eight with Ann Mackneal. He died in 1827, aged sixty-five. At that time he was probably the wealthiest man in New South Wales.

Unlike his more respectable son William, D'Arcy Wentworth was a bit of a rake who, according to Professor John Ritchie, was ready to *flirt with any pretty wench or agreeable trollop* and had at least six mistresses during his lifetime. The suburb of Wentworth Point is named after him.

William Wentworth

In 1816 William went first to Paris and then to England to study law at Cambridge University. He met up with John Macarthur there and, in his typically optimistic fashion, told Macarthur that he intended to marry his eldest and most delicate daughter, Elizabeth. William foresaw a marvellous union between two great families of New South Wales.

Unsurprisingly, Macarthur was not particularly keen on his daughter marrying a dishevelled, illegitimate son of a convict woman and a highwayman, who had a badly turned eye. Some time later, after William had quarrelled with Macarthur's son John over some money,

William received a letter from Macarthur telling him, rather tersely, that he could not marry Elizabeth.

In 1819 William became the first Australian-born author to have a book published. It had the rather grandiose title: *A Statistical, Historical, and Political Description of the Colony of New South Wales, and its Dependent Settlements in Van Diemen's Land: with a Particular Enumeration of the Advantages which these Colonies offer for Emigration, and their Superiority in many Respects over those Possessed by the United States of America.*

He was still in England, strutting about London, the proud son of a gentleman who owned an extensive country estate, when a pamphlet criticising Governor Macquarie was published. It accused Macquarie of exploiting the colonists' desire for rum in order to build a palace for the principal surgeon (D'Arcy), whom it alleged had been transported for highway robbery. William was outraged at such slander about his father and he immediately sought a public apology—but in the process he discovered that, while his father had never actually been convicted, he had indeed been tried for highway robbery on three occasions.

William was called to the bar in 1822. He submitted an epic poem, *Australasia*, for the chancellor's medal at the University of Cambridge (it was awarded second place). The poem contains the now-famous lines:

And, O Britannia! . . . may this—thy last-born infant—then arise,
To glad thy heart, and greet thy parent eyes;
And Australasia float, with flag unfurl'd,
A new Britannia in another world!

William returned to Sydney in 1824 (aged thirty-four) and was welcomed as a hero by the *Sydney Gazette*. When D'Arcy died three years later, William inherited property at Bringelly, Parramatta and Sydney. He bought more land in eastern Sydney where he built a mansion called Vaucluse House.

William became the colony's leading political figure, advocating self-government, trial by jury, a free press and the abolition of convict transportation. He was a director of the Bank of New South Wales and co-founded the *Australian* newspaper (not today's publication). He was elected to the Council for the City of Sydney, became a member of parliament, and helped to draft a constitution for self-government. He also pioneered primary school education and helped to found the University of Sydney.

With his work done, in 1854 he returned to England where he died in 1872. In accordance with his wishes, his body was brought back to Sydney. There, he was given the first state funeral service (in St Andrew's Cathedral). The day was declared a public holiday and his body was laid to rest at Vaucluse House. The town of Wentworth in country New South Wales and Wentworth Falls are named after him.

John and Elizabeth Macarthur

In 1817 the British Government finally gave permission for John Macarthur to return to New South Wales, unconditionally and without charge. He was even provided with free passage for himself, his two sons, some bulky agricultural equipment, a load of stores and a green-house full of plants.

Once back in Sydney, he pushed on with his vision for a thriving wool industry—and Elizabeth withdrew from the management of their estate. Macarthur was a founding investor in both the Australian Agricultural Company and the Bank of Australia (which was formed by 'exclusives' to rival the Bank of New South Wales).

As he aged, his temperament became increasingly erratic. He served on the New South Wales Legislative Council until he was suspended due to his deteriorating mental health. He subsequently became paranoid about his family and ordered Elizabeth out of the Elizabeth Farm house. She moved to Sydney to live with her daughter Mary. Macarthur died in 1834. Elizabeth moved back to Elizabeth Farm, where she lived for another sixteen years until her death in 1850.

The Australian electoral division of Macarthur was named in honour of them both.

Susannah and Henry Kable

The Kables continued to manage five farms at the Hawkesbury and another one at the Cowpastures, in addition to several Sydney properties. Susannah died in 1825, aged sixty-three. Henry lived for another twenty-one years, dying in 1846 aged eighty-four.

Colbee

It is thought that Colbee died following a payback battle in 1806, as he is not mentioned in any records after that time.

The Forest Red Gums

The two forest red gums (*Eucalyptus tereticornis*), which were spared from the original land clearing in Farm Cove, and which Esther and Elizabeth Macquarie would have admired as they walked past, still stand on Bennelong Lawn in the Royal Sydney Botanic Gardens, now overlooking the Sydney Opera House. They form a living link to Sydney's colonial past.

Acknowledgements

Many people have encouraged and helped me to create this book. Thank you to John Haines for your early technical support; to Carol Odell, Nigel Foote, Dawn Egan, Belinda Pring, David Whitehouse and Robin Walsh for your excellent feedback on my early drafts; and to the anonymous historian who evaluated a later draft.

As the final manuscript came together, the following people were also unfailingly helpful and I thank you all: Robyn Dryen, President of the Australian Jewish Genealogical Society; Tinny Lenthen, Librarian at the Sydney Jewish Museum; Sabrina Elias, Senior Archivist at the Australian Jewish Historical Society; Dr Anthony Joseph, President of the Jewish Genealogical Society of Great Britain; Rabbi John Levi; Jo Nicholson at the British Ministry of Defence; Jon Shepherd at the Kent History and Library Centre; Irina Fridman at the Chatham Memorial Synagogue; Kathryn Fehon at the Parramatta Heritage Centre; Jennie Rayner at Sydney Living Museums; Fiona MacFarlane at the Tasmanian State Library and Archive Service; the librarians at the State Library of New South Wales; UK genealogists Laurence Harris and Alexander Poole; and Calvin Johnston.

Geoffrey Lemcke, it was lovely to meet you when I was in the middle of my research; I hope you are looking down with approval. Alan Roberts, thank you for taking the time to meet with me and assist with introductions. Ann Varley, it was so kind of you to invite me into your beautiful home and I was delighted to shake hands with some of Esther's DNA.

Christopher Tobin, thank you for your meticulous review of the Indigenous aspects of my story; Esther Kahn, I thank you for sharing your painstaking research into the Abrahams family; Peter Walker, thanks for passing on Young George's painting and the information about its significance.

Irina Dunn, this book would never have happened without your expert review and guidance, and your unrivalled network of contacts. Thank you for championing my manuscript. Richard Walsh, your generous mentoring and incomparable editing were absolutely invaluable. To the team at Allen & Unwin—Elizabeth Weiss, Angela Handley, Hilary Reynolds and Lu Sierra—thank you for your wise advice and stewardship through the final stages of production.

To my children, Alex and Tristan, thank you for always letting me detour to see the Customs House flag whenever we were anywhere near it. And to my husband, Stephen, loving thanks for putting up with so many years of my preoccupation with the people and events of early Sydney, and for continuing to inspire me with your ever-optimistic outlook on life.

A note about sources

If you would like to find out more about any of the people in this book, the (online) *Australian Dictionary of Biography* is a great place to start. The most well-known record of Esther's life is George Bergman's 1966 article 'Esther Johnston: The Lieutenant-Governor's Wife' in the *Australian Jewish Historical Society Journal*. Three other publications that I used extensively are Iris Nesdale's *The Fettered and the Free*, Geoffrey Lemcke's *Reluctant Rebel* and Alan Roberts's *Marine Officer, Convict Wife*.

Biographies of other people I found particularly useful include Michael Duffy's *Man of Honour* (about John and Elizabeth Macarthur), Hazel King's *Elizabeth Macarthur and Her World*, Michelle Scott Tucker's *Elizabeth Macarthur*, Paul Kable and June Whittaker's *Damned Rascals?* (about Henry and Susannah Kable), Lysbeth Cohen's *Elizabeth Macquarie*, George Mackaness's *The Life of Vice-Admiral William Bligh* and John Ritchie's *The Wentworths*.

Bennelong and Barangaroo, and all the events I recount about them, are described in detail in the journals written by John Hunter and Watkin Tench. I found additional information about Indigenous society at the time in Keith Smith's article 'Bennelong among his people' and his book *Bennelong: The coming in of the Eora, Sydney Cove, 1788–1792*.

You will find all the titles and publishing details for those sources in the bibliography, along with many others that provide information about Esther's life.

A note about Esther

There are many aspects of Esther's life about which we will never know all the details, including her name, her upbringing and her Jewishness.

Her name continues to be a puzzle. On her convict record she was listed as Esther Abrahams, but a few years later she used the surname Julian. We don't know which one was her maiden name. Unfortunately, very few records were made of the births of Jewish girls at the time, and not all Jewish marriages were recorded either. Many historians have searched for Esther among the genealogical records without success.

When George Bergman wrote about her in his 1966 article and her entry in the *Australian Dictionary of Biography*, he assumed that her maiden name was Abrahams and that Julian was the surname of Rosanna's father. He added that Julian 'is a Hispano-Jewish name, fairly common among Maranno-Sephardic families' in England at the time. Since then, most historians have accepted his assumption, but there appears to be little documentary evidence for it.

On the other hand, there is some evidence for her maiden name being Julian. The Mitchell Library in Sydney holds a nineteenth-century photograph of Esther's portrait with a handwritten inscription on the back: *Esther Julian daughter of a Major Julian of New Folkestone, Kent*. It's true that some colonists told lies about their origins in order to make it appear that they came from better families than was actually the case, but there is another piece of evidence for Esther's surname being Julian. In 1897, Esther's grandson, Edward Charles Johnston, was reported in the *Evening Standard* as having named his property near Stanmore 'Folkestone', presumably following the local custom of naming properties after British places that have family significance. And did Esther name her daughter Julia in honour of her father?

There *was* a Major Julian who was born about 1751 and who served in the American War of Independence. He would have been about eighteen when Esther was born. There is a record of him marrying later, in 1788 (aged thirty-seven), after which he had three children. There was also a Michael Julian who enlisted in the British Marines in 1770, around the time Esther was born, and a George Julian who died in 1802 after serving on HMS *Orion*. But no links to Esther can be found.

The British Naval Historical Branch has confirmed that Jewish men joined the British Marines during the eighteenth century and some went on to become officers, even though that required them to publicly receive the sacrament according to the rites of the Church of England. British Marines follow the ranks of the army, rather than the navy, so they include the rank of Major.

There is also some evidence for the surname of Rosanna's father being Abrahams. When Rosanna married in 1805, she did not accept the surname of Julian. Her name was originally recorded in the marriage register of St Philip's Church as Rosanna Julian, but it looks as though she crossed out the name Julian herself and wrote Abrahams above it. Then she signed as Rosanna Abrahams.

There are two other tantalising shreds of information, neither of which is conclusive. In 1824 a convict named Julia Ann Julien was recorded as being a Jewish 'niece to Mrs Colonel Johnston' when she was transported to New South Wales. Esther may have been her aunt by marriage to Julia's uncle, or she may have been a blood relative.

Then, in 1837, a Michael Abrahams, who had come to Sydney as a free settler, committed a crime and was sentenced to fourteen years' transportation to Van Diemen's Land (Tasmania). His mother, Phoebe Abrahams, wrote from her Regent Street address to the Colonial Secretary at the time, pleading for her son to be returned to England, and claiming that he was a 'relative' of George Robert Nichols (Rosanna's second son, a prominent lawyer and part-owner of the *Australian* newspaper). Abraham Abrahams—Michael's father and Phoebe's second husband—may have been a brother or cousin of Esther's, or he might have been Rosanna's father.

At that time, a Jewish couple could be considered married if two valid witnesses saw the husband give the bride an article of value (usually a ring) and heard him declare to her: *Behold you are betrothed to me by this ring.* The marriage must then be consummated. According to Jeremy Pfeffer, in *From One End of the Earth to the Other*, such marriages were sometimes entered into by 'playful unthinking Jewish adolescents'.

Whatever her background, Esther appears to have had no contact with her family following her arrest. During the years her three children were at school in England, several of Johnston's friends kept in contact with them and had them to stay, but there is no mention of anyone from Esther's family doing so.

On balance, I decided that there was more evidence for Esther's maiden name being Julian rather than Abrahams, so that is how I have presented her in my narrative.

The second aspect to consider is Esther's upbringing. Esther could read, but not write (she signed the marriage register with a cross). In England at that time, fewer than half of the women were literate and Jewish girls were particularly poorly educated. Esther's convict record shows her to be a milliner, although it is possible that she supplied an occupation to avoid being taken for a prostitute. Milliners at that time made clothing as well as hats, but Esther was never assigned to mending clothes in the colony.

It is also interesting that someone close to her was wealthy enough to pay for a barrister at her original trial—unusual at the time—and also her accommodation in the Master's Side in Newgate Prison.

Indeed, she behaved in a manner consistent with a fairly good upbringing. She certainly raised her own children to be able to conduct themselves in polite society—they were welcomed into the homes of the most exclusive families and to stay at Government House. Mrs Atkins, wife of the deputy judge advocate, considered by some at the time to be the most well-connected lady in the colony, apparently 'delighted' in looking after Esther's two youngest daughters, Maria and Isabella, when they were small children. It is most unlikely that Mrs Atkins would have babysat the children of a lower-class convict. And when Esther was thirty-five, she was described as a 'genteel and pleasant lady'.

She was also capable of managing Johnston's large agricultural estate for many years while he was absent. The sales from the estate to the government were recorded in Esther's name and she was the person named responsible for Johnston's estate in all the associated court cases, even when her eldest son, George, was at home.

Then there is the consideration of Esther's Jewishness. Todd Endelman, in *The Jews of Georgian England, 1714–1830*, points out that by 1771 in England 'large segments of the [Jewish] community had already shed much of Jewish tradition and were on their way to becoming Englishmen in social and cultural terms'. Jeremy Pfeffer adds: 'The newly emancipated Jews of eighteenth-century London had become so enamoured with the ways of English society that there was nothing any rabbi could say that would bring them back to traditional Judaism.' So it seems that Esther's family is unlikely to have strictly observed Jewish customs.

Esther's children were baptised as Anglicans, and she herself was married and buried as an Anglican. Nevertheless, it is clear that her Jewish religion was important to her, that she maintained close friendships with other Jews in the colony and that she passed on a respect for the Jewish religion to her grandson, George Nichols.

Chapter notes

Chapter One: *Guilty!*

The most reliable source for Esther's age is the Home Office list of female transports compiled on 1 January 1787 which gave her age as seventeen, meaning she was born in 1769. If her birthday was in the second half of the year, she would have been only sixteen when she stole the lace. Arthur Bowes Smyth, the *Lady Penrhyn*'s doctor, recorded her age as twenty, but it is likely that she wanted to seem older on the ship for her own protection. Subsequent records of her age vary.

Esther has been described as an 'attractive young woman', an 'exceptional beauty' and a 'handsome woman'. A copy of her portrait hangs in the office of the Australian Jewish Historical Society. It is not very flattering to modern eyes, but is remarkably similar to a portrait of Elizabeth Macarthur.

Details of Esther's crime and trial can be found in the online Old Bailey session papers. It is not known *why* Esther stole the lace, and I have imagined a possible family background and the circumstances leading up to her crime. She is unlikely to have known that she was about six weeks pregnant at the time. Esther's address was recorded as St James, Westminster. Newgate Prison is described in Sheehan's article 'Finding Solace in Eighteenth Century Newgate'.

King George III later became known as Mad King George after suffering several bouts of insanity which may have been the result of bipolar disorder. His decision to send convicts to Botany Bay is recorded in a letter from Lord Sydney to the British Treasury in the *Historical Records of NSW*.

The British Marines did not become the Royal Marines until 1802. Moore's *First Fleet Marines* provided valuable details for this chapter. The *Lady Penrhyn* is described in Bateson's *Convict Ships* and beautiful models of all the First Fleet ships are on display at the Museum of Sydney. At one hundred and three feet long, the *Lady Penrhyn* was smaller than many of today's inner Sydney Harbour ferries.

Nelly Kerwin (also known as Eleanor Kirvein) as Esther's cellmate in the Master's Side of Newgate Prison, and the birth of Nelly's baby, are described in Rees's *Floating Brothel*. I have supposed the friendship between the two women. The identity of Rosanna's father remains a mystery, but it's possible that it was Abraham Abrahams. I created the events surrounding Esther's liaison with him.

The decision on Esther's appeal for Royal Mercy was not made for over a year, and then it stated that the jury, by acquitting her of 'private stealing', had already given her as much mercy as she deserved. It is recorded in the Home Office Judge's Reports of 1788.

Chapter Two: *To the Other Side of the World*
The details and descriptions of events during the First Fleet's voyage come from the journals of Clark, Collins, Hunter, King, Smyth, Tench, White and Worgan, plus Bateson's *Convict Ships* and Phillip's accounts in the *Historical Records of NSW*. The habit of the British settlers of referring to the native people as 'savages' is seen in the letters they sent home.

Isabella Rosson's experience is described in Gillen's *Founders*. The ship's surgeon, Arthur Bowes Smyth, mentions her baby's birth and death in his journal but provides no details. Ann Smith's life is discussed in Gray's article 'Ann Smith of the Lady Penrhyn'. I imagined the interactions between Esther, the other convict women and Johnston. His purchase of a she-goat is recorded but I have supposed Esther was asked to milk it. Arthur Bowes Smyth mentions bringing geraniums to Sydney on the *Lady Penrhyn*; Johnston may have done the same.

I found descriptions of the Indigenous people in the personal journals mentioned above and the State Library of NSW's *Eora*. Some historians believe the local Indigenous clans around Sydney Cove made up a larger Eora tribe. Others believe there was no Eora tribe but, when asked 'Whose land is this?', the native men replied in coastal Darug language, 'eora', meaning 'our people'. When the Indigenous people called out 'Warra, warra', they were saying 'go away!'

The small beach where the explorers camped is now called Camp Cove, the reedy bay is Rushcutters Bay and Van Diemen's Land was later renamed Tasmania.

Chapter Three: *A New Beginning*

The descriptions of the early colony and its events come from the journals of Bradley, Clark, Collins, Hunter, Smyth and White, plus Phillip's letters in the *Historical Records of NSW*, and Moore's *Marines*. James Ruse carrying Johnston ashore is discussed in Roberts's *Marine Officer*.

Small round brass plaques in the paving leading to the Sydney Opera House indicate the position of the original shoreline, which was much further inland than it is now, and extended to about where Customs House now stands. A flag of the original design that was raised on 26 January 1788 flies on a small flagpole on the western side of Customs House to mark the place where the first flag flew.

The location of Johnston's tent is shown on the map of 'Sydney Cove' drawn in 1788 by Francis Fowkes. The adjacent cove, where the first crops were planted, became known as Farm Cove and is now part of the Royal Botanic Garden, Sydney. The swampy ground that gave rise to the stream running into Sydney Cove was near what is now Hyde Park. Today the stream runs between George and Pitt Streets. High Street became George Street. The Navigator Islands, where Comte de La Perouse's men were attacked, are now known as Samoa.

Many people believe that Phillip made a long, rousing speech on either 26 January or 7 February 1788 that included the words

'How grand is the prospect which lies before this youthful nation', because such a speech was reported by Roderick Flanagan in his book *The History of New South Wales* (1862), and many other authors have reproduced it since then. However, such a speech is not mentioned in any of the original journals, nor is it included in any historical records. It appears to have been written instead by William Bede Dalley and given as a hoax to Flanagan who included it in his book.

I have imagined Ann Smith's hostility towards Esther, though her refusal to accept clothing and her escape from the colony is recorded in Smyth's journal, as is Ann Inett's move to Norfolk Island with King. The cabbage tree palms that grew around Sydney Cove, and whose fronds were used for making hats, were *Livistona australis*.

I drew much of the detail about Susannah Holmes and Henry Kable from original court records and Kable & Whittaker's *Damned Rascals?* Kable's three applications to marry Susannah are recorded in the *Australian Biological & Genealogical Record*. John Simpson's mercy dash is related in the *Norfolk Chronicle*, Neal's *Rule of Law*, and the *Scot's Magazine*. Squire Jacob Preston also wrote a letter of appeal on 29 October to Lord Suffield, the Norwich representative in parliament, after which Lord Suffield wrote to Under Secretary Evan Nepean.

Susannah's parcel has usually been referred to as belonging to Henry Kable, but Thomas Trimmings, Steward of the *Alexander* transport, declared in his sworn testimony that it was to be handed to Susannah on her arrival in New South Wales. Over two hundred years after the first civil court case in New South Wales, the *Bulletin* magazine listed Susannah Kable in the top one hundred most influential people in Australia's history because of the ruling.

Currey's *Mary Bryant* was my main source of information about Mary Broad. A description of Barrett's hanging is found in Cobley's *Sydney Cove 1788*. The island of Pinchgut is now known as Fort Denison.

I have imagined how Esther's relationship with Johnston may have initially developed.

Chapter Four: *A Hut to Call Home*

The journals that provided much of the detail for this chapter include those of Bradley, Collins, Tench, Hunter, Nagle, Smyth, White and Worgan. Phillip's letters in the *Historical Records of NSW* were also very informative. The native canoes are described in Smith's *Bennelong*. The method used by the Indigenous women to cut off their little fingers is described in Mathews' *Culture in Translation*. The native sarsaparilla vine, which the colonists used to make tea, is *Smilax glyciphylla*. Government House was built where the Museum of Sydney now stands, at the corner of Phillip and Bridge Streets, and the area known as the Brickfields was near today's Haymarket.

I drew on Neal's *Rule of Law* for the details of Susannah Kable's court case, but I supposed Johnston's involvement in it. The lagoon mentioned in the expedition from Manly Cove is Narrabeen Lagoon and the tip of the peninsula is today's Palm Beach. The explorers camped near today's Mona Vale. Arabanoo's capture by Johnston is described in Tench's journal.

While we do not know if Esther milked Johnston's goat, the death of his goat is recorded. We also don't know when Esther moved in with Johnston. Many have assumed it was as soon as the First Fleet arrived, or even on board the *Lady Penrhyn* but, as their first child was not born for another two years, it would seem more likely to have been much later. I have suggested how it might have come about.

Chapter Five: *Hunger*

I found much valuable information for this chapter in the *Historical Records of NSW*, particularly Fowell's letters to his father. The journals of Bradley, Collins, Hunter, King and White provided further information. Tench's journal added extra details about Arabanoo, including his nature, skill as a mimic and rapport with children. Phillip wrote that he was 'about 24 years of age'; Hunter thought he was about thirty. I have supposed the closeness of Johnston's friendship with him, but all the officers knew him well. Smith's *Bennelong* proved a rich source of information about both Bennelong and Colbee.

I gleaned details of Bryant's theft of fish and his associated sentence from Cobley's *1789–1790* and Currey's *Mary Bryant*. Floggings are described in Holt's *Memoirs* and also Silver's *Battle of Vinegar Hill*. The route taken by the convict men who walked from the Brickfields to Botany Bay was along today's Oxford Street.

How the Indigenous population was infected with smallpox remains controversial. It had been seventeen months since the colonists had left the Cape, where they had seen the last case; the French ships had been gone for twelve months, and they had had no other contact with the outside world.

Some believe the smallpox epidemic arose from bottles of smallpox virus brought to New South Wales by Dr White to inoculate children born in the settlement; others that the illness was actually chicken-pox, which at the time was considered a mild form of smallpox and can be a serious illness for adults. It is thought that due to the stress caused by the harsh conditions in the colony, some of the settlers may have developed shingles, which causes blisters containing live chickenpox virus. When the Indigenous people came into contact with it, they would have had no natural immunity against the disease. This issue was discussed on ABC Radio in *Ockham's Razor*, 13 April 2014. Tench and King both refer to the Indigenous people's belief that the spirits of their dead ancestors were in the sky.

Mackaness's *Bligh* provided the details of his seamanship. The area explored by Captain Tench is near what is now Penrith. I found information about the climate at the time in Karskens' *Colony* and descriptions of HMS *Guardian*'s fate in Cobley's *1789–1790*, Rees's *Floating Brothel* and Fitchett's *Nelson and His Captains*. Fitchett claims Bligh and Riou met at Cape Town, but Mackaness describes Bligh arriving at the Cape five days after Riou had left.

Chapter Six: *An Island of Surprises*
I drew heavily on the journals of Bradley, Clark, Collins, Hunter, King, Nagle and Tench for this chapter. I found extra information, particularly about the Second Fleet, from official letters recorded in the *Historical Records of NSW* plus Karskens' *Colony*.

Johnston often referred to Esther as 'Hetty' in his personal diary, which is quoted in Nesdale's *The Fettered and the Free*. His diary also notes that Esther and the two children accompanied him to Norfolk Island. Some sources mistakenly report that Rosanna was left behind in Sydney.

The wild birds eaten on Norfolk Island were two species of petrels: *Pterodroma melanopus*, which Clark called Mount Pitt birds, and *Pterodroma solandri*, which were known as Providence Petrels and were eaten to extinction on the island (though they survive on Lord Howe Island and Philip Island). Clark recorded the number of birds caught each night, which was occasionally over six thousand. Charlotte Field was later renamed Queensborough. Bergman notes that on Norfolk Island Esther was treated not as convict, but as a 'privileged person'. Rees's *Floating Brothel* describes the *Lady Juliana* and Nelly Kerwin's arrival on Norfolk Island.

Wentworth's use of the alias Henry Fitzroy in London is described in John Ritchie's *Wentworths*. There is no evidence for a relationship between Esther and Wentworth, either in England or New South Wales. However, they were in the same places at the same times of my narrative, so it remains a possibility.

Chapter Seven: *An Uncertain Future*

Once more, it was the journals of Clark, Collins, Hunter, Nagle and Tench that provided most of the background information for this chapter. The possibility that the spearing of Governor Phillip was arranged as payback is discussed in Karskens' *Colony*. Smith's *Bennelong* continued to provide helpful information about both Bennelong and Barangaroo. Bennelong's cottage was built on what is now called Bennelong Point, the location of the Sydney Opera House. I placed William Bryant in the boat going to Rose Hill. Moorooboora's lands covered the modern suburb of Maroubra. Elizabeth Macarthur wrote about Daringa visiting with her new baby; she may also have visited Mary.

I again relied on Moore's *Marines* for detailed information about the marines and their activities on Norfolk Island. Johnston's diary, quoted in Nesdale's *The Fettered and the Free*, documents his return to Sydney in May with Esther and the two children. (Others show Johnston returning in February, probably mistaking him for John Johnson.) The New South Wales Corps became known as the Rum Corps.

Mary Bryant's escape is described in Currey's *Mary Bryant*. Tench includes a detailed description of the buildings at Parramatta in his journal. John Macarthur's disdain for convicts is well documented, although I created Esther's encounter with him and Elizabeth. Johnston's letter to Clark about returning to England is recorded in Clark's *Letterbook*.

Chapter Eight: *The Annandale Estate*
For this chapter, I relied particularly on the journals of Collins, Hunter, King, Tench and Worgan, plus the *Historical Records of NSW*.

The string bags carried by the native women are described in Smith's *Bennelong*, and their method of drawing sickness through a string is recorded in the journals of both Collins and Tench. No one knows what became of Ann Smith after she initially escaped from the colony. I have imagined her confrontation with Esther. Johnston's diary, quoted in Nesdale's *The Fettered and the Free*, documents the birth of Esther's stillborn baby but provides no further details.

Enoch's death has been mistakenly reported elsewhere as occurring in 1792. The inscription on his grave can be seen online in the inventory of burials for the old Sydney burial ground (now the site of the Sydney Town Hall). Long Cove is now known as Darling Harbour.

Bergman, and many subsequent historians, wrote that Robert was born in 1792 (probably because of an error in his death notice in the *Sydney Mail*). However, Johnston's diary clearly records more than once that it was in 1793. Some historians have also claimed that Robert was Arthur Phillip's godson. However, I could find no evidence for this claim, and the fact that Robert was actually born three months after Phillip had left the colony makes it seem unlikely.

Much of the detail about Mary Bryant's epic voyage came from Tench's *Account of the Settlement* and Currey's *Mary Bryant*. Kable acting as an agent for the officers is noted in the *Australian Dictionary of Biography*. Rees's *Floating Brothel* describes Nelly Kerwin's successful return to England.

The original part of Johnston's Annandale estate (on the southern side of Parramatta Road) became the suburb of Stanmore. The additional grant of land he received in 1799 (on the northern side of Parramatta Road) became the modern suburb of Annandale. His lease on High Street was on what is now Lower George Street, between Essex and Alfred Streets. Cowpasture Plains became Camden.

Chapter Nine: *Managing Alone*

Annandale House was situated on what is now Macaulay Road, halfway between Northumberland Avenue and Percival Road in Stanmore. Its driveway led down to Parramatta Road, where gates were situated almost opposite Johnston Street. Alan Roberts includes detailed information about Annandale House and the estate in *Marine Officer, Convict Wife*. Grose Farm is now Camperdown, and the University of Sydney sits on Petersham Hill.

A letter from Hunter to Portland in the *Historical Records of NSW* plus Collins's journal describe the bushfire, and I found additional information about eucalypts and fire in both Hay's *Gum* and Pyne's *Burning Bush*. I have imagined the effect of the fire on the properties at Elizabeth Farm, Annandale and Sydney.

HMS *Supply*, which sailed with the First Fleet, had been sold by the Royal Navy in 1792. The HMS *Supply* that was sent to the Cape by Hunter was an American ten-gun storeship (originally the *New Brunswick*), which had been purchased as a replacement.

Colbee's payback battle and Bennelong's reaction to the events are recorded by Collins. Johnston's arrest and trial are recorded in the Parliament of Great Britain's *Report from Select Committee 1812*. Wentworth's decline is well documented, but I have supposed his meeting with Esther. The civil court case *Esther Julian on behalf of Captain George Johnston against Anthony Richardson*, 5 August 1801, is recorded in the NSW State Archives.

Chapter Ten: *Night Terrors*

The court cases in this chapter are also recorded in the NSW State Archives: *Julion v Biggars* (spellings vary), 30 August 1802; *Biggers v Julian*, 3 September 1802; and *Smyth v Biggars*, 3 September 1802. Later, a clerk named Michael Robinson demanded from Biggers a gallon of rum for the return of his bond. Biggers appealed to Governor King who found Robinson guilty of perjury and sentenced him to seven years' hard labour on Norfolk Island.

As usual, I discovered details about the other main events in this chapter in the *Historical Records of NSW*. As well as the usual sources for Johnston, I found extra detail about the Vinegar Hill uprising, and Johnston's role in it, from Silver's *Vinegar Hill* and reports in the *Sydney Gazette*. I imagined what Esther and Wentworth did during that event. Pendant Hills became Pennant Hills, the Coal River was renamed the Hunter River, and King's Gift became Horsley Park.

Esther's sales of meat and grain to the commissariat are recorded in tables at the back of Roberts's *Marine Officer, Convict Wife*. He also remarks upon Johnston's possible relationship with Bridget Edwards. John Grant, an educated convict, wrote to his mother that the judge advocate's wife 'delighted' in looking after Maria and Isabella. Rack's *Reasonable Enthusiast* describes how Samuel Marsden was heavily influenced by Wesleyan teaching. Extra details about the fate of the colony's sheep and cattle, including the fascinating story of how the first Merinos arrived, is described in Garran & White's *Merinos*.

The handwritten entry in the St Philip's Church marriage register for Rosanna and Nichols's wedding (in February 1805) is located in the middle of the December 1806 entries. It would appear that it was written nearly two years after the event. Perhaps the Reverend Samuel Marsden simply forgot to register the marriage at the time. Considering Rosanna's first child was not born until 1807, it might also be possible that they were actually married in February 1806 and, when Marsden made the entry ten months later, he wrote the wrong year by mistake.

We know that Mary Gilbert was Esther's servant at the time of the assault by Biggers and I have assumed that she remained with Esther throughout the following years. Jinny Grigg as a nursemaid at Annandale House is noted by Roberts.

Chapter Eleven: *The Trouble with Bligh*
As usual, the major events in this chapter are recorded in the *Historical Records of NSW*. While we know Isabella died in 1806, no cause for her death was recorded. I have imagined it was from the bite of a redback spider. Robert Johnston was the first person born in Australia to join the Royal Navy. Hunter's letter to him is located in the Johnston Family Papers in the Mitchell Library, Sydney.

The Blaxland wives and Elizabeth Macarthur are recorded as associating with female emancipists (such as members of the Parramatta Bible Society).

I gleaned much information about Bligh from Mackaness's *Bligh*, Fitzgerald & Hearn's *Bligh* and Currey's *Bligh*. I found even more about Bligh and Macarthur in Duffy's *Man of Honour*. And I discovered more details about the Blaxland brothers in Hyde's *Gregory Blaxland*.

I was able to calculate at skyviewcafe.com that the moon had not yet risen when Johnston was driving home in his buggy. The parade ground where the soldiers assembled is now Wynyard Park.

Chapter Twelve: *First Lady*
Duffy's *Man of Honour*, Lemcke's *Reluctant Rebel*, Ritchie's *Wentworths*, Mackaness's *Bligh*, and Fitzgerald & Hearn's *Bligh* are among many books that provide details about the Rum Rebellion. The *Historical Records of NSW* includes the associated letters.

Bligh later denied that he had hidden under a bed, but Duffy supports the accusation, noting that it took at least an hour to locate Bligh within the small house. Mackaness's *Bligh* includes a full account of the various witness statements.

I have supposed that Johnston used a pigeon to send a message to Annandale House. There has long been a belief that the Macarthurs used carrier pigeons between their various properties, although some now think that is a myth. Pigeons were brought out by the First Fleet, possibly for both food and communication within the colony.

The term 'First Lady' would not have been used at the time but I have included it in my narrative for modern readers. The King's birthday celebrations are reported in the *Sydney Gazette*. There is no record of the attendees, but it is likely that Esther was there. The dishes that were served are based on records of similar events, including those in Cohen's *Elizabeth Macquarie*. Esther is also likely to have attended the ball hosted by Paterson.

Johnston's worn leather notebook, which includes the handwritten lists of items he hoped to bring back from England—his 'Castles in the Air'—plus lists of all the furniture at Annandale House, resides today in the Mitchell Library in Sydney. The powdering room mentioned at Annandale House was used for powdering hair. The Mitchell Library also holds the letter Collins wrote to his brother which includes his remarks about Bligh.

By this time, it was not uncommon for women to be managing farms alone. When Governor Macquarie toured outlying districts in 1810, he wrote that some of the better farms he saw were managed by women. Esther's grant of land along the George's River was bounded by today's Milperra and River Roads. Paterson writes about the flood in a letter to Lord Castlereagh in the *Historical Records of NSW*.

Chapter Thirteen: *Mrs Johnston*

As usual, I drew on the formal records of this time, which are collected in the *Historical Records of NSW*. I found additional material in Karskens' *Colony*, including helpful detail about the colony's buildings.

The court case, *Rosetta Marsh v Esther Julian*, 20 March 1810, is recorded in the NSW State Archives. The *Sydney Gazette* reported Macquarie's declaration about rewarding good citizens; Mackneal's notice about his wife; Harry taking over the Kables' businesses; and the first horse races at Hyde Park, including William's ride to victory.

The friendship between Young George and William Wentworth, and also Macquarie's dinner with Wentworth and Redfern, are described in Ritchie's *Wentworths*. Macquarie's belief that Johnston would be executed is reported in Duffy's *Man of Honour*. The road that took Esther to George's Hall became the Hume Highway. The exact location of Bennelong's grave is not known, but Peter Mitchell's research places it in front of a house in Watson Street, Putney. Wentworth's Sydney Hospital became New South Wales Parliament House and the Mint Museum. The area known as South Creek became the suburb of St Marys.

I found details about the Blaxlands and the discovery of a route across the Blue Mountains in Hyde's *Gregory Blaxland* and Mackaness's *Journeys*. The route that George Caley discovered, which followed the ridges and was part of an existing Aboriginal pathway, was later developed into Bell's Line of Road. William Wentworth's poem 'Australasia', which contains 'The boundless champaign ...' was printed in the *Australian Town & Country Journal*. The intended recipient of his love poem is not known—but it might have been the pretty Julia Johnston.

We do not know if Esther was ever married to Rosanna's father. If she was, she would normally have required a GET (a Jewish divorce document) from her husband before she could legally marry again. However, as she was entering into an Anglican marriage with Johnston, he may have convinced her to take advantage of the English common law rule that 'a person could be presumed dead who had not been heard of for seven years by those who would be most likely to hear of him were he alive'. Certainly, most ex-convicts at the time believed that they were released from any previous matrimonial obligations.

In 2011 one of Esther's descendants contacted the Sydney Jewish Museum, offering for sale the jewellery box that had been 'presented to Esther Abrahams by Mrs Macarthur on the occasion of Esther's marriage'. The resulting correspondence can be found in the archives of the Australian Jewish Historical Society.

Esther's daughters staying with the Macquaries at Government House, Parramatta, is described in Cohen's *Elizabeth Macquarie*.

Select bibliography

ABC Radio, *Ockham's Razor*, 13 April 2014

Australian Biographical and Genealogical Record, Society of Australian Genealogists, Sydney, 1985

Australian Dictionary of Biography, National Centre of Biography, Australian National University, http://adb.anu.edu.au

Barton, G.B., *History of New South Wales from the Records*, Volume I 'Governor Phillip', Government Printer, Sydney, 1889

Bateson, Charles, *The Convict Ships: 1787–1868*, Brown, Son & Ferguson, Glasgow, 1969

Bergman, G.F.J., 'Esther Johnston: The Lieutenant-Governor's wife', *Australian Jewish Historical Society*, Volume 6, Part 2, 1966

Bradley, William, *A Voyage to New South Wales, December 1786–May 1792*, original manuscript. Collection 02, Safe 1/14, State Library of New South Wales

Broadbent, James & Hughes, Joy (eds), *The Age of Macquarie*, Melbourne University Press and Historic Houses Trust of New South Wales, 1992

Clark, Ralph, Letterbook, 3 April 1787 – 30 September 1791, Mitchell Library, State Library of New South Wales

——, *The Journal and Letters of Lt Ralph Clark, 1787–1792*, P.G. Fidlon & R.J. Ryan (eds), Australian Documents Library, Sydney, 1981

Cobley, John, *Sydney Cove 1788*, Angus & Robertson, Sydney, 1962

——, *Sydney Cove 1789–1790*, Angus & Robertson, Sydney, 1963

——, *Sydney Cove 1791–1792*, Angus & Robertson, Sydney, 1965

——, *Sydney Cove 1793–1795*, Angus & Robertson, Sydney, 1983

——, *Sydney Cove 1795–1800*, Angus & Robertson, Sydney, 1986

Cohen, Lysbeth, *Beginning with Esther: Jewish women in New South Wales from 1788*, Ayers & James Heritage Books in association with the Australian Jewish Times, Sydney, 1987

——, *Elizabeth Macquarie: Her life and times*, Wentworth Books, Sydney, 1979

Collins, D., *An Account of the English Colony in New South Wales, with Remarks on the Dispositions, Customs, Manners, etc. of the Native Inhabitants of that Country*, Volume 1, Cadell & Davies, London, 1798

——, *An Account of the English Colony in New South Wales, with Remarks on the Dispositions, Customs, Manners, etc. of the Native Inhabitants of that Country*, Volume 2, Cadell & Davies, London, 1802

Currey, C.H., *The Transportation, Escape and Pardoning of Mary Bryant (nee Broad)*, Halstead Press, Sydney, 1963

Currey, John (ed.), *William Bligh: Account of the rebellion of the New South Wales Corps*, The Colony Press, Malvern, 2003

De Vries, Susanna, *Historic Sydney: The founding of Australia*, Pandanus Press, Brisbane, 1983

——, *Females on the Fatal Shore: Australia's brave pioneers*, Pirgos Press, Brisbane, 2009

Donohoe, James Hugh, *Captain Bligh's Petticoat Mutiny*, J.S. Shaw North Publishing (Kindle version), 2012

Duffy, Michael, *Man of Honour*, Macmillan Australia, Sydney, 2003

Dyster, Barry, *Servant and Master: Building and running the grand houses of Sydney 1788–1850*, UNSW Press, Sydney, 1989

Edinburgh Review, February 1823 – May 1823, Volume XXXVIII, Edinburgh

Ellis, M.H., *Lachlan Macquarie: His life, adventures, and times*, Angus & Robertson, Sydney, 1965

Endelman, Todd M., *The Jews of Britain 1656–2000*, University of California Press, Oakland, 2002

Endelman, Todd M., *The Jews of Georgian England, 1714–1830*, University of Michigan Press, Ann Arbor, 1999

Fitchett, W.H., *Nelson and His Captains*, Smith, Elder & Co., Waterloo Place, 1902

Fitzgerald, Ross & Hearn, Mark, *Bligh, Macarthur and the Rum Rebellion*, Kangaroo Press, Sydney, 1988

Flannery, Tim, *The Birth of Sydney*, Text Publishing, Melbourne, 1999

Forbes, Morris, 'Esther Johnston Revisited: Revisionism in her story', *Journal of the Australian Jewish Historical Society*, Volume 17, Number 2, 2004

Garran, J.C. & White L., *Merinos, Myths and Macarthurs: Australian graziers and their sheep, 1788–1900*, Australian National University Press, Canberra, 1985

Gillen, Mollie, *The Founders of Australia: A biographical dictionary of the First Fleet*, Library of Australian History, Sydney, 1989

Gray, A.J., 'Ann Smith of the "Lady Penrhyn"', *Journal of the Royal Australian Historical Society*, Volume 43, Part 5, 1957

Hay, Ashley, *Gum*, Duffy & Snellgrove, Sydney, 2002

Hill, David, *1788: The brutal truth of the First Fleet*, Random House, Sydney, 2008

Historical Records of New South Wales, Volumes 1–7, Part 1, Government Printer, Sydney, 1893–1901

Holt, Joseph, Thomas Crofton Croker (ed.), *Memoirs of Joseph Holt: General of the Irish Rebels, in 1798*, H. Colburn, London, 1838

Hunter, John, *An Historical Journal of the Transactions at Port Jackson and Norfolk Island with the Discoveries which have been made in New South Wales and the Southern Ocean, since the publication of Phillip's Voyage, compiled from the Official Papers; including the Journals of Governors Phillip and King, and of Lieut. Ball; and the Voyages from the First Sailing of the* Sirius *in 1787, to the Return of that Ship's Company to England in 1792*, Libraries Board of South Australia, Adelaide, facsimile edition, 1968

Hunter, John, *Governor Hunter's Remarks on the Causes of the Colonial Expense of the Establishment of New South Wales etc., Hints for the Reduction of Such Expense, and for Reforming the Prevailing Abuses*, S. Gosnell, London, 1802

Hyde, Victor, *Gregory Blaxland*, Oxford University Press, London, 1958

Johnston Family Papers, Mitchell Library, State Library of New South Wales, Sydney

Johnston, George, Letterbook 1803–7, Mitchell Library, State Library of New South Wales, Sydney

Kable, Paul & Whittaker, June, *Damned Rascals? A chronicle of Henry & Susannah Kable 1764–1846*, privately published, 2007, available from http://damnedrascals.com

Karskens, Grace, *The Colony: A history of early Sydney*, Allen & Unwin, Sydney, 2009

Kercher, Bruce, *Debt, Seduction & Other Disasters: The birth of civil law in convict New South Wales*, Federation Press, Sydney, 1996

King, Hazel, *Elizabeth Macarthur and Her World*, Sydney University Press, Sydney, 1980

King, Jonathan & King, John, *Philip Gidley King: A biography of the third governor of New South Wales*, Methuen Australia, North Ryde, 1981

King, Philip Gidley, Letterbook, Norfolk Island 1788–1799, C187, Mitchell Library, State Library of New South Wales, Sydney

——, Letterbook, Volume 3, Mitchell Library, State Library of New South Wales, Sydney

Lemcke, Geoffrey, *Reluctant Rebel: Lt. Col. George Johnston 1764–1823*, Fast Books, Sydney, 1998

Levi, John S., *These Are the Names: Jewish lives in Australia 1788–1850*, Miegunyah Press, Melbourne, 2013

Levi, J.S. & Bergman, G.F.J., *Australian Genesis: Jewish convicts and settlers 1788–1850*, Rigby, Adelaide, 1974

Macarthur Onslow, Sibella (ed.), *Some Early Records of the Macarthurs of Camden*, Angus & Robertson, Sydney, 1914

Mackaness, George, *Admiral Arthur Phillip: Founder of New South Wales*, Angus & Robertson, Sydney, 1937

——(ed.), *Fourteen Journeys Over the Blue Mountains of New South Wales, Part I, 1813–1815*, Review Publications, Dubbo, 1950

——, *The Life of Vice-Admiral William Bligh*, Angus & Robertson, Sydney, 1951

Macquarie, Lachlan, *Diary, 1 March 1820 – 8 March 1821.* Original held in the Mitchell Library, State Library of New South Wales, Sydney

Martin, Ged (ed.), *The Founding of Australia*, Hale & Iremonger, Sydney, 1978

Mathews, R.H., *Culture in Translation*, ANU E Press, Canberra, 2007

Moore, John, *The First Fleet Marines*, University of Queensland Press, St Lucia, 1987

Nagle, Jacob, *The Nagle Journal: A diary of the life of Jacob Nagle, sailor, from the year 1775 to 1841*, John C. Dann (ed.), Weidenfeld & Nicholson, New York, 1988

Neal, David, *The Rule of Law in a Penal Colony: Law and power in early New South Wales*, Cambridge University Press, Cambridge, 1991

Nesdale, Iris, *The Fettered and the Free*, Orchid Publications, Adelaide, 1987

Parker, Derek, *Arthur Phillip: Australia's first governor*, Woodslane Press, Warriewood, 2009

Parliament of Great Britain, *Report from the Select Committee on Transportation*, House of Commons, 10 July 1812

Pfeffer, Jeremy I., 'From One End of the Earth to the Other': *The London Bet Din, 1805–1855, and the Jewish convicts transported to Australia*, Sussex Academic Press, Eastbourne, 2010

Pyne, Stephen J., *Burning Bush: A fire history of Australia*, Henry Holt & Co., New York, 1991

Rack, Henry D., *Reasonable Enthusiast: John Wesley and the rise of Methodism*, Epworth Press, London, 2002

Rees, Sian, *The Floating Brothel*, Hodder, Sydney, 2001

Ritchie, John, *The Wentworths*, Melbourne University Press, Melbourne, 1997

Roberts, Alan, *Marine Officer, Convict Wife: The Johnstons of Annandale*, Annandale Urban Research Association in association with Barbara Beckett Publishing, Paddington, 2008

Rusden, G.W., *History of Australia*, George Robertson, Sydney, 1883

Ryan, R.J. (ed.), *Land Grants 1788–1809*, Australian Documents Library, Sydney, 1974

Schama, Simon, *The Story of the Jews, Volume 2: Belonging, 1492–1900*, Bodley Head, London, 2017

Sheehan, W.J., 'Finding solace in eighteenth century Newgate', in J.S. Cockburn (ed.), *Crime in England 1550–1800*, Methuen, London, 1977

Silver, Lynette Ramsay, *The Battle of Vinegar Hill, 1804: Australia's Irish Rebellion*, Watermark Press, Sydney, 2002

Smith, Keith Vincent, 'Bennelong among his people', *Aboriginal History*, Volume 33, 2009

——, *Bennelong: The coming in of the Eora, Sydney Cove, 1788–1792*, Kangaroo Press, Kenthurst, 2001

Smyth, Arthur Bowes, *The Journal of Arthur Bowes Smyth: Surgeon, Lady Penrhyn 1787–1789*, P. Fidlon (ed.), Australian Documents Library, Sydney, 1979

State Library of New South Wales, *Eora: Mapping Aboriginal Sydney 1770–1850*, State Library of New South Wales, Sydney, 2006

Jack, Sybil, 'Who did she think she was—Esther Abrahams', *ISAA Review*, Volume 10, Number 2, 2011

Sydney Gazette, available online at: http://newspapers.nla.gov.au/ndp/del/title/3

Taylor, Peter, *Australia: The first twelve years*, Allen & Unwin, Sydney, 1982

Tench, W., 'A Narrative of the Expedition to Botany Bay', printed for J. Debrett, London, 1789

——, 'A Complete Account of the Settlement at Port Jackson', printed for J. Debrett, London, 1793

The Times, digital archive, accessed via the State Library of New South Wales

Tink, Andrew, *William Charles Wentworth*, Allen & Unwin, Sydney, 2009

Tucker, Michelle Scott, *Elizabeth Macarthur: A life at the edge of the world*, Text Publishing, Melbourne, 2018

Vigilante, T., Dixon, K., Sieler, I., Roche, S. & Tieu, A., *Smoke Germination of Australian Plants*, Rural Industries Research and Development Corporation, West Perth, 1998

Walsh, Robin (ed.), *In Her Own Words: The writings of Elizabeth Macquarie*, Macquarie University and Exisle Publishing, Wollombi, 2011

White, John, *Journal of a Voyage to New South Wales*, J. Debrett, London, 1790

Whittaker, June, *Kable: The story of Henry Kable, First Fleet convict extraordinaire*, privately published, Tumbarumba, 2002

Wilkerson, Marjorie, *Past-into-Present Series: Clothes*, Batsford, London, 1970

Worgan, George B., *Journal of a First Fleet Surgeon*, Library of Australian History, Sydney, 1978

Yarwood, A.T., *Samuel Marsden: The great survivor*, Melbourne University Press, Melbourne, 1977

Index

Kable, Henry *continued*
  Rum Rebellion, 182
  trading, 122, 133, 143, 154
  at Windsor, 217
Kable, James, 122, 217
Kable, Susannah *see* Holmes, Susannah
Katoomba, 223
Kemp, Anthony, 179
Kent, William, 132, 135, 162, 194
Kerwin, Nelly, 4–7, 8–9, 10, 91, 122, 252, 259
King, Anna, 108, 146, 154
King, Norfolk, 82, 109, 148
King, Philip, 28, 82, 170, 197, 207
  at Botany Bay, 32
  convict uprising, 156, 158
  government, 134, 139–40, 147, 153, 260
  with Macarthur, 148, 165
  Norfolk Island, 32, 108, 127
King, Sydney, 108, 109
King's Gift, 162, 231, 236, 260
Kingsgrove, 161

Lady Juliana, 86
Lady Madeline Sinclair, 168
Lady Penrhyn, 7–8, 21, 9–25, 27, 29–30, 48, 268
Lawson, William, 179, 194
Laycock, Thomas, 161, 179, 187
Linden, 223
Liverpool, 216
Lock, Maria, 237
Lockwood, 234
Long Cove, 118, 258
Lord, Simeon, 175, 184
Lovell, Henry, 43, 44

Macarthur, Edward, 104, 148, 200
Macarthur, Elizabeth, 103, 105, 121, 154, 192, 261
  children sent to school, 148
  convict uprising, 156
  death, 241
  fire, 130

gift for Esther, 226, 263
manages estate, 202
Macarthur, Elizabeth (junior), 148
Macarthur, James, 196
Macarthur, John, 104, 193
  with Bligh, 169–70, 176–7
  Brush Farm, 226
  death, 241
  duel, 147, 195
  in England, 148, 165, 218, 239
  fire, 130
  grants, 119, 162
  with Hunter, 134, 140
  with Johnston, 196
  with King, 147
  later years, 241
  merinos, 132
  Nichols trial, 135
  with Paterson, 147
  returns to Sydney, 165
  Rum Rebellion, 180, 184
  Secretary of the Colony, 190
  trial, 179, 189
  at Young George's death, 230
Macarthur, John (junior), 148
Macarthur, William, 196
Mackellar, Neil, 147
Mackneal, Ann, 214, 238–9
Macquarie Gift, 230–1
Macquarie, Elizabeth, 209, 211–12, 225
  arrives in Sydney, 207
  baby dies, 213
  gives birth, 224
  with Johnston girls, 228
Macquarie, Lachlan, 213, 262
  arrives in Sydney, 207
  Bank of New South Wales, 237
  with Bligh, 208
  death, 238
  government, 206–25, 236
  with Johnston, 213, 224
  later years, 236
  Native Institution, 236
  with Young George, 227, 229
  at Young George's death, 230